DK small business *guides*

working
from home

DK small business guides

working from home

PETER HINGSTON & ALASTAIR BALFOUR

A Dorling Kindersley Book

Dorling Kindersley

LONDON, NEW YORK, SYDNEY, DELHI, PARIS,
MUNICH, and JOHANNESBURG

Senior Art Editor Jamie Hanson
DTP Designer Julian Dams
US Consultant Stuart Gittleman
US Editors Gary Werner, Margaret Parrish
Production Controller Michelle Thomas

Managing Editor Adèle Hayward
Senior Managing Editor Stephanie Jackson
Senior Managing Art Editor Nigel Duffield

Produced for Dorling Kindersley by
Grant Laing Partnership
48 Brockwell Park Gardens,
London SE24 9BJ

Managing Editor Jane Laing
Project Editor Helen Ridge
Project Art Editor Christine Lacey
Picture Researcher Jo Walton

First American Edition, 2001

00 01 02 03 04 05 10 9 8 7 6 5 4 3 2 1

Published in the United States by
Dorling Kindersley Publishing, Inc.
95 Madison Avenue
New York, New York 10016

Library of Congress Cataloging-in-Publication Data

Hingston, Peter.
    Working from home / Peter Hingston & Alastair Balfour.
        p. cm. – (Small business guides)
    Includes index.
    ISBN 0-7894-7200-7 (alk. paper)
        1. Home-based businesses. I. Balfour, Alastair. II. Title. III. Series.
HD23333 .H56 2000
658.02'2--dc21
                                                            00-066019

Color reproduction in Italy by GRB Editrice
Printed and bound by Mondadori in Verona, Italy

see our complete catalog at

www.dk.com

CONTENTS

INTRODUCTION

Working from home is the dream of many people. It offers the possibility of greater control over your life and enhanced family relationships. Every day some people act on that dream, deciding to leave the conventional workplace and to set up a business of their own at home. The "open-collar" revolution is becoming increasingly popular as stress rates climb among pressured employees, commuting becomes more tiresome, and lifestyle becomes more important.

Although many may regard this shift in working patterns as a new development, in fact the people who choose to work from home today are doing precisely what their ancestors did in the age before the Industrial Revolution. It is somehow a very natural way to live. While this concept belongs to a previous era, the technology that has allowed the latest revolution is definitely of the present age. The computer, improved telecommunications, and the internet have been the liberators this time around.

Working from Home begins by setting out the practical issues you will need to consider before starting a home-based business, and outlining the personal qualities you will need to develop if you are to succeed. The book looks at the different ways you can get into business and investigates the many opportunities available because of the internet. It discusses the location options for your work space and provides advice on designing and equipping it to suit your particular requirements. Next, the fundamental skills involved in running a business are outlined, including step-by-step instructions on preparing a business plan. The book then tackles issues specific to working at home: how to get the right balance between family life and business responsibilities, and between working hard and staying healthy and motivated.

Working from Home is suitable for the self-employed, partnerships, and corporations, and for all businesses operating from domestic premises. Due to the many complexities involved when starting or running a business, you would benefit from getting sound professional advice before making any important decisions.

GETTING ready to begin

*T*his section introduces the concept
of becoming a home entrepreneur, and
investigates the most common types of
home business. It explains the practical
issues that you need to consider before
starting out, and provides a simple
self-assessment exercise to enable you
to evaluate whether you are well
suited to running your own business
from home. Finally, it offers tips and
techniques for organizing the daily
running of your business efficiently,
managing your time effectively, and
minimizing stress.

TAKING STOCK

Employment can be stressful, as surveys across the Western world show. Most people who are employed today say that they find work more demanding, more tiring, and more pressure-filled than ever before. This chapter highlights how far-reaching changes in corporate culture and technological advances have affected the job market, and reveals why many employees are re-examining their careers and choosing to work from home. It will also help you to determine whether making the break and pursuing a home business venture is the right move for you.

The most significant factor contributing to the increased pressure experienced by employees has been the gradual disappearance of the "job for life" culture within most businesses and markets. Although this culture has been with us for a relatively short period of time – 100 years or so – generations have grown up knowing only one employer and one type of job. Yet today they are faced with the fact that a growing proportion of jobs on offer are short-term, designed to bridge a gap, or deliver a specific objective for the employer. It is also becoming relatively common for people to find that conventional salaried employment is simply unavailable in their particular skill or geographic area. They are therefore forced to join the ranks of temporary contract workers, moving from project to project as demand dictates.

Work from home whenever it suits you, any time of day or night

Accompanying this trend has been the shift by major employers – who provide more than half of private sector jobs in most Western economies – to pare down their operations and outsource a growing range of business services. The main target areas for this treatment include accounting and payroll systems, cleaning services, catering, office administration, marketing and public relations, computer maintenance, installation of furniture systems, car fleet maintenance, and recruitment.

The internet age has brought us on-line buying and selling, enabling the business cycle to take place electronically. As a result, costs are slashed and many jobs lost.

CASE STUDY: Deciding to Go It Alone

JENNY HAS BEEN fired for the third time in four years. Employed as a full-time newspaper photographer, she has been on the receiving end of continual takeovers in the fast-moving media business. She knows that, while she could easily find another job because of her reputation and good contacts within the industry, the chances are that history would repeat itself. Jenny decides to explore self-employment opportunities and discovers that there is no one else in her field providing a news photography service to press agencies. Since she is cautious by nature, she checks out payment rates and finds that it should be possible to earn as much as before as a freelancer – and tax savings will mean that she ought to be better off.

The result of this determined attack on corporate bureaucracy has been the development of the modern business organization: lean, focused, and driven with great energy and speed by a dedicated leadership team. For those that stay with them, the rewards can be great. So are the pressures. Welcome to the information age.

The Results of Outsourcing

As the huge outsourcing trend, also described as "downsizing," has displaced millions of staff employees, it has also created many new job and business opportunities. New jobs are being created daily as the growing network of business services companies supply the corporate world's every need. Temporary staffing is now big business everywhere.

There are two important consequences of outsourcing. The first is the fresh energy that has poured into the entrepreneurial sector of business. Over the past decade owner-managed companies have recorded dramatic growth rates, which make them the major creators of new employment. They are flourishing on the back of surging demand for a vast array of specialized services, many of which are now delivered on the internet.

The second is the equally dramatic growth in the number of people now choosing to work from home, whether they are running their own business, being a self-employed contract worker, or telecommuting for a large company. This seismic shift in working patterns is changing more than just the employment market: it is impacting on car usage, shopping trends, computer sales, and house design. In turn, it is generating still more demand for home-based business services.

The Home Business Explosion

Experts call the home business explosion the most profound transformation ever to hit business markets. Throughout the developed world, home-based businesses have become the fastest-growing sector of the economy.

This "open-collar" revolution has been driven on one hand by the escalating outsourcing practices of big business, and on the other by the readily available technology to run a business from your spare bedroom or garage.

WHO IS DOING IT?

The simple answer is everyone! It is not just people who have lost their jobs or become disillusioned with the pressures at work.

WHY PEOPLE HEAD FOR HOME

There are a number of reasons why people leave their jobs and set up on their own at home. The following are the most common:

- They worked for aggressive bosses.
- They did not like office politics.
- They were tired of relentless deadlines.
- They wanted more autonomy.
- They were uncertain about their role.
- They experienced sexism in the office.
- They experienced racism in the office.
- They disliked commuting.

Home businesses are also being started by retirees, mothers, part-timers, students whole families – in fact, anyone who wants to gain control over their own life and carve out a new future on the basis of their own skills, energy, and imagination. A small but rapidly growing group of new entrepreneurs comes from those who have simply decided to give up their careers and opt for the convenience of working from home, particularly mothers with young children. Surveys show that, unlike the male-dominated world of big business, home businesses are run by men and women in equal proportion. In the U.S., 1997 was the year in which the number of new home-based businesses overtook those new-starts launched in conventional business properties, such as offices, factories, and stores. The trend has continued to grow ever since.

Organize your time effectively between childcare duties and work

WHAT ARE THEY DOING?

It is easier to list what home entrepreneurs are not doing! Their vast sprawl of activity falls into four main categories:

1 OFFICE-BASED PROFESSIONAL SERVICES, such as information, publishing, training, financial advice, consulting, and software programming.

2 DOMESTIC SERVICES AND TRADES, from landscaping, decorating and plumbing to car repairs and childcare.

3 DIRECT SELLING, such as party plan, direct mail, and door-to-door retailing.

4 CRAFT BUSINESSES, producing batches of artwork, clothing, jewellery, and other items, often for local retail outlets.

WORKING PARENTS
It can be a liberating experience working from home, particularly for parents who can fit their business hours around caring for their children.

COULD YOU BE A HOME ENTREPRENEUR?

Assess your readiness to run a business from home by answering the questions below. Score 1 for "No", 2 for "Not sure", and 3 for "Yes". Mark the options closest to your instincts, and be honest. Then add your scores and refer to the results at the end of the questionnaire to see how you scored and to check your potential. Whatever your

score, remember that this type of self-assessment test is general. It is designed only to give an indication of whether you have the basic attitude, instincts, and capabilities to make a success of launching a home-based business. If your score is low, the chances are that you do not. If it is high, the opposite is true.

	No	Not sure	Yes
Do you aspire to run your own business?	1	2	3
Do you have a specific business idea to turn into reality?	1	2	3
Are you willing to commit five years or more to a business?	1	2	3
Are you able to work happily on your own?	1	2	3
Are you prepared to work long hours by yourself?	1	2	3
Are you comfortable with responsibility as the boss?	1	2	3
Is it important to you to make a great deal of money?	1	2	3
Are you an instinctive risk taker?	1	2	3
Can you get really enthusiastic about projects?	1	2	3

	No	Not sure	Yes
Are you good at thinking up new ideas?	1	2	3
Are you creative at solving difficult problems?	1	2	3
Do you like making decisions?	1	2	3
Can you work to deadlines?	1	2	3
Are you outgoing and self-confident?	1	2	3
Are you comfortable working with figures?	1	2	3
Do you have computer skills?	1	2	3
Do you have experience of dealing with customers?	1	2	3
Can you sell?	1	2	3
Are you able to put budgets together?	1	2	3
Are you ambitious?	1	2	3

RESULTS

Up to 25 points
The odds are that you would face an uphill struggle going it alone at this stage. Why not try persuading your employer to let you work from home?

26–40 points
It is entirely possible that you could make a success of a business venture. You would probably be best suited to one with rigid and systematic processes, such as hairstyling, accounting and bookkeeping, or landscaping.

41–50 points
Your instincts are probably in the right place, but take a look at the areas where you answered "No" and assess whether a relevant course or program might help get you up to speed.

51 points or more
You have the drive, the ambition, and most of the skills required. Take a course to improve any weak skill areas, such as using a computer. Then go for it!

HOW ARE THEY DOING IT?

Some home entrepreneurs can work only in a dedicated space, such as a bedroom converted to a home office or an outbuilding turned into a craftshop. Others are equally happy operating from the kitchen table or a corner of their living room. What they all have in common is access to virtually the same computing and communications technology as their larger competitors, giving them a low-cost base, good

ADVANTAGES AND DISADVANTAGES OF RUNNING A BUSINESS FROM HOME

ADVANTAGES	DISADVANTAGES
Independent lifestyle	The buck always stops with you
Control over your own destiny	More difficult to take vacations
Personal satisfaction	Isolation and boredom
No commuting	Inevitability of longer working hours
Lower stress levels	More pressure over longer periods
Flexible working hours	Difficult to know when to stop working
Blending business with family	Clash between business and family
Range of opportunities	Difficult to assess competition
Low investment required	Poor financial returns at first
Power of affordable technology	No corporate computer support

efficiency, and the ability to market worldwide, if necessary. They also have a strong desire to succeed by working in a way that does not compromise their quality of life. Surveys consistently show that the greatest motivation for home entrepreneurs comes from the desire to maintain a balanced and healthy lifestyle, without the pressures of the corporate workplace or the hassles of daily commuting.

The Impact of Home Working

The home-working revolution is impacting increasingly on all Western economies, covering both home-based entrepreneurs and employees able to work from home.

In the U.S. one worker in three now operates from home for more than one day a week. The equivalent figure in the U.K. is one in four, where some six million people are now officially designated as working from home. In Europe there are over 20 million home offices and over 30 million professionals working at home. An additional 45 million Europeans are employed in micro-businesses, employing two people on average, which are mostly run from home.

A particular trend is for large companies to equip home offices so that their key people can operate flexibly between home and office while maintaining full communication with their teams at the central office. For example, U.K. telecom giant BT has over 25,000 employees who work from home via the company's website.

Third-age Entrepreneurs

A rapidly growing number of home businesses are being started by people over 50. With the trend toward early retirement and job loss, more older people with energy and cash are taking the plunge to become their own bosses. In the U.K. over 10 percent of new home-based businesses are being started by this group, known as third-age entrepreneurs.

Their average turnover and earnings are less than those of similar businesses run by young entrepreneurs, but that is largely because many such companies are run more as hobbies and to supplement retirement pensions. However, there is no doubting the determination of their owners to prove that, despite their years, they are healthy, ambitious, and ready for anything but the scrap heap.

Because third-age entrepreneurs often convert long-standing hobbies into businesses, this is likely to mean that their start-up costs will be lower than for others starting from scratch with no existing materials or machinery.

TAILOR-MADE PROFESSIONS

Although many over-50s today find themselves without jobs, there are skills that can easily be transferred from the corporate office or factory to the home. Tailoring is one such profession, requiring a minimum of overhead.

The flip side is that it can be traumatic for people going out on their own after being cushioned in a large company or government department. There can also be unpleasant consequences for the tax treatment of pensions if people over 65 are making good livings from their new business ventures.

But it seems unlikely that these negatives will affect the trend toward home enterprise by the over-50s. Many who have been successful have discovered a fresh vigor and enthusiasm through their business that bodes well for a lengthy retirement – once they reach it.

Considering Your Business Options

Before making any serious commitment to running your own business from home, even to the point of starting to research an idea, consider the full implications of such a move.

Be honest; this may well be the biggest decision you ever make in your working life. If the business is successful, it could set you and your family on a new path that offers prosperity, quality of life, as well as freedom from the rigidity of employment and the workplace. But if the potential rewards are high, so, too, are the risks. These fall into five main categories:

1 family life
2 finances
3 personality
4 technology
5 your home.

FAMILY LIFE

It is a simple truth that life at home is never the same once the main breadwinner makes the decision to work from home. It is inevitable that working and living under the same roof will result in collisions and conflict. Studies

BURNING THE MIDNIGHT OIL

Working all hours, late into the evening and on weekends, is very tempting when you first set up your business at home. Although it requires a great deal of self-discipline, try to set aside quality time for your family and friends.

show that the three major disadvantages are:
■ not being able to get away from work
■ being interrupted by family
■ having work interfere with family.

On one level, there is the inevitable competition for space and quiet; on the other, there is the potential for disruption when business visitors arrive for meetings.

If there are no children in the household and it is a case of two partners with quite different working patterns – one at home and the other with a conventional job – there is still considerable opportunity for tension.

Although in an advantageous situation from the point of view of disruption, a couple setting up a business together from home will find it remarkably difficult to establish clear barriers between work and home life.

FINANCES

Starting a business means that you effectively become self-employed, at least until it reaches the size where you become an employer and start hiring others. The consequences are that you will have none of the following:

■ monthly pay checks
■ paid sick leave
■ paid vacations
■ life insurance
■ health insurance
■ company car.

In addition, your fortunes are entirely dependent on your own efforts and abilities, more so than at any previous time in your life.

You may also be putting at potential risk much of what you have already built up by way of investment in your home and other assets. Securing business loans from a bank may necessitate having to pledge your house as security, with the risk that you lose it if you cannot afford to repay the loan.

PERSONALITY

Like never before, your strengths and weaknesses will be pushed to the limits as you strive to launch and build up your own business. You will end up wearing more hats than you thought possible. As well as being the boss, you will also have to be the following:

■ marketing whizz kid
■ financial genius
■ super-salesperson
■ efficient secretary
■ astute administrator
■ level-headed production controller.

You will also work long hours, at least 50 hours a week and probably well over that when you first set out, so stamina will be important. You will have to keep on top of perhaps dozens of projects and tasks all at the same time. And you will have to counter the inevitable effects of being lonely; you will be working on your own for a great deal of time, especially at the outset.

Above all, you will have to cope with the pressure of knowing that the success or failure of your business rests entirely on your shoulders. The buck stops at your desk or workbench, and nowhere else.

> *Consider other locations if an office at home is likely to cause family problems*

KEY SUCCESS FACTORS FOR HOME ENTREPRENEURS

1 Hard work, energy, and stamina: ability to work when you least want to.

2 Self-motivation and drive: being confident in your abilities is a must.

3 Ability to set and achieve goals: know what you want and how to get it.

4 Willingness to take measured risks: recognize which risks are worth taking.

5 Good streetwise judgment: instinct and knowledge both play a part.

6 Experience in chosen business: insider information is invaluable.

7 Strong communication skills: being articulate about your business.

8 Natural sales ability: selling is vital to the success of any business.

9 Comfortable with uncertainty: you can never be sure of anything.

10 Passion for your business: customers react well to genuine enthusiasm.

TECHNOLOGY

Whatever your likely type of business, whether you plan to make things or sell ideas, you will be heavily dependent on technology, and more so than any previous generation of home entrepreneurs. In addition to the ubiquitous computer for word processing and accounting, you will need a printer and possibly a photocopier. Communications equipment such as a mobile phone, fax, and email are essential, while it is increasingly hard to ignore the internet, if only as a cheap method of marketing your business.

All of this means that you will require a basic competence in operating all this equipment, which is not something that comes easily to

everyone. Indeed, if you struggle to master keyboards, let alone equipment-operating manuals, you should seriously consider bringing in someone to help you manage your technology while you concentrate on running the business and satisfying customers. That, of course, means an immediate additional cost for the new venture to bear.

Your Home

The best scenario for home entrepreneurs is to find a separate space where they can operate undisturbed by the rest of the household. This is easier said than done in many homes,

particularly if space is tight and the "office" has to be in a corner of the living room or bedroom. The situation is worse if the business involves noisy or dirty manufacturing processes. You may also have to find storage space for materials or finished goods, at the same time trying to fit in meetings around the kitchen table. Basing yourself at home is not always an easy option. Some people find that the only workable solution is to rent a furnished office nearby.

There are also official complications to setting up a business from home. If the property is rented, the landlord's approval will be needed, and insurance companies will need to be notified. If you plan to carry out building alterations, local government planning permission is needed. And if one or more rooms are reserved exclusively for business purposes, you may face a tax charge when selling the property.

Setting Objectives

If you are still convinced that working from home is right for you, start setting key personal and business targets to guide you toward launch day and beyond. This process will be increasingly useful as your business grows and develops, so it is valuable to become familiar with it now. However, also remember that things will change, often quickly, so keep your targets broad and flexible.

When considering these targets, it is essential that you include the rest of your household in your calculations. After all, they will be involved almost as much as you, even if they actually play no part in the business, simply because they live under the same roof.

PERSONAL

More people are choosing to run a business from home because it suits their desired lifestyle. But, as many discover, it is too easy to work even longer hours than previously because the desk or workbench is so close at hand. A certain level of income is also needed to support that lifestyle. So, the first decisions you must make are linked inextricably together:
■ How much do you want to work?
■ How much do you want to earn?
The choice here will obviously influence the type of business that you establish. But it makes sense to view these decisions from a personal standpoint, rather than rushing into setting up a venture simply because you want

Decide whether you want to work full- or part-time before you start

to have your own business. The chances are that if you do that you will find yourself working harder than you ever have before but without experiencing the main benefits that working from home offer.

There are many home entrepreneurs who happily run part-time businesses, especially if the aim is to achieve a second income. They work when they can in between other commitments, such as childcare. If this is the case, you might choose to work only during school hours and perhaps again in the evening.

On the other hand, you might have a hobby or a sport that you wish to pursue at the same time as running a business. Although a difficult compromise to make, such a balance is not impossible. The most important thing to do is to set a structure for your working day – and keep to it. Remember that in the heat of battle it is only too easy to let good resolutions waver and end up working every available hour.

As far as income goes, if your new venture is intended to replace the main breadwinner's job in the household, then the amount you wish to make will probably be at least as much as you earned before. Achieving this is easier said than done. Any new business will take at least six months to establish, if not a year or more, to the point where it can support a full salary. What is beyond doubt is that adopting this target will involve a major full-time commitment to establishing a sizable business.

To some extent your potential income will be decided by the type of business you choose. A self-employed market consultant, for example, can earn high fees, giving him or her the option of working fewer days, while a sales agent or caterer may need to work long hours for a basic income. This is because of the different pay scales that different types of job attract.

Fact File

The exciting thing about becoming a home entrepreneur is that it opens up the whole spectrum of possibilities: from building a successful business that delivers more income than you could previously have hoped to attain from a job to enjoying a part-time venture that brings in enough to fund a couple of good vacations a year.

Business Meetings

The type of business meeting area you will need at home depends to a great extent on your profession. In the informal world of graphic design, it is quite acceptable to conduct meetings at the dining room or kitchen table.

Business

The key decision here – which business to pursue – is dealt with in more depth in the next chapter. But at this early stage, before making any final commitment, you need to be clear about the type of venture you are best suited to tackle. This is not a decision that can be made in isolation. For example, your home may be unsuitable to any form of manufacturing or production, perhaps because it is an apartment or a duplex with no separate accommodation for noisy or smelly operations, or you cannot get planning permission. But if that is the type of business with which you are most familiar and want to pursue, you might have to consider moving.

Another relevant issue is whether you are likely to hold business meetings at home. As well as needing to have a suitable private space available, consider whether parking will be a problem and whether this might be the cause of future conflict with neighbors.

From the decision on the type of venture stems the likely location of the space you will use. In turn that will influence the impact on the rest of the household. It is good to settle all these matters before going any further. There is nothing worse than to be well down the road toward the launch of your new home business only to discover that it is impractical in your present house.

The final decision to make at this stage is equally important, even if it may now seem a little irrelevant: how long do you give your venture? This issue impacts on all kinds of lifestyle matters. If you make an open-ended commitment to a home business for primarily lifestyle reasons, you may well find it succeeding to the point where it consumes your life and your free time, leaving you no easy means of escape back toward a more leisurely existence. Better to give it, say, five years now and then undertake a fundamental review with the rest of the household. Business

DOS AND DON'TS OF HOME WORKING

✔ Do evaluate your home as a potential business base before making big decisions.

✔ Do discuss the big issues with your family and friends before making decisions.

✔ Do consider the risk that you will work harder at home than you did in your last job.

✔ Do set realistic objectives for your home business so that you will not be disappointed.

✘ Don't expect a home business to deliver your desired lifestyle immediately.

✘ Don't underestimate the new pressures that will fall on your shoulders.

✘ Don't imagine that you know it all – a new home business will require new skills.

✘ Don't forget the importance of setting goals at the outset – and sticking to them.

can be a seductive pastime, especially for those with incipient workaholic tendencies; and it is all too easy to find the years slipping by and feeling a great deal of satisfaction with what you have achieved, but having no time in which to enjoy the fruits of your success.

Preparing Yourself

Now that you have made the commitment in principle to pursue a home business venture, you will need to prepare financially, organizationally, and, of course, mentally for the journey ahead. The major issues to consider concern your finances, the extent of your skills and knowledge, and deciding which business to pursue.

Starting a new home-based venture is both an enormous commitment and a huge shift in circumstances, especially for those who have known only traditional employment. It can be scary to become the boss, particularly if you are the main breadwinner in the home. Despite your determination to win, a new business will only be as good as the planning, research, and detailed thought that go into its creation. Prepare thoroughly for the adventure ahead; once you launch your business you will be fully committed to driving it forward.

Dos and Don'ts of Finance

✓ Do spend time assessing and planning your personal finances.

✓ Do minimize your living costs.

✓ Do ensure that your home and its contents are adequately insured for business use.

✓ Do set up a financial cushion to protect against unexpected delays in payment.

✓ Do think about running your business part-time at first.

✗ Don't leap into a business venture without considering the personal implications.

✗ Don't take on heavy personal borrowing.

✗ Don't forget the importance of planning personal as well as business cash flow.

✗ Don't leave yourself without adequate life insurance coverage.

✗ Don't assume you have to commit everything to a new venture.

Creating a Strong Financial Base

A high degree of financial planning for you and your household is essential when you start up your own business. It is crucial that you approach the launch from the strongest possible personal financial situation. The inevitable risks have to be minimized and costs controlled so that you can concentrate 100 percent on the new venture without distraction.

The following key points will need to be taken into consideration:

■ **Salary** You will not have a salary at least until the business can afford to pay you one, which could take a year or more. Even then, income is likely to be sporadic, depending on how customers pay. So you must work out the personal cash-flow consequences of giving up your present work to go solo. Home business advisers recommend having an emergency fund of six months' living expenses tucked away in a high-interest account. If just contemplating this scenario worries you, it may be that even at this early stage you have to face up to the issue of whether you can handle the inevitable money worries that running a business involves. An interim solution could be to keep your day job and start the venture on a part-time basis, until it grows large enough to require and fund a full-time commitment. Alternatively, your partner could take on more work to bring in additional income during the critical start-up phase.

CASE STUDY: Making Your Way Through the Financial Minefield

PAUL, WHO HAD BEEN a financial controller with a large company, decided to set up a home business providing accounting services to other home businesses. Methodical by nature, he went through his own personal financial checklist before committing himself, but forgot to speak to his bank about borrowing for the venture until after he had registered his new business with the appropriate authorities.

Although Paul had been with the same bank for 20 years, the new business was refused an overdraft, and he had to extend his mortgage to get the money to launch the business and cover his first few months' operation until customers began to pay his invoices. He also had to pay more for his house and car insurance, as they were to be used for business purposes. Even accountants can be caught off guard by the complexities of setting up a home business!

▓ **BORROWING** You will need personal cash to develop your home base, as well as a computer, car, tools, and so on, to fund your outgoings until the business takes off. Arrange these things, whether through a bank loan or by refinancing your mortgage, while you are still employed and have a regular income. Be warned: banks and savings and loans are wary about lending to newly self-employed people. Borrowing to fund the business is done on the basis of a business plan (see pp. 88–101).

▓ **BUSINESS BANKING** Open at least one new checking account solely for your business (this does not have to be with your existing bank) for customers to pay into, for paying your suppliers, and for paying yourself a "salary." Ideally, choose an account that can be managed electronically, by phone or over the internet, so that you can access it at all times. Also consider setting up a high-interest business bank account into which you can regularly transfer surplus cash to cover quarterly sales tax, Social Security, and other payments.

▓ **OUTSTANDING LOANS** If you are making heavy monthly payments with sizable interest payments, consider borrowing enough to pay them off. It is usually much cheaper to borrow from a bank or savings and loans.

Plan your finances carefully before you launch your home business

▓ **MORTGAGE** Consider extending the repayment term of your mortgage to reduce your monthly outgoings.

▓ **HOME INSURANCE** Your existing home insurance is unlikely to cover business equipment or stock. Worse, in some cases if you start up a business from home without telling your insurer, it could invalidate your entire policy on the property and its contents. Be sure to tell your insurer about your plans; you may have to pay a higher premium, and even switch to another insurer, as some firms provide only basic coverage for home office equipment.

▓ **LIFE INSURANCE** Once you are out on your own, you have no employer coverage for life or health insurance. Ask an independent financial adviser to recommend the best deal for new policies giving sensible levels of coverage. As your health and well-being will be critical for the success of the new venture, consider the best level of personal accident and disability insurance you can afford.

▓ **SAVINGS** If you have savings plans, investigate whether you can "park" them without making further payments for a period of time. Alternatively, find out whether you can borrow against them on better terms than you can obtain elsewhere.

■ **PENSION** The best option is probably to transfer an employee pension into your own self-employed plan. Seek professional advice. You may be able to borrow against such a plan in the future.

■ **CREDIT CARDS** Apart from minimizing your personal credit card bills, the only sensible approach to them when you are also running a business is to repay them immediately to avoid any interest charges. This will put extra strain on meager cash flow, particularly if you have a large outstanding balance at present, but to do otherwise merely adds to your overall debt at a time of financial strain. You may also need the full borrowing powers of your cards for business purposes, such as to tide over a cash-flow gap. Be sure to maintain separate card accounts for business and personal expenditure.

Assessing Your Practical Skills

To be a successful home entrepreneur, you will need skills you probably never thought you had. Some people possess them instinctively but have never really used them in

TRAINING

Both the government and the private sector produce training and personal development packages and programs. Before committing to a course or program, ask to see testimonials from previous users to satisfy yourself that it is relevant to your needs; as yet there are few aimed directly at future home entrepreneurs. The best courses usually feature practical lectures and case studies from people who have done it before, instead of concentrating on theory.

Places to seek help and information include:

■ **BANKS** Most have specialized advice services for small business, although few specifically for home entrepreneurs, available in print and on the internet.

■ **GOVERNMENT ENTERPRISE AGENCIES/BUSINESS LINKS** These offer guides to training courses available in their specific area. Their online information services can also be extremely helpful.

■ **JOB CENTERS** As well as providing information on locally available training programs, job centers are also possible sources of funding, such as grants.

■ **LIBRARIES** These are useful for reference books, videos, and, increasingly, online services.

■ **BUSINESS SCHOOLS AND COLLEGES** Most offer a range of relevant programs, many available in the evenings.

■ **CHAMBERS OF COMMERCE** These organizations often maintain databases of local training courses available from both community colleges and private sector providers.

■ **YELLOW PAGES** These are good sources of information about companies that specialize in business training, particularly computer and internet courses.

Take an appropriate training course before you launch out on your own

employment, and so need to work on them. Others need to acquire them from scratch.

The key business skills you will need are:

- general management
- planning
- people management
- communication
- marketing
- sales
- financial management
- time management
- negotiating
- production control
- making decisions
- delegating.

Taking each of these points in turn, ask yourself the following questions:

- Do I have any experience in this area?
- If so, do I feel comfortable with handling these issues for my own business?
- If not, do I instinctively feel able to cope with them?

If your answer for any of these areas is two "Nos" out of three, you would be wise to seek relevant skills training before launching your venture. And if you feel uncertain about coping with more than half of these issues, you should once again reexamine your feelings about setting up a home-based business to see if you still feel confident about your future success.

Evaluating Your Personality Traits

For a number of years, business development experts have recognized that there is more to good managers than their skills, even though these may have been honed over the years to an extremely high standard. Equally important, in their view, is the personality of the individual, which dictates how those acquired skills are deployed.

There are various methods, mostly patented, of analyzing the personality to identify the main attitudes and the behavior patterns that result. These so-called psychological profiles are increasingly used by employers to find the most suitable people for their culture and work teams. Given that new home entrepreneurs will rely as much on their personalities as their skills to build a business, it is worth finding out where your basic strengths lie. Use the chart on p. 26 to help you.

LIBRARY RESEARCH
Having all the right skills for running your own business from home is essential. Local libraries are excellent sources of training information, supplying not only books for reference or borrowing but also videos.

WORK DEFINITIONS

The following definitions are useful for assessing the various activities which you will need to undertake within your business. They are taken from the Margerison-McCann Team Management Systems approach to organizational effectiveness developed by Dr. Charles Margerison and Dr. Dick McCann.

The Margerison-McCann types of work model displays nine key activities, or "types of work," identified as being essential to successful teamwork. If you are considering setting up on your own, no matter what your proposed type of business, you need to think about how you will address each area.

■ **ADVISING** Obtaining and disseminating information

■ **INNOVATING** Creating and experimenting with ideas

■ **PROMOTING** Searching for and persuading others of new opportunities

■ **DEVELOPING** Assessing and testing the applicability of new approaches

■ **ORGANIZING** Establishing and implementing ways of making things work

■ **PRODUCING** Operating established systems and practices on a regular basis

■ **INSPECTING** Checking and auditing systems to make sure everything is working

■ **MAINTAINING** Ensuring that standards and processes are upheld

■ **LINKING** Co-ordinating and integrating the work of the team

Margerison-McCann Types of Work Model

APPLYING THE MODEL

Consider which types of work will require the most input at the start of your venture, and how this bias might change as your business evolves. Next determine whether you are going to try to cover all these work areas yourself, or whether you will turn to a partner, close friend, or external support for help on an occasional basis.

By knowing at the outset where you need to direct your energies, you can identify what skills and attributes you are likely to need. However, remember that many people actually develop these attributes under the pressure of their new commitment. You may find that your skills and attributes change significantly as you climb the inevitable learning curve of personal development on the road to becoming a highly successful, all-round business achiever.

Finding the Right Business Idea

Some people have a clear idea from the outset about which kind of home-based business to start. Others do not have a clue, but just know that they want to do it. The best way to go about researching the best idea for you is to have a clear idea of the personal objectives

you wish to attain through running your own business. The most important goals include:

■ how much money you want to make

■ how hard you want to work

■ how long you want to work at it.

Set these objectives down on one side of a sheet of paper. Then think about the type of business that would feel most comfortable.

The chart at right is a guide to the most popular kinds of home-based businesses. There are hundreds of different ventures included under these broad descriptions. For example, many come already packaged by franchisors, and there is also a whole genre of business ideas that have evolved as a result of the internet.

One thing is for sure: if you have no fixed idea about what type of venture to try, there is no shortage of options. This makes it all the more important that you approach the task of researching these options methodically, based on your personal objectives as already defined.

If you now have a clearer idea of the type of business you want to pursue, set it down on your notepad across from your list of objectives. Then use that as your basis to assess the various options in that category.

THE MOST POPULAR TYPES OF HOME-BASED VENTURES

SERVICES	DESCRIPTION	EXAMPLES
PROFESSIONAL SERVICES	Qualified specialized services meeting a specific need	Consultants, accountants, architects, lawyers, trainers, fundraisers
PERSONAL SERVICES	Helping individuals with their daily lives	Childcare, landscaping, beauticians, hairstyling
BUSINESS SERVICES	Servicing local businesses with specialized needs	Consultants, maintenance, graphic design, computers, outsourcing
HOSPITALITY SERVICES	Accommodation, catering	Bed and breakfast, small restaurant
RETAILING	**DESCRIPTION**	**EXAMPLES**
IMPORT/EXPORT	Handling overseas buying and selling of goods	Craft goods, jewelry, books, watches, wine, clothing
CATALOG SALES	Direct marketing of specialty products	Beauty products, health products, baby clothes
DIRECT SALES	Acting as agent for branded-goods maker	Tupperware, lingerie, books, household products
MANUFACTURING	**DESCRIPTION**	**EXAMPLES**
CRAFT AND HOBBY PRODUCTS	Using your own skills to make individual items	Pottery, toys, jewelry, furniture, textiles, art
BUSINESS SERVICES	Supplying unique products for local businesses	Publishing, boardroom art, trade services, product design
CATERING SERVICES	Making food for retail or own sale	Jams, wine, buffets, cakes, business lunches

YOUR INTERESTS

Last of all, before beginning any in-depth research, think about your own interests and hobbies; you may have developed skills in areas that could serve you very well in a business context. Gardening, cooking, repairing bicycles, making clothes – even painting – are just a few of the hobbies that people have turned into successful home-based businesses.

Carrying Out Thorough Research

No matter how vague your thoughts might be at this stage, it is important that you investigate every avenue. You never know when a concept might suddenly appear to click into place, fitting your ambitions and skills like a glove. Done well, the research process can be fun and open your mind to lots of possibilities that you might not otherwise have considered. There are three elements to this research process:

■ evaluating your experience
■ doing a systematic search
■ asking around.

EVALUATING YOUR EXPERIENCE

Identify the skills and special knowledge you have acquired during past jobs and hobbies. Everyone accumulates and absorbs underlying abilities over the years that they often do not use or just take for granted. Research shows that this is the major source of business ideas, and not just for home entrepreneurs. So it is important to recall methodically the many things you have done over the years, starting with the subjects in which you did best at school or college, following with hobbies and sports, and finishing with jobs and skills or qualifications.

Set all these down on paper, listing what you liked about each, and add any business ideas

that occur as a direct result. You will probably be surprised by the extent of your activities and the range of skills that they required. You might just find one or more potential ventures staring you in the face at this stage of your preparation.

DOING A SYSTEMATIC SEARCH

Use the many sources of public information available about business opportunities. The most prolific and most easily accessible is now the internet, with its millions of pages of information. The problem is how to cut to the chase and find the websites that are most relevant to you. Some of the best are listed at the end of this book (see pp. 184–6). A useful method is to focus on sites from another country – for example, look at Europe or England to find out what new business ventures are being launched there. Many people have been highly successful at importing business concepts from elsewhere and then being the first to develop them in their own country.

There are also a growing number of entrepreneurial publications with lots of ideas available on the news stands. If you have a notion about a particular area or type of business, buy the relevant trade magazines and make a point of attending trade exhibitions and fairs. Specialized exhibitions for the SOHO market (Small Office, Home Office) are starting to appear. And do not forget your local library, which can be a goldmine of useful information.

Make sure that your home business idea will use your skills to the full

ASKING AROUND

Consulting friends and family, as well as local businesspeople, is an important part of the research process, yet it is quite alarming how often budding entrepreneurs miss this trick. There are two aspects to this type of research.

■ Find out what friends and family really think about your plans. The people who know you best can often surprise you with their insight into your potential. Often their opinions are

FIVE COMMON RESEARCH MISTAKES

1. Asking loaded questions that only confirm your own ideas.

2. Failing to speak to a range of potential customers.

3. Inexperience at getting the best out of the internet.

4. Ignoring trends that are about to undermine a favorite plan.

5. Letting your enthusiasm overwhelm negative feedback.

unexpected; they could perhaps be fundamentally negative about what they perceive as a risk-laden venture, which could cost you, and possibly them, dearly if it all goes wrong. They could come up with strong reasons why a particular idea is not, in fact, so bright. They may also reveal an inherent lack of faith in your ability to be successful at all. By themselves these messages might not be enough to convince you that you are barking up the wrong tree, but they should certainly make you think long and hard about whether your

dissatisfaction with your situation at work is pushing you in a direction that you are ill-equipped to handle. Equally, people close to you can be an excellent source of inspiration and ideas. If they like what you eventually decide to do, they could even be involved in your chosen enterprise or invest money – friends and family are often potential backers of new home-based businesses.

■ Talk to local businesspeople and find out how, in general, they are faring. You are unlikely to receive specific information, particularly if they perceive you are thinking of a venture which, for all they know, might offer competition. By the same token, it would be wise not to be too candid about your ideas if you have some at this stage. But do ask if there are specific services they need that are not being currently supplied locally.

Making a Good Business Match

At this stage of the preparation process, you should be ready to create a shortlist of suitable business ideas with which you feel comfortable. This involves matching your personal ambitions and skills with any

OPPORTUNITIES CHECKLIST		RESULTS
Is there some service or product that you and neighbors want but is not currently available?	☐Y ☐N	*If you answered "No" to three or more of these questions, you should think seriously about your ability to generate ideas that could work. Having an instinctive feel for business opportunities is a characteristic that will become very important once your venture is up and running.*
Have you talked to local businesses to find out if all their needs are being met?	☐Y ☐N	
Think of the last time you experienced really bad service. Could you do any better?	☐Y ☐N	
Is there any service you regularly use but which you feel is too expensive?	☐Y ☐N	
Can you recall a newspaper article about a business venture that you liked the sound of?	☐Y ☐N	
Think of what you most like doing. Could you make a business out of it?	☐Y ☐N	

particular interests you have that are likely to produce compatible business concepts. Research shows that if you fail to play to your strengths in this way, your chances of making a success of a venture are greatly reduced.

Decision Matrix

Making a decision matrix will help you to assess a shortlist of business ideas. It will allow you to match your work targets with your skills and interests. On one side of a sheet of paper, set down your personal targets for each key business area (as shown below). Then, along the

top of the sheet, note your strongest business-orientated skills and interests. Below each put a related business idea that appeals to you and makes the most of that skill or interest. Then work down each column of the matrix, thinking carefully about your specific targets and whether that particular business idea can help you to

Sample Matrix

The individual who drew up this matrix has four business possibilities each centered on a different skill or interest. The website designer idea scores highest by a narrow margin and the cycle repairs idea the lowest.

SAMPLE DECISION MATRIX

KEY BUSINESS AREA	TARGET	SKILL 1 MARKETING	SKILL 2 FINANCE	INTEREST 1 COMPUTING	INTEREST 2 CYCLING
		BUSINESS IDEA: AUTHOR OF MARKETING BOOKS	BUSINESS IDEA: FINANCIAL CONSULTANT	BUSINESS IDEA: WEBSITE DESIGNER	BUSINESS IDEA: CYCLE REPAIRS
FINANCIAL	Earn $50,000 a year	Possibly	Yes	Yes	No
WORKING HOURS	Work full-time	Yes	Yes	Yes	Yes
GROWTH POTENTIAL	The business has large growth potential	No	Possibly	Possibly	No
LEVEL OF STAFFING	None, at least not at the outset	Yes	Yes	Yes	Yes
MOBILITY	Spend half of each day away from home	No	Possibly	Possibly	Possibly
LEVEL OF INVESTMENT	Maximum of $5,000	Yes	Yes	No	Yes
LOCATION	Work in attic office	Yes	Possibly	Yes	No
MARKET SIZE	National	Yes	Possibly	Yes	No

achieve those targets. Mark the matrix with "Yes," "No," or "Possibly," as appropriate.

Carry out this exercise more than once, perhaps allowing a day or two to pass between each one. You may be surprised at how your perceptions can change as soon as you really start to think seriously about the sort of business you might like to embark upon.

Once you have completed the decision matrix, the business idea with the most positive answers is the one that shows the best match between your skills or interests and your personal business targets. The next step is to research that most promising business idea. How to go about this is covered in the next section (see pp. 56–60).

Paying Heed to Your Dreams

It is helpful to remember the importance of instinct and inspiration when making such a big, life-changing decision as starting your own home-based business. Setting down goals and analyzing your skill base is valuable, not least because it forces you to be precise about aspects of your personality and knowledge about which you may be vague. Studies show that people who go through this exercise are more likely to be successful than those who prefer an abstract, less precise approach to making such decisions. But everyone has their dreams, too!

Look for a business idea that you will enjoy and find satisfying

Dreams and flashes of ideas are often your subconscious striving to get a message through. In ways that we do not yet fully understand, the brain is capable of coming up with more answers than we usually allow.

As your shortlist of ideas starts to come together, take some time out to think more reflectively about this big adventure. Visualize yourself in your home office or workshop, working at a business, being the director, making decisions, clinching sales, and so on, and ask yourself the following questions:

◼ Does it feel natural?
◼ Will I enjoy working on my own?
◼ Will I be confident and comfortable making all the decisions?
◼ Will I miss the workplace, my colleagues, even the daily commute?
◼ How will my domestic setup be affected?
◼ How will the rest of the household react?

Once you start your own business from home, you will be working all the hours you have set aside for it – and almost certainly more when you first embark on the venture. You will be on a continual and rapid learning curve, and there will be precious little time for reflection. So, it's far better to dream those dreams now, before you commit yourself, and see if you can visualize yourself in the role of home entrepreneur. If not, it is certainly a sign that you still have some way to go to cross the mental watershed between employee and business owner.

THE E-REVOLUTION

An estimated 150 million Americans can access the internet from their home, and tens of millions more can get on the web at work or at school – and the numbers are rising rapidly. This means that about two out of three Americans can use this global computer network for work, education, and play. It is a similar picture worldwide. The world of business is undergoing the most fundamental revolution since the invention of the telephone. Home businesses have also been affected by the e-revolution, and this chapter outlines how the internet can be made to work for you.

Instant, inexpensive global communications have spawned a new generation of companies that operate on-line, bypassing traditional means of selling products and buying goods and services. These companies are operating with new processes and working faster; they describe a year in the internet market as equal to five or seven years in conventional business.

The consequent explosion in electronic communications, particularly email, has had dramatic effects. In 1999 data communications overtook voice traffic on BT's U.K. phone network. It is no surprise that the arrival of the internet offers more options for a home business, including:

- upgrading the marketing of an existing business (see case study on p. 35)
- radically rethinking an existing business (see case study on p. 37)
- trying a completely different type of on-line business (see case study on p. 39)

Make sure you understand how the internet works before you use it in business

What the Web Can Do for You

It is important to understand fully the internet phenomenon, even if you think that it is unlikely to feature in the planning and launch of your own enterprise. No one in business today can forecast long-term trends because of the rapid advances made in technology, so you

---

INTERNET TERMINOLOGY

BROWSER A software program that reads web pages.
DOMAIN NAME Your website's address on the internet.
EMAIL Electronic mail, sent from computer to computer, worldwide and instantly.
HTML The most widely used code by which software programmers lay out the content of a website.
INTERNET The global network of computers that exchanges data, images, and words.
ISDN (INTEGRATED SERVICES DIGITAL NETWORK) High-speed data transmission on phone lines.
ISP (INTERNET SERVICE PROVIDER) A branded company that connects you to the WWW via its own computers.

MODEM A box or card in your computer that connects your computer to the internet.
PORTAL A branded website that attracts you to click on and find a wide range of different products and services, such as Amazon.com and Yahoo.com.
SEARCH ENGINES Sophisticated computers that search the web automatically for requested information.
WEBSITE A computer file containing pages of specific information about an organization or topic.
WORLD WIDE WEB (WWW) The computer network that presents transmissions on your monitor in a usable format.

ADVANTAGES AND DISADVANTAGES OF A HOME INTERNET BUSINESS

ADVANTAGES	DISADVANTAGES
A web business can be launched quickly and cheaply in comparison with a conventional commercial venture.	You need to be reasonably computer-literate to operate a web business.
It is relatively easy to make your website appear just as professional as those of much larger competitors.	Putting up a website opens you to communication, some of it unwanted, from anywhere in the world.
You can use the internet to create a business that targets a tiny niche market.	It can be difficult to make buying decisions on the internet because of the wide range of options open to you.
Websites can be changed instantly if a new competitor appears on the scene or new products become available.	There are many internet scams, which sometimes makes it risky to distinguish one offer from another.
There is a huge amount of information available on the internet to help you plan your business.	Some clients may not want to do business over the internet and, for those, you have to offer viable alternatives.
There are numerous sites offering free downloads of useful software, including publishing and planning programs.	It is easy to become confused and overwhelmed by the sheer volume of information available on the internet.
Web businesses can market, sell, and buy goods and services all on-line without a scrap of paper being used.	Once you put up a website, everyone can see your business and quickly copy it.
You do not need to spend years training to be able to design and operate your own website.	Using the internet potentially exposes your computer to global viruses that can wipe out all your information in a second.
Technology allows your business to be mobile, whether you are in the car, hotel, or airport.	Personal relationships, which are critical to many business transactions, may suffer.

cannot assume that the internet will never play a part in your venture; indeed, the internet may become critical to your business's success. Using the internet for a start-up business can give you a huge advantage over existing conventional competitors. In addition, you need to recognize that there are very few businesses that cannot be effectively run and marketed on the web. This is what makes the internet so appropriate for home-based concerns.

In these days of highly sophisticated websites and advanced software programs that enable you to watch video and download music over the internet, the prospective home entrepreneur has a wide variety of options for going on-line. There are four basic stages of doing so with your own website:

1 Putting Your Marketing Literature on the Web
"Brochureware", as it is often called, can be achieved relatively easily and cheaply. You can either design the site yourself or employ a web designer to do it for you. This type of simple marketing ranges from a single page of basic information about your business, complete with contact email addresses and phone numbers, to a more sophisticated setup offering a number of choices of where to look for specific information. Remember that your "home" or front page should be

Remember you can access the internet almost anywhere and at any time

designed to download within seven seconds to prevent browsers from clicking away from your site out of boredom or irritation.

2 Creating an Interactive Website Here, visitors can make on-line inquiries and bookings, download your catalog onto their own computers, and work out schedules and timetables using your services. An interactive site will be more expensive, whether you host it on your own computer or – more popularly – buy the service from an Internet Service Provider (ISP), but it can dramatically increase business inquiries and sales.

3 Having Full E-commerce Ability With this, it is possible to sell your finished

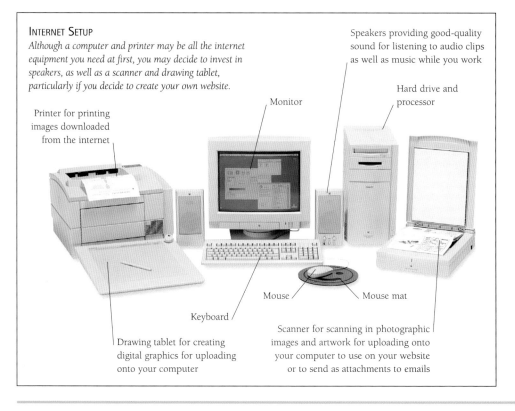

INTERNET SETUP
Although a computer and printer may be all the internet equipment you need at first, you may decide to invest in speakers, as well as a scanner and drawing tablet, particularly if you decide to create your own website.

Speakers providing good-quality sound for listening to audio clips as well as music while you work

Hard drive and processor

Printer for printing images downloaded from the internet

Monitor

Mouse

Mouse mat

Keyboard

Drawing tablet for creating digital graphics for uploading onto your computer

Scanner for scanning in photographic images and artwork for uploading onto your computer to use on your website or to send as attachments to emails

CASE STUDY: Upgrading the Marketing of an Existing Business

PENNY HAS BEEN running a home-based aromatherapy business for five years. Although the enterprise has been successful, she finds the cost of gaining new clients through advertising and leaflets quite expensive. After researching the web, she decides that it offers good opportunities for her to reach new clients at a lower cost, and persuades a friend who works in an internet design business to create a basic website consisting of two pages. She puts the site onto a new portal that is being launched by a local newspaper, and has an encouraging response, gaining a third more clients at a quarter of the cost normal advertising would have cost. She feels confident enough to recruit a part-time assistant, which she does through a notice on her website.

product or service with on-line financial transactions and also to source suppliers on-line. This is the stage where the internet's remarkable ability to cut swathes of cost out of existing business processes really comes into its own. There is no more time-consuming invoicing and checking and paying of bills. Combined with an on-line network of secretarial and financial support, the result can be a particularly efficient operation capable of achieving sales several times that of a paper-based business with similar resources.

4 HAVING A PURE ON-LINE E-BUSINESS
Internet companies aim to compete aggressively with existing "bricks-and-mortar" organizations. Amazon.com, priceline.com, and several banking and discount stock brokerages are examples of this pioneering type of business. Sophisticated data-tracking software enables such companies to identify the interests and habits of prospecitve buyers. This, in turn, allows them to e-market buyers with precisely tailored offerings in the ultimate one-to-one customer relationship.
While many home businesses will start their on-line life with brochureware websites, perhaps then moving on to running an interactive site, and later to having a full e-commerce setup, a growing number of start-up ventures operate as on-line companies from the outset. Popular markets for this type of operation include mail order and agencies or broking services.

Popular Home-based Web Businesses

There are a number of web businesses that are particularly well suited to being run from home. The following are probably the most well known:

▓ **PUBLISHING** The ready availability of publishing software, from page makeup to circulation lists, combined with on-line information transmission, makes it practical to produce even quite sophisticated publications from home, both as printed and electronic matter.

▓ **MAIL ORDER** Acting as an internet middleman, assembling printed and/or on-line catalogs of products and marketing them to a database of prospects. Effective at targeting niche markets that are too small for larger players.

▓ **FINANCIAL ADVISER** Using the internet as an information source for financial products, home-based advisers specialize in serving local investment and savings markets. They can deliver advice electronically, too.

▓ **SOFTWARE CONSULTANT** Working on-line to provide solutions to clients' computer problems, remote-accessing their programs, and analyzing their performance. Some specialists serve their niche markets around the world from home.

▓ **WINE SALES** Wine buffs handle the importing and marketing of fine wine on the

IS A HOME INTERNET BUSINESS RIGHT FOR YOU?   RESULTS

Question	Y	N
Are you skilled enough working with computers that you could fix a software problem?	☐Y	☐N
Do you track the progress of on-line businesses as an observer or investor?	☐Y	☐N
Are you able to surf the web, to research other businesses producing work of interest in your area or market?	☐Y	☐N
Do you enjoy email contact with business associates as well as with friends?	☐Y	☐N
Have you bought products over the web?	☐Y	☐N
Are you capable of forming on-line working relationships with people whom you will probably never meet?	☐Y	☐N
Do you have a flexible attitude to working hours?	☐Y	☐N
Can you communicate well via the keyboard?	☐Y	☐N
Could you manage your own website?	☐Y	☐N
Are you disciplined and well organized?	☐Y	☐N

If you can answer "Yes" to seven or more of these questions without thinking about the issues for more than a few seconds, you have the basic mind-set required to operate happily on-line. If you also have the right attitude to run a business – determined, assertive, focused – you have the mental ammunition to turn ambition into reality!

internet, maintaining an on-line list, and receiving payment over web-based financial services. They also carry out marketing and organize delivery on-line.

■ **LEGAL SERVICES** Home-based lawyers can consult and provide documentation, from wills to contracts, through the internet. They maintain a database of basic documents, which they can then personalize according to the needs of their clients.

■ **MARKET RESEARCH** Ready availability of databases around the world makes it feasible to provide a custom research service from home for business clients. Specialized experts can offer this service globally, adding regular emails and newsletters.

■ **FREELANCE** Covers a wide range of professional services, based on a specific skill and good contacts in the relevant industry. The publishing industry in particular relies on a good network of artists, cartoonists, editors, photographers, and so on.

■ **ACCOUNTING AND BOOKKEEPING** Using popular accounting and spreadsheet programs available on the internet, accountants and bookkeepers handle paperwork for private clients and small businesses, turning their documentation into regular statements. They also complete tax returns and submit them on-line.

■ **VIRTUAL ASSISTANT** Providing phone-answering, secretarial, and organizing services for busy people and small businesses, using phone and email for normal work and the internet for research and documentation. Can handle a number of clients anywhere in the world.

Keeping Up with the Internet Revolution

The internet revolution will continue to change the way we do business, as well as the way we live, for years to come. Experts are all agreed on that, but they cannot agree on what the situation will be like in, say, three years' time, let alone a decade away.

CASE STUDY: Radically Rethinking an Existing Business

DAN RESTORES AND SELLS classic cars, working from a garage and workshop at his rural home. His business is growing but he finds sourcing spare parts increasingly time-consuming. After analyzing his purchasing patterns, he discovers that he buys 90 percent of his parts from only three suppliers. He persuades them to put their catalogs on the internet, together with an on-line ordering system offering rapid despatch. At the same time he establishes a website that carries photographs of the cars and a list of vehicles available for sale. This allows Dan to do his administration in the evenings, leaving the days free for building and selling cars. After three months Dan finds that he has increased his turnover by 20 percent and that his website is attracting people interested in selling their cars to him for restoration.

While you may at the present time be thinking of starting a basic on-line business from home by establishing a brochureware-type website, it is useful to know where technology is heading. With that knowledge you can be more confident about when to upgrade your site, take advantage of new cost-effective processes, and stay ahead of competitors or react to their moves.

There is a wide range of information sources available to help keep you up to speed on the technology and the business processes relating to e-business. You should be able to find companies in your area that specialize in software to enable your business to run electronically, so that you can buy supplies, sell your products, and do your recruitment and administration – all on-line. These companies will be eager to tell you how they could help your venture cut costs, and run faster and more efficiently. In addition, they will be able to build in attractive features such as the ability to show streaming video footage (downloading video from a website to your computer). If you are unsure about handling particular kinds of software and are unwilling to employ anyone to explain operating procedures or figure out any problems, there are training courses available. One thing is certain: if you go down the e-business route at the outset of your business, you will have to keep abreast of advances in technology so that you can take advantage of new software that will allow you to give better service to customers, cut costs, or – ideally – do both.

The eight main business opportunities offered by the on-line revolution are:

KEEPING ACCOUNTS

Accounting and bookkeeping are two professions that can be pursued effectively from home. They have also benefited enormously from the e-revolution, taking advantage of the many popular accounting and spreadsheets available on-line.

■ **Attracting Customers** No longer is marketing to prospective buyers a hit-and-miss affair. The arrival of enormous databases and profiling software means that not only can target customers be identified precisely, but their likely needs can also be anticipated. A flow of suitable new customers can also be guaranteed through tapping into other websites.

■ **Informing Customers** Once prospective buyers have arrived at a website, they need to be able to see well-presented and relevant information that will persuade them to stay on the site and buy. Web content software enables complex product lines to be displayed simply and clearly, so that browsers can quickly gain a picture of exactly what is available.

■ **Customizing the Product** Once a customer has been persuaded to enter his or her requirements, configuration programs construct a product or service that precisely meets their needs. At the same time the programs check whether the components are actually in stock and on which day the item can be delivered.

■ **Transaction** Once the product or service is defined and available, the price has to be negotiated and agreed. Market-making software enables deals to be done through auction, exchange, and even barter in addition to the provision of good old cash.

■ **Payment** If money is to change hands, this, too, can be done instantly on-line in a variety of ways through secure transmission channels. Web-based credit can be obtained

Personal Issues to Consider Before Working with the Internet

Attitudes		Skills	
Do you feel comfortable and confident working with computers?	You should feel totally at ease with your home computer; it is your most important work tool.	Are you familiar with the main types of software programs?	You should be skilled with word processing, spreadsheet, and graphic design programs.
Do you use the internet now?	You should have a range of experience in on-line information-gathering and making purchases.	Have you used email for business purposes before?	Email should become your preferred form of communication, including document transmission.
Do you believe in the internet as a business opportunity?	You need to be aware of the types of ventures being established on the internet – and how they work.	Can you use peripheral equipment, such as printers and scanners?	You should be able to scan images and insert them into documents for printing and binding.
Can you handle the process of working on-line day in, day out?	It should seem natural to spend most of each day at the computer dealing with clients whom you never meet.	Can you fix computer system problems?	You should be able to analyze the cause of most basic network problems and fix them yourself.

using underwriting software. It is now often easier to secure credit through the internet than it is from your traditional bank.

- **SUPPORT** Once the transaction has taken place, customer-interaction software swings into action to provide information on the progress of the order, to resolve any outstanding problems, and to see if any other sales are possible. On-line tracking of order progress is now routine.

- **DELIVERY** Fulfillment and delivery systems ensure that the goods not only arrive at the customer's premises on time and in proper working order, but that any installation requirements are met. Often it will take months after actual delivery to ensure that systems are working properly.

- **PERSONALIZATION** Now that a new customer has been acquired, data-mining and filtering software analyzes every scrap of information, including personal behavior patterns, to ensure that the next time the customer logs on to the website his or her experience will be improved, and that another purchase is likely to be made.

Thinking of Selling Your Business?

It is one thing starting an internet-based business from home and another knowing what to do with it, apart from improving its performance and increasing profits. The business climate today is one in which companies are bought and sold with bewildering speed as managements strive to build strong positions in markets and capture the latest technology. Some on-line businesses end up being bought before they have achieved profit or even secured any customers.

While the motivation of many people in starting a home business is to provide a secure means of earning a living under their own control, they also have the option of establishing a venture with the specific objective of selling it. The end result could be a healthy capital sum which, after taxes, is enough to provide for you and your dependents into retirement.

If selling your business is an appealing option, consider the following three key issues:

CASE STUDY: Trying a Different Type of On-line Business

SUZY WORKED FOR a consumer organization, dealing with complaints from the public about shoddy goods and poor service; but after becoming increasingly frustrated with her working conditions she decided to set up on her own at home. Through the internet she researched similar private sector businesses and found a formula for establishing an on-line complaints venture. She also checked whether there was such a service already in existence in her region; there was not. Once her own website was up and running, people throughout the country began to email Suzy with their complaints. Suzy pursues these through the websites of the relevant companies and government departments, using phone calls and faxes as backup, where necessary. After six months she has handled 40 cases, with a success rate of over 50 percent. This unusual on-line service has brought Suzy a lot of press coverage, which, in turn, brings in more business.

■ Is your prospective business based on unique technology?

■ Is the venture aimed at a "new economy" market that is still developing?

■ Is this market primarily that of other companies rather than consumers?

If the answers to these three questions is "Yes," you may be able to create a business with the specific objective of selling it in a year or two's time. If you have no previous experience of this scenario, seek early advice when planning the launch of your venture from a lawyer or accountant, probably with a large city-based firm with a track record of such deals. You could also attend regular networking sessions for e-commerce entrepreneurs. First Tuesday (www.firsttuesday.com) is probably the largest of these on-line organizations. It provides an

FACT FILE

There are two types of likely purchasers for your business: other companies or professional investors. The former will look for products or services to reinforce their offerings, perhaps with a strong brand behind them, together with a good customer list. The latter will be more interested in a good, sound business idea, effective management, and a healthy financial performance.

entrepreneurs' website and email service, and acts as a forum for people to meet the first Tuesday of every month and exchange contacts, share information, and discuss investment.

REGISTERING YOUR DOMAIN NAME

If you have your own website, you will need to choose a domain name, which is the first part of a website address. You must register this name with ICANN (Internet Corporation for Assigned Names and Numbers) before you have the legal right to use it.

■ It is important to choose the best name to describe your business, but on the internet this is not easy. At the end of 2000 there were more than eight million sites on-line around the world, and over 18 million registered domain names. The obvious names were registered in the mid-1990s before most of us had even heard of the internet.

■ Choose a name that can also be used for everything else related to the venture: business name, trademark, bank account, product or service name, as well as your domain name.

■ A full internet address always ends with a suffix describing the type of organization and the country where it is registered. The most popular is .com. Originally created to describe a business, it is now used almost

exclusively by US companies. Other widely used suffixes are .net and .org, which are both open to anyone.

■ To make it easier to find the right name for your venture, so-called second-level domain names are now available to give a more prosaic description of purpose. They are: .firm, .shop, .web, .arts, .rec, .info, and .nom.

■ You can register your domain name through a registry service, for which there may be both initial and recurring charges. You can find a registry service on most portals, such as AOL, Yahoo, MSN bCentral, about.com, or office.com, or you can find one at icann.org. Type in your preferred name to see if it is available. If it is available, register it in your name immediately! If it is not, log on to www.betterwhois.com to see who is the registered holder. You may find that it is worthwhile contacting the holder to find out if they are genuinely using the name for business or whether they are hoping for a sale. It may be possible to use the name under an agreement, or to create a link between their website and yours.

DECIDING THE SCALE OF YOUR INTERNET VENTURE

ISSUES	SIMPLE VENTURE	COMPLEX VENTURE
DETERMINING THE LEVEL OF SOPHISTICATION OF YOUR ON-LINE BUSINESS	Set up a basic marketing "brochureware" site listing all your products.	Establish an integrated e-commerce site, with on-line payment facilities.
DESIGNING AND DEVELOPING YOUR WEBSITE	Buy inexpensive software to design the site yourself.	Use a major ISP with comparable experience in similar projects.
CREATING THE CONTENT OF THE PAGES OF THE SITE	Write up a lively description of your products with photos.	Develop streaming video and audio to make it stand out.
OBTAINING A DOMAIN NAME THAT WILL ATTRACT CUSTOMERS	Select an available name closest to the one you really like.	Research the best name and buy it if it is already registered.
PROMOTING THE SITE TO THE WEB WORLD	Register your site with some of the major search engines.	Use website registers and software to link with hundreds of search engines.
CREATING AN EFFECTIVE ON-LINE MARKETING CAMPAIGN	Email as many friends as possible about your new site.	Offer incentives to encourage registrations, then send voice messages to those who register.

MANAGING YOUR TIME ALONE

You have almost completed the essential preparation processes for deciding which home business to launch. Before you make any firm commitments, though, think about how you will manage your time. After all, this will probably be a totally new experience, and resources are likely to be scarce. Organization is the key to success, and you will need to be in full control of your affairs if you are to manage a thriving business without your home life suffering. This chapter outlines a series of techniques and tips to help you become an organized business manager.

Picture the scene: you are six months into your new life as a home entrepreneur and everything seems to be going reasonably well. You are working all the hours you used to put in for an employer, sometimes more, and still there are pressing deadlines for the completion of various projects and proposals. But, it is a beautiful day, the dog is desperate for a walk, and you would love a swim. What do you do?

The right answer is to reward yourself with a nice break, so that you can return refreshed to your desk or workbench later in the day. After all, what is the point of going to all the trouble of establishing a home business if you cannot exercise more freedom over what you do, whenever you like?

Such freedom does not come easily, however. Like most things in life it has to be paid for, and in this case the price is organizing your business life so that you make the most of the only real commodity you have: time.

The Importance of Personal Discipline

Many home entrepreneurs undergo a substantial change in attitude once they start their own business. The sheer pressure of work and the necessity of meeting deadlines force them to become quite ruthless about not wasting time and more focused on what they

CASE STUDY: Switching from Notebook to Palmtop

CORINNE HAD ALWAYS used wire-bound notebooks to jot down everything of significance in her business life. But once she started her own venture the amount of information that she had to record increased dramatically, and she realized that something much more sophisticated than pen and paper was required to keep her on top of her business affairs. Because Corinne liked to be organized and also enjoyed working with computers, she decided to buy a palmtop computer to look after her calendar, contacts list, notes, and financial accounts. After spending two hours a day for a week practicing the computer's inputting process using a plastic stylus, she was able to switch from notebooks to this electronic form of organization. Corinne reports that using the palmtop has made her more efficient and given her an extra hour a day of productivity.

MAKING A DATE
Keeping an up-to-date business planner, whether the old-fashioned paper kind or a state-of-the-art palmtop computer, is as important to the home entrepreneur as it is to the chief executive of a global corporation.

need to do and by when. The big difference is that, previously, when in employment, they were used to a corporate support structure of secretaries and personal assistants, as well as various departments, such as personnel and computer support, which took care of the administrative and technical details.

Once you work for yourself at home, the buck for everything stops right at your desk, which is why it is important to absorb and apply new organizational principles. Anyone can become better organized, even the most chaotically disorganized among us.

WORK IN A WAY THAT SUITS YOU

Decide when you work best. When are you at your sharpest, capable of keeping lots of different balls in the air at once, at the same time making crisp decisions and operating at your persuasive best with potential customers?

Most people know themselves well enough to be able to identify these crucial high-performance periods in their working days. For many it is the period between ten and 11

DOS AND DON'TS OF ORGANIZATION

✓ Do manage paperwork ruthlessly.

✓ Do make only essential phone calls.

✓ Do establish a process for identifying and listing priority tasks.

✓ Do most of your newspaper and magazine reading in your spare time.

✓ Do make proper use of filing cabinets.

✓ Do use time-saving systems, such as buying your stationery on-line.

✗ Don't waste time chatting on the phone.

✗ Don't work on tough jobs at less productive times of the day, such as straight after lunch or at the end of a long and tiring task.

✗ Don't feel that you have to do all the routine administration yourself if you can afford to outsource the work.

✗ Don't forget to take regular breaks and to get exercise.

o'clock in the morning when they are still feeling fresh from a good night's sleep; for others it is dawn; and for probably a minority it is the middle of the night. It is important to acknowledge the existence of these energy patterns and to allocate your prime daily tasks accordingly. For example, if you have a difficult proposal to prepare for a demanding customer and your peak energy period is dawn, then get up early and ignore all distractions while you work through the project. The end result will be of a much higher caliber.

Some people hate noise of any kind while they are working, while others positively thrive on listening to their favorite music as they concentrate on projects. If you are among the latter, then consider installing a good-quality stereo in your home office or workshop. After all, you will be working on your own – at least until the business grows large enough for you to need assistance – so why not create the ideal working environment for yourself? Choice of music is, of course, personal, although some say that the smoother, softer rhythms of classical and chamber music are conducive to reflective work, while rock music is better if you have a busy, active day ahead working on a number of different projects all at once.

FIT FOR WORK?

Health and fitness should matter a lot to busy business people. Being in good physical shape gives you more energy to meet challenges and helps you to think more quickly and be more productive (see also pp. 154–6). But, as ever, the issue is how to fit in regular exercise routines with a hectic work schedule. The obvious first answer is to plan them into your

KEEPING FIT
A healthy body helps keep the mind sharp for business. Regular exercise, such as swimming, should be made an intrinsic part of your working week.

weekly planner, whether it is a bike ride or jog around the neighborhood or a visit to a local gym or swimming pool. The second trick is to find a training partner for a regular session, a commitment that should prevent you from reneging under pressure of business. And the third solution is to get out of bed half an hour earlier for a workout before heading down to the desk or workbench.

Time Management Techniques

According to the experts, controlling the use of your time is the single most effective way of maximizing your personal productivity. It is all too easy, when running a business venture, to get caught up in detailed administration to the point where the big issues are not being addressed. Then deadlines start to be missed, customers are perhaps let down through late delivery, and, before you know it, your reputation suffers and you find it difficult to make new sales. Suddenly, your precious business is in danger – but it is all very avoidable if you manage your time more effectively. The key issues are to:

■ plan ahead to make the most of your days
■ control the way you spend your time working
■ manage the amount of time you spend communicating by phone, letter, and email
■ contract out routine work

PLANNING PRIORITIES

There are no substitutes for lists in helping you to prioritize what has to be done each day. Running a business involves a variety of tasks of different importance to the overall objective of building a profitable and satisfying venture. Compiling a weekly list of things to be done, from which a daily list can be drawn up, is

Plan your working days in advance for maximum productivity

TIME SAVER
Once you have a established a work routine, keep a daily log for a couple of weeks. Break the day down into 30-minute segments, and analyze what you do and for how long. Most people find they spend too much time communicating through phone and email or fiddling with administrative jobs, and not enough time doing their basic work. With your survey, you can identify the time-wasting parts of your day and tackle them.

essential to separate the important wheat from the detailed chaff. It is also vital in avoiding the feeling that is familiar to many home entrepreneurs: being overwhelmed by work and not knowing where to start tackling it all.

It is worth sitting down at the start of each week to draw up a list of tasks that must be done during the next week. If you do this on a Sunday evening, it will give you a flying start for the following day. Some of the tasks on your list, probably to do with longer-term projects, will be hanging over from the previous week, while others will be "must-dos."

Once your list is complete, prioritize the tasks into the following three categories:

1 ESSENTIAL Apart from projects with an imminent deadline, which are clearly urgent, include anything to do with meeting your customers' requirements and sales development. Successful entrepreneurs focus on keeping their customers happy, and seeking ways to push the business forward.

2 ROUTINE These are the "day-job" tasks involved in actually creating and delivering your service or product.

3 BIG ISSUES Opportunities, ideas, and challenges occur all the time to the entrepreneur. It is worth actually setting aside time to think about these seriously; otherwise they will remain just thoughts, rather than actions, which could be decisive in moving your venture up to a new level of performance and profitability.

Be ruthless when you embark on this prioritizing process, particularly when you draw up the list of "Essential" tasks. Ask yourself whether each item is really essential, or whether it will keep for another week. You may find it surprising how many nonessential jobs there are on your list, which in turn will help you focus attention on the crucial tasks.

It may be worth investing in one of the business planners on the market. Usually available in bound folders, they comprise daily pages, "To do" sections, project management sheets, and other scheduling items. Some entrepreneurs run their entire lives from such planners; others use personal electronic organizers such as palmtop computers; while there are those who prefer to use good old-fashioned notebooks and engagement calendars. Whatever works for you is best.

CONTROLLING YOUR DAY

There is no point in drawing up lists unless you are able to control the way you do things. This means creating a structure for your working day and sticking to it, in precisely the same way that you would if you were working in an office with lots of other people.

Running a home business often means that you are alone during the day and vulnerable to all kinds of distractions, such as wandering through to the kitchen to make a cup of coffee, selecting some music to play on the stereo, buying a newspaper…. The list goes on. If you give in to such distractions, your precious time will simply disappear.

With the prioritized task list that you have created, assign jobs to each day, working in blocks of an hour or whatever time component

Employ people to do your routine work if you are too busy to do it yourself

makes sense for your business. Leave enough time for communications, but allow for interruptions, and take at least two 20-minute breaks each day, which will refresh you both physically and mentally. Last of all, at the end of each day, briefly review progress on the week's list and adjust your priorities for the next day accordingly.

Running a home business is no different from working at a regular job. Aim to keep sensible hours, avoid distractions, and stay focused on the key tasks.

MANAGING COMMUNICATION

Communication is such a vital part of business that it is easy to spend too much time talking and writing to other people. Phone calls have a habit of interrupting you in the middle of a major project, and it is tempting to check your email constantly for new messages. Managing your communications effectively is vital, and the first priority is to assign specific times each day for dealing with the phone, email, and correspondence (see right).

CONTRACTING OUT

If you expect to be very busy once you launch your new business, consider subcontracting routine work to specialists – the cost may well be outweighed by the extra benefit to your business as you focus more of your time on producing top-quality work and keeping customers happy.

Examples of well-established specialist services include:

■ **BOOKKEEPERS** They will provide monthly statements and keep track of your cash flow. You should always keep an eye on the accounts, too.

■ **ACCOUNTANTS** They will do the above as well as produce annual statements and handle tax returns.

■ **SECRETARIAL SERVICES** These services cover the complete secretarial spectrum, from handling your correspondence to

Suggestions for Managing Communications Effectively

Type	Suggestion
Telephone	■ Use an answering machine or voice-mail service to take messages, rather than be at the mercy of incoming calls. Leave a short greeting asking callers for a detailed message, so that you are prepared for the return call. ■ Make or return calls during a set block of time, either first thing or late afternoon, when people are most likely to be at their desks. ■ Restrict your time on each call. Once the main business has been dealt with, politely finish the conversation. ■ Buy a speaker phone or headset, so that you can do other work while making calls. ■ Do manual work such as signing letters, stuffing envelopes, assembling reports, and so on while you are on the phone. ■ If you are away from the office a great deal, use a mobile phone with a headset to make and receive calls while traveling. ■ When you go away for a lengthy period, leave a message on your answering service asking callers to phone you on your return. This will cut down the message backlog.
Mail	■ Establish three in-trays for your mail, labeled "Essential," "Routine," and "Big Issues," or whatever prioritization codes are appropriate for you. ■ Distribute your daily mail between these trays as soon as you receive it, and act accordingly. ■ Answer letters by phone or email – it is quicker. ■ Every week at a set time – perhaps Friday afternoon – check each tray to make sure that nothing important has been ignored. ■ If you are going away, take unanswered mail with you and compose your replies while traveling, ready for inputting into your computer on your return.
Email	■ Check your inbox no more than twice a day – when you start work and at the end of the day – unless you are in the middle of a dialogue that requires immediate action. ■ Deal immediately with messages that require a quick response. ■ File less urgent messages in their relevant folders according to customer, project, or other appropriate category. ■ Establish an action folder for messages requiring a response within, say, a week. ■ Establish another folder for messages you have sent that requested action. ■ Print out messages and attached files that require more leisurely consideration. Set aside time later for reading them. ■ If you are not proficient in using a keyboard, take a class; it will speed up productivity. ■ Use email as an inexpensive, instant way of marketing. ■ Observe "e-tiquette," using clear, polite language in your messages.

answering the telephone and dealing with general office administration. Sometimes these services may be organized by a "virtual personal assistant," who is based hundreds of miles away and stays in touch by phone, fax, and email.

■ **REPORT WRITERS** They will take your scribblings and transform them into a professional document, incorporating graphics where appropriate.

■ **PROFESSIONAL ORGANIZERS** These are the latest recruits to the burgeoning ranks of home business subcontractors. They are consultants who will visit your home and carry out a review and reorganization of your desk, paperwork, and filing systems. They will recommend processes for keeping your business organized, keeping on top of your correspondence, and, above all, maintaining a clear desktop. If you find it impossible to keep track of paperwork, it may be worth calling in such an expert.

PAPER MANAGEMENT

Of all the challenges facing the new home entrepreneur, managing the tide of paperwork that will be produced by a business venture is one of the toughest – unless, that is, you are one of those superorganized people who always has a clear desk and immaculate filing

EMPLOYING A SECRETARY
If you expect to be inundated with administrative work, consider employing a secretary. This will allow you to concentrate your efforts and expertise on building up the business and fulfilling your customers' needs.

cabinets. However, research shows that over 90 percent of people in business have trouble coping with the constant flow of paper and information into and out of their office or desktop. In U.S. corporate offices, for example, employees spend an average of 100 hours a year looking for lost paperwork! Tax authorities report that one of the major excuses for not filing tax returns on time is that the necessary papers have been lost.

Forecasts made a few years ago about the computer revolution leading to the paperless office have been decisively proven untrue. Inexpensive printers, faxes, and email have caused the opposite problem, and it is now entirely possible to lose control of your business and, indeed, your personal affairs, amid a mountain of paperwork in which you simply cannot find what you need.

The major sources of paperwork for the home business entrepreneur are:

■ **BUREAUCRACY** The government machine churns out forms and questionnaires on issues from health and safety to social security and tax registration.

■ **MEDIA** You are likely to find yourself perusing a growing volume of business press, from newspapers and magazines to specialist newsletters, generating a flood of information that has to be managed.

STEMMING THE PAPERWORK TIDE

To prevent your new venture from being submerged by a relentless tide of paperwork, there are some important basic principles you should consider implementing at the same time as you are setting up the business. These are to:

1 Review all paperwork as soon as it appears, from whatever source.

2 Decide on what action to take immediately, rather than leaving papers piled on a corner of your desk.

3 Recognize that you have only three options for dealing with any paperwork: throwing it away, acting on it, and filing it for future reference.

THROW IT AWAY Be ruthless about trashing material you know that you will not need. Adopt a similar approach for unsolicited material, which is unlikely to ever be relevant to your needs, and for items of such marginal interest that you are unlikely to want to refer to them. If you are in doubt about anything, leave it in a pending file for a week, then review it. You will almost certainly end up throwing it away!

ACT ON IT Set up an action file to keep material that you know you need to do something about, such as responding to invitations, thanking clients for their business once the work has been completed, or writing the first draft of a proposal document.

FILE IT Establish a filing system that covers each client, central administration issues such as stationery orders, tax receipts, bank details, and general reference material.

4 Create a process for finding relevant information among the flood of media that will cross your desk and computer screen. If it is a newspaper, quickly scan the headlines and cut out anything interesting for filing or action; if it is a magazine, scan the contents and cut out or photocopy the relevant pages. Internet information and emails can either be printed out and filed, or transferred to an appropriate folder in your documents file on your computer.

TRASH IT!
Paperwork is the scourge of many home-based businesses. Keep a large trash can or recycle bin at the side of your desk to encourage you to throw away unwanted material.

■ **UNSOLICITED MARKETING MATERIAL** As soon as your name appears on the databases of phone companies, banks, and business equipment suppliers, you can be sure to receive an ever-increasing volume of unrequested mail shots, brochures, junk faxes, and other literature from people eager to sell you things.

■ **YOUR BUSINESS** Finally, there is the unavoidable correspondence, reports, and administration material generated by you and your business in the course of providing your service or product!

DOS AND DON'TS OF PAPERWORK

✓ Do act immediately when paper comes into your home office, otherwise the paper mountain will inevitably begin to grow.

✓ Do use one notebook or planner to keep track of everything that happens, so you will always have a source of referral for information, phone numbers, and so on.

✓ Do be ruthless in throwing away or recycling letters, magazines, old reports, and other documents, unless you are firmly convinced you will need them again.

✓ Do set aside time in your planner every week – or, at worst, every month – to go through outstanding piles of paper to prevent mountains of it from accumulating.

✗ Don't use those ubiquitous yellow stickers to leave messages all over your correspondence, files, computer monitor, and desktop; they are messy and do not encourage action.

✗ Don't be stingy with filing space when establishing your home office, because as your business grows so too will your need to store paperwork.

✗ Don't allow your desk to become a refuge for paper awaiting action, filing, or simply a decision on what to do about it.

✗ Don't print out all your emails unless you really need to, as you then have the job of deciding what to do with them.

A NEAT DESK

Once you have selected your office desk, whether a new, custom-built work surface with a drawer unit or the corner of the kitchen table, be sure to make the most of it – and that means keeping that work space as free as possible for work, rather than as storage for piles of paper and other clutter.

If you have drawers in your desk, put your ancillary stationery equipment, such as staplers, rulers, and floppy disks, out of sight in them. If you have one, use a desk organizer.

Think about adding a side table to your office layout for reports, newspapers, and magazines awaiting reading, and other non-critical paperwork.

Buy a big trash can or recycle bin. Home entrepreneurs consistently underestimate the amount of paper refuse they will generate and the unsolicited material they will receive – and having a big bin encourages you to throw material away instead of keeping it.

CRISIS ACTION PLAN

Despite your best efforts, it is entirely possible that after a few months of running your business you will end up with the home entrepreneur's classic nightmare: a desk piled high with paper, equipment, and knick-knacks, and no place actually to do your work. To compound the situation, the floor may be

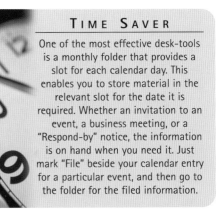

TIME SAVER

One of the most effective desk-tools is a monthly folder that provides a slot for each calendar day. This enables you to store material in the relevant slot for the date it is required. Whether an invitation to an event, a business meeting, or a "Respond-by" notice, the information is on hand when you need it. Just mark "File" beside your calendar entry for a particular event, and then go to the folder for the filed information.

SURVIVING THE PAPERWORK

Paperwork needs to be controlled on a regular basis. Putting off doing your filing is counterproductive and serves only to demoralize and make you less efficient.

strewn with old magazines and newspapers, reports and documents awaiting filing. There is only one thing to do: set aside a substantial chunk of time, either half a day at the outset or at least an hour a day for a week, and start to clear up the mess as follows:

1. Make a decent working space for yourself on your desk. If you have allowed ornaments, pictures, and stationery equipment to encroach upon it, move them to a side table, desk drawer, or window ledge. If you cannot face throwing away old reports, catalogs, binders, and so on, find a bookshelf for them. Ideally, if you have the wall space, erect shelving to accommodate what is certain to be a heavy load of

Keep your desk clear of unnecessary papers, to give you plenty of space to work

documentation. Be ruthless in getting rid of old material. It is highly unlikely that you will ever need it again.

2. Reestablish control over your desktop by ensuring that your filing system is adequate for the task and that you know where everything is.

3. Ensure that you have the most frequently used materials and items on hand – planner, notepad, sticky notes, stapler, and so on – beside the phone and your computer keyboard, leaving you enough room to spread out documents for reading.

4. Tackle any remaining piles of paper and sort them out according to the principles outlined above.

5. Establish a daily routine for dealing with new paperwork. As soon as any appears, move it to the relevant destination – trash/ recycle, act on it, or file for reference (see p. 49). Never allow it to accumulate.

TAKING
the plunge

Now that you have decided on the type of home business that you would like to start, and thought about some of the substantial issues involved in making this move, it is time to take decisive steps. If you are not already clear about which market to enter, this section offers some of the more popular options, then guides you through all the basic processes involved in running a business, from doing market research to handling cash flow. Finally, it provides a comprehensive checklist enabling you to create a detailed business plan.

GETTING INTO THE RIGHT BUSINESS

You may have left your last job with the specific purpose of establishing a certain type of business. But if you did not, now is the time to choose your venture. Even if you have already narrowed down your list of options, you will still need to research each one to ensure you make an informed decision. This chapter details some of the most innovative home businesses and suggests some basic research processes that will enable you to find out what the opportunities are likely to be in your preferred market.

To start with, it is important to recognize that the world of business is changing very rapidly under the twin pressures of the internet and global competition. Every business, no matter how small or how local, will be affected in some way by these pressures. What this means for the new home entrepreneur is that there is more opportunity! Existing businesses may not have recognized certain trends, giving you the chance to create a different type of venture aimed at the same market. And new types of business are springing up all the time, some completely fresh and some imported from elsewhere in the country or, indeed, the world.

Research your chosen option thoroughly before going ahead

NEW BUSINESS CONCEPTS

One such example of a relatively new type of business is car valeting, which five years ago was virtually unknown and now is becoming increasingly popular. All it takes is a driveway, if you are operating from home, or a van to take the washing and polishing equipment to the customer's house or office, if you are going to them.

Other examples of new business concepts include:

■ **DISPUTE MEDIATION** Trained people, often with a law degree, settle civil conflicts between individuals or organizations without the parties concerned having to go to court and suffer the associated high costs and delays.

CASE STUDY: Finding a Business Opportunity

IONA, A FORMER home economics teacher, was in between jobs and on the lookout for a business opportunity. While at her local supermarket, she watched harassed businesspeople and parents with children diving into the store in the evenings to stock up when, clearly, they would rather be elsewhere. She then decided to place an ad in her local newspaper offering a personal shopping service, and was very surprised by the number of replies she received. She gave herself a two-week trial doing people's shopping for a fixed fee, and discovered how easy it was to assemble combined shopping lists, so that she could carry out four or more jobs on one visit. Now she plans to launch her unusual service formally by mailing leaflets in her area.

COMPLAINTS SERVICE Tackling people's problems with big businesses or the government, complaints services fight through red tape and bureaucracy to sort out issues that inexperienced individuals would struggle to resolve.

FUND-RAISING Fund-raisers offer expert help to an increasing number of organizations, including charities, schools, arts foundations, and churches, all of which depend on the general public for funding.

FINANCIAL PLANNING Planners assist others in coping with life's financial complexities, perhaps by showing them how to regain control over their personal budgets or by teaching them the essentials of financial management.

PARTY COORDINATION This involves the organization of various celebratory events, such as birthdays, weddings, and graduations. The work ranges from assembling the guest lists to preparing the food and providing the decorations.

HELPING THE ELDERLY

As the average life expectancy increases, so does the demand for geriatric care. Independent carers not only help the elderly to take care of themselves in their own homes, but also help to make them feel less isolated.

GERIATRIC CARE Carers in this area help take care of the elderly by providing a range of support services for them, including home management and transportation.

BUSINESS NETWORK ORGANIZATION This service sets up groups of noncompeting small business owners that meet regularly, exchange views and experiences, and help each other to find customers.

ANTIQUE LOCATION With their specialized knowledge of the markets, antique locators help home owners and decorators to find the antiques they want.

FITNESS INSTRUCTION Personal trainers help those who are eager to keep healthy and in shape but do not have the time, motivation, or commitment to organize their own workouts or diets.

What is important about this list of new business ideas is not so much the specific concepts described, but the wealth of diverse opportunity available that is based simply on tackling an identified need.

ESTABLISHED BUSINESS CONCEPTS

Most existing businesses, whether run from home or a commercial space, have been in existence for some years. It is natural that they concentrate on their proven way of meeting someone's need for a specific product or service. Established businesses are traditionally reluctant to change a winning formula, unless they are forced to through fresh competition or a change in the dynamics of their particular market. But that does not restrict you, the new entrepreneur, from looking at that need and working out how to meet it differently.

Further information on these types of business can be found in the publications and websites listed on pp. 186–7.

The more established home-based businesses fall into two categories. These are:
- ▪ **BUSINESS SUPPORT SERVICES** Secretarial, financial, marketing, consulting, training, computer maintenance, publishing, couriers, and communications
- ▪ **DOMESTIC SUPPORT SERVICES** Cleaning, maintenance, decoration, landscaping, childcare, architecture, furnishing, computers, entertainment, and catering.

Doing the Market Research

To help you answer the fundamental question – Is there a market for my product or service, and is it big enough to support me? – you need to do some market research. With almost any business, you will be able to make some sales, but you really need to know that you will be able to sell enough to make a decent living. There are also other aspects that your market research needs to consider, such as any regulations pertaining to your proposed line of business and the competition.

Basic market research can be broken down into three parts:
1. analysis of the market
2. analysis of competitors
3. testing the market (before you commit yourself fully).

ANALYZING THE MARKET

By analyzing the market you will get an inside picture of the trade you are thinking of entering, the trends both nationally and locally,

RAKING IT IN
If you love the outdoors generally and gardening in particular, then setting up as a landscaper could be the ideal home-based business. The work can vary from basic garden maintenance to formal design.

and an understanding of the needs of your potential customers. Much of this can be done by desk research, partly on-line and partly at your local library. Many industries are described in market research reports.

Other sources of market research information are trade magazines, trade associations, and their exhibitions. Your local library should be able to give you the names of trade magazines and the addresses of relevant trade associations. From these you can find details of exhibitions, some of which will only allow admission to members of that trade. Speak to as many people as you can in the trade concerned, but be careful how much information you divulge about your proposed venture.

If possible, travel to another part of the country – or even another country altogether, perhaps combining market research with a vacation – to see how the trade in question is handled there. You will often find distinctive regional variations in the way that the same markets are organized and served, and you may discover a new approach that you could import into your locality.

You also need to consider the "target market," which is the term used to describe the section of the population that could potentially use your product or service. For your business to succeed you obviously need customers, but have you stopped to think just who those people are, what exactly their needs are, and what benefit they will get from using your product or service? They are obviously surviving without you right now, so why will they want to use your business? Also, are there enough potential customers within reach of your business?

If your target market is business customers, first prepare a list of some or all of the companies whom you believe may be interested in your business. Find them in the Yellow Pages or a trade directory, and then contact them to find out their views on what you have

Research your target market thoroughly and be realistic about how likely you are to fare

FIVE GOLDEN RULES OF CONDUCTING QUESTIONNAIRES

1 Ask between five and 10 questions, and keep them short and simple.

2 Do not "weight" the questions; you are less likely to get a valid answer.

3 Minimize open questions in order to have focused replies.

4 Ask only likely customers to complete a questionnaire.

5 Aim to finish with between 50 and 100 completed questionnaires.

to offer. Before you make such an approach, you will need to work out your prices. The technique then is to get an appointment, either by phoning first or writing a letter, which you then follow up with a phone call.

If your target market is private individuals, determining who will buy what from you is much more difficult to do. Start by asking those already in the trade and who are not direct competitors. The next step is to speak directly to likely customers. The most thorough way of doing this with the general public is with a carefully compiled questionnaire (see box above).

ANALYZING YOUR COMPETITORS

The close observation of potential competitors can provide you with a great deal of interesting and useful information. In one sense your competitors are doing today what you are planning to do tomorrow. They should have already refined their product or service and discovered how to do things in a more effective way, and this knowledge will be of enormous benefit to you if you are able to tap into it. Furthermore, since they will become actual competitors it makes good sense to be aware of their strengths and weaknesses.

To learn about competitors, first consult the Yellow Pages and any trade or business directory. Next do a search of the internet. Where possible, talk to people in the industry. Then read the trade magazines and, finally, attend relevant trade or consumer exhibitions.

Obtain pamphlets, sales literature, and price lists whenever available, by writing, phoning, or asking for them at trade shows or exhibitions where the competitor has a stand. Your competitors are at their most vulnerable at such events, as their goods are on display and you can usually walk straight on to their stands. Also, look at their advertisements and check out their internet website.

If a competitor is a publicly traded corporation, it has to file annual and quarterly reports with the U.S. Securities and Exchange Commission. These reports, available at many public and business libraries, and on the internet at www.sec.gov/edgarhp.htm, give the names of directors and financial details, although you may need an accountant to interpret the figures for you.

Try testing the quality of your competitors' service. If, for example, you are thinking of starting a bookkeeping service, contact the existing competitors in your area and ask them about their service and request a quote. This will not only provide you with valuable information about their pricing, but also give a good indication of how professional they are at responding to your inquiry. You will get a measure of the quality of their people, which in turn establishes a benchmark for you to beat.

You should aim to work out how you can compete successfully with existing competitors, who have all the benefits of being established; that is, having a client base and a reputation in key areas such as:

▓ quality
▓ price
▓ speed
▓ reliability
▓ friendliness.

You may discover that there is a particular service that your competitors are not currently providing. If so, find out why. There may be a good reason – little demand, or a national chain does it more quickly and cheaper than a local company could – and it is far better to have that information now.

TESTING THE MARKET

If your initial market research is rather inconclusive, you may want to test the market. Although not always possible, test marketing can be very useful; it can be thought of as

COMMON ERRORS TO AVOID IN MARKET RESEARCH

1. Speaking to everyone except the actual potential buyers.

2. Failing to notice warning signals as you are convinced your project will work.

3. Asking "weighted" questions encouraging answers that confirm your ideas without revealing the interviewee's thoughts.

4. Ignoring the fact that often 20 percent of the customers provide 80 percent of the turnover.

5. Assuming you will compete effectively just because your prices will be lower.

6. Being influenced by your contacts who promise to supply you with lots of work when you start. (Ask yourself how they are getting by without you now.)

7. Underestimating how long it can take to enter a market and take a reasonable market share; it is more likely to be years, not months.

8. Failing to recognize the strength and the reaction of the competition.

9. Basing your likely sales estimates on the simple assumption that you will take a certain percentage of the total market.

10. Forgetting that new products or ideas take time and money to introduce to the market.

putting a toe in the water. Its function is simply to test the market reaction to a new product or service with the minimum of investment, and it is usually done at an early stage before a full commitment is made to the project. It acts as a bridge between "having the big idea" and launching a full-scale business. It can also provide useful, possibly essential, feedback, but it may reveal your hand to a competitor.

Test marketing is a very common practice and takes a number of forms:

▩ **ADVERTISING** The simplest way to check market response is to place an advertisement or, if you prefer, a series of advertisements as if the product or service were actually available (even if you are not quite at that stage) to see what reaction it produces. But note that your ad must not be misleading and should not therefore request any cash but simply invite a response for more information. Its main limitation is that you get minimal feedback unless people take the trouble to respond, so the advertisement needs to be particularly stimulating. You may just get a deafening silence from which it is difficult to draw useful conclusions.

▩ **SAMPLE** If it is a product you are making, which is to be sold to the trade, you could take samples to potential buyers or exhibit them at a trade show. That way you could take orders before committing yourself to full production. This practice is common in the fashion, gift, and craft trades where buyers are used to placing orders many months before receiving the goods.

▩ **MAILSHOT** In this case you send a letter to a potential customer requesting a response, which would indicate their interest in what you have to offer. This can be an effective technique, especially if the customers are businesses and the letters are addressed to named individuals. It will probably still need a telephone follow-up to obtain the information you seek. Rather than distributing letters like confetti, spend time creating a quality mailing list. For national coverage you can rent such mailing lists, although you are probably the best person to create a local one.

▩ **LEAFLET DROP** This is a less personal version of the mailshot, best suited to the general public, where leaflets are slipped into mailboxes. Leaflet drops can also be used for trade customers. Leaflets that are inserted loose into newspapers or magazines are referred to as an "insert."

▩ **EXHIBITION OR TRADE SHOW** Yet another way to judge market reaction to your product or service is to rent a stand at suitable exhibition or trade show. This is particularly useful because, unlike all the previous options (except the sample above), you get immediate feedback from potential customers. This can be crucial in helping you to fine-tune your product or service, establish prices, and so on, or conclude that there is an inadequate market. The importance of this market intelligence cannot be overstated, but it does, of course, reveal your venture to other businesses, some of which could become competitors or try to copy aspects of your idea. If you are exhibiting samples, you may be ready to take orders. If not, at least look for serious buyer interest rather than simply curiosity. Note that participating in exhibitions can be very costly in terms of cash as well as time.

▩ **FOCUS GROUP** This technique is often used by companies whose customers are the general public. Selected people are invited to a meeting where they are shown prototypes of new products, or a new service is fully described. They are then asked prepared questions, and there is some open discussion, which is controlled by a

Check that your chosen market is growing and likely to keep on doing so

moderator. All responses are carefully recorded, often on video, for later analysis. Participants are usually paid a small sum, and are served light refreshments.

In most test marketing an element of bluff is essential, particularly if you have not yet launched the business and are trying out the market before you commit yourself.

Starting Up in Direct Selling

One way to start your own business within an existing structure is by direct selling. This is where a manufacturer skips the retailer by selling direct to the consumer. Sales are usually made by self-employed people, who are generally home-based and often work part-time. The manufacturers give their salespeople various titles, such as "distributors," "associates," "consultants," or "demonstrators," which are sometimes prefixed by the word "independent." Many products are sold in this way, including clothes, cosmetics, household goods, jewelry, books, and dietary and nutritional products. Almost 90 percent of sales are made on a person-to-person basis, with the balance being by party plan. Ideally, to enter direct sales, you need to know a lot of people who can be your initial sales contacts.

THE ADVANTAGES

Being involved with a direct-selling company has many advantages over setting up a business on your own. Doing the market research, developing and testing new products, planning, pricing, and working out sales techniques are done by the company. All you need do is to absorb their sales training and sometimes buy a starter pack of goods to sell. The sales procedure has been written by experts, so by following the training you should, in theory, be able to make sales.

Consider direct selling only if you are self-motivated and confident

	WHAT TO AVOID IN A DIRECT SALES COMPANY
1	The company promises that you will "get rich quick."
2	Products are unsalable, unattractive, overpriced, or of poor quality.
3	You would not choose to use their products yourself.
4	It is not clear exactly what you will be getting from the company until you have made an initial payment.
5	Earnings are primarily made by recruitment of new distributors rather than by selling actual products.
6	The company asks you to make fixed, regular payments.
7	The company is relatively new and has not been in business for very long.

THE PITFALLS

There are a number of reasons why people have difficulties making sufficient sales and fail to earn a living from direct selling.

▪ They do not follow the company's instructions.

▪ They do not give the process enough time; you need to commit yourself for 12 months.

▪ They become disenchanted with selling and absorbing the company hype.

▪ They work for a company that does not have a code of ethics; if goods are shoddy or fail to arrive as promised, customers become disgruntled.

▪ They work for a company that has unsalable goods (a not-uncommon problem).

CHOOSING A COMPANY

Joining a direct-selling company is usually quite easy. The relevant trade associations can give you the names of their member companies

HOW IS DIRECT SELLING DONE?

Before getting involved in direct selling, it is important to know the main types of selling and how each one of them works.

■ **DOOR TO DOOR** This type of selling tends to operate by the salesperson leaving a catalog and then returning a few days later hoping to take an order and pick up the catalog. Success tends to rely on repeat business. Typically the salesperson gets about 20 percent commission on each sale.

■ **SELLING TO CONTACTS** This is also known as "personal referral." You find the people who are interested in obtaining the product, visit them, and try to make a sale. The idea is that by making contact before you visit you know they are interested in the product, so it is not "cold calling," and you have a reasonable chance of making a sale. The key is to know a lot of people and be prepared to approach them all. You might contact neighbors, friends, relatives, people who are in clubs that you belong to, people in a religious group of which you are a member, parents of children with yours at school, and (where applicable) contact lists that you receive from your company. Be warned, though, that not everyone likes to be on the receiving end of this form of selling, so choose whom you approach carefully.

SELLING DOOR-TO-DOOR

Some of the most successful door-to-door selling is done when a salesperson has built up a foundation of regular customers to visit.

■ **PARTY PLAN** This form of selling is still sometimes referred to as "Tupperware parties," after the company that first popularized it. A host – the salesperson or a friend of theirs – invites a group of friends and relatives to his or her home. The salesperson (or "demonstrator") brings samples of the items for sale, demonstrates them, and encourages the guests to place orders. Some people who sell in this way prefer to hold stock so that customers can take away their goods. Others take orders and then supply the goods later, collecting the money when the goods are handed over. Party-plan selling relies on good demonstration rather than a hard sell.

or you may already know a distributor. It is important that you like what the company has to sell and will use the products yourself.

NETWORK MARKETING

Some, though not all, direct-selling companies operate a multilevel system of sales where a salesperson can recruit other salespeople and will then receive bonuses depending on how well their recruits perform. This way of selling is called network marketing (networking) or multilevel marketing (MLM for short), and it accounts for about a quarter of total direct sales. It works like this: you sell the products to friends and contacts. One or two of them might think they can sell it to their friends and so

ASSESSING A FRANCHISE

WHAT TO LOOK FOR

A proven business format that is viable, with advertising support and an operations manual.

The use of a business name and/or trademark.

Training in both trade and business skills.

A contract that clearly defines the rights and obligations of both parties.

Long-term market research to ensure that the business keeps up with marketplace changes.

An exclusive territory large enough to generate an adequate income.

Full support before, during, and after start-up, including ongoing advice and troubleshooting.

WHAT TO AVOID

Only one outlet in the country (the franchise is not fully proven).

A sales pitch based on the success of the franchise in another country.

The franchisor does a hard sell on you.

Huge projected profits from a small setup fee.

A large initial fee is demanded.

Claims that there is little selling to do.

Mapped-out territories that have not been researched in terms of regional variations and differing markets.

A dismissive attitude toward competitors.

agree to become distributors. By recruiting them, you earn bonuses that are dependent on their sales. If those new distributors recruit more people, you get a share of their sales bonuses, too. This continues as the network expands. The people who recruit you are your "uplines," and the people you recruit are your "downlines."

To promote high levels of sales and recruitment, most direct-selling companies offer incentive prizes such as household appliances, vacations, even cars. A small minority of people do achieve impressive incomes from this type of selling, and the companies they work with are huge multibillion-turnover organizations. Network marketing, along with other aspects of direct selling, is regulated by law (see p. 172).

Taking On a Franchise

In franchising, you copy someone else's business, with their full approval and support, under a license agreement called a franchise. The franchise-giver (the franchisor) allows you to use their name, provides training and backup, and gives his or her expertise with all its benefits. In exchange, you as the franchisee have to pay the franchisor an initial fee, then ongoing royalties. The major advantage of this method is that you get into business more quickly and possibly with less risk.

The franchise you take on should be a well-proven business idea; unfortunately, the success of franchising has attracted many unscrupulous business people who are offering franchises of dubious value. There is, therefore, a need for caution and independent professional advice. Franchising was developed in the U.S. in the 1950s, and many of the well-known franchise names are still American.

HOW DOES FRANCHISING WORK?

Setting up any business takes money, but with a franchise operation it costs more, because you are also paying for the business experience and proven product or service of the franchisor. In return, the franchisor may set up the whole business for you, including taking care of all the legal work, training you and any partners and staff, and helping you to select stock or tools. In some cases this hand-holding is very complete, but you need to decide if the extra cost of a franchise is worthwhile.

The franchisor provides an operations manual, which lays down the whole format of how to run the business. There is also a contract, which forms the basis of the close association between you and the franchisor. It is very important that you check this document carefully, no matter how well-known the franchisor. Read all of it and ensure you understand it. Ask questions about any part that is unclear. Before you sign the contract, consult a lawyer; some contracts have hostile clauses that, if you have a problem running the business, are likely to work in favor of the franchisor rather than you.

HOW TO ASSESS A FRANCHISE

Many franchisors are members of a national association (see p. 185), which you can contact for information, and there are a number of franchising magazines available. Attend the various franchise exhibitions that are held annually to meet franchisors. When you have found several franchises that interest you, request their free information packs (also called prospectuses); each should describe the company in detail. If your bank has franchise advisers, get their advice. The next step is to visit the franchisor's head office.

If satisfied so far, ask to see a specimen contract and take it away to read carefully and then show to your lawyer. After the meeting, visit at least two of their franchisees (of your own choice) and get their viewpoint. Now do your own market research (see pp. 56–60). You need to find out just how strong the market demand is for such products or services, what customers think of the franchise, and the strength of the competition in your area.

QUESTIONS TO ASK A FRANCHISOR

When you visit a franchisor, ask probing questions – even if some are answered in their prospectus – and note the answers.

◼ When was the business established?
◼ Are they members of the national franchise association? If not, why not?
◼ How many outlets are there in the country?
◼ How many outlets have ceased operation, and why?
◼ What are the credentials of the people behind the franchise?
◼ How good is the company's financial performance?
◼ What is the initial capital required?
◼ What are the addresses of franchisees you can visit?
◼ How is the royalty calculated?
◼ What do you get for your money?
◼ What ongoing support do they give?
◼ Are there other charges, e.g. advertising?
◼ What are the long-term prospects for the franchise?
◼ What is the length of the agreement and how can it be terminated?
◼ Who is the competition?

A common complaint is that franchisors understate the necessary capital to start the business. They sometimes entirely omit your living costs prior to the business making a profit, they may quote a low figure to purchase a second-hand van or other piece of essential equipment, and omit your own legal and accounting fees. Sales tax is also often omitted; you will have to pay this and can claim it back only if you are going to be sales tax-registered.

Taking on a franchise does not guarantee success. Some franchises fail altogether, while others do not meet projected turnover figures. A franchisor's membership in a national franchise association does not lessen the need for careful checking on your part. Even if you join a good, well-managed, ethical franchise, your own business could still have problems due to local competition and business circumstances. Franchising works for many thousands of people, but it is essential to choose your franchise very carefully indeed. Even if it is successful, the business will require plenty of hard work and some considerable time to become established.

Choosing a Business Name

For any new business, the choice of name is a critical issue. It is the key way to project a clear image and allow your venture to stand out from the competition. The name may also tell people what you do and even hint at how well you might do it, for example, including "Quick" in the name, where relevant. The name can also sound prestigious and imply that it is more than just a little home-based business.

Choosing the correct business name is a simple, yet very successful marketing strategy, but it can also be one of the most difficult challenges you will face in establishing your new home business. The obvious name choices in your market sector will almost certainly have been taken already, and it can be remarkably difficult to come up with a name that achieves at least some of the following major objectives:

■ It is distinctive.
■ It describes the business.
■ It implies positive attributes, such as quality or size.
■ It is easy to fit on business cards and in letterheads.
■ It is available for registration on the internet.

The final objective can be decisive in your choice of business name, particularly if your venture is aimed specifically at the on-line market. We have already become familiar with names made up of several words joined together, primarily because they are readily found through the search engines used by the

DOS AND DON'TS OF CHOOSING A BUSINESS NAME

✓ Do consider using a name that explains the kind of work you do.

✓ Do consider using a name that reflects your proposed image.

✓ Do consider using made-up words to make your name unique.

✓ Do consider the suitability of the name for the internet.

✓ Do consider using a name that people can say easily. (There is a counterargument, however: if you use an unusual name and people have some difficulty saying it initially, then once they have mastered the pronunciation it will stay in their minds.)

✗ Don't use a name that clashes with an incorporated company's name.

✗ Don't use a name that clashes with a registered trademark.

✗ Don't use a name that clashes with an existing website domain name.

✗ Don't use a name that could be confused with an existing local business.

✗ Don't use a name that could be confused with an existing business in your industry.

✗ Don't use a name that could be confused with a nationally known business.

majority of web surfers. It is best to find a name that works well on the internet as well as in the conventional world. Needless to say, that is easier said than done.

BRANDING YOUR BUSINESS

It is sometimes the unconventional that is the most effective. Who, for example, would have thought that Virgin could make a strong brand name before Britain's Richard Branson thought of it? And who would have chosen Apple for a record label or personal computer? Specialized consultants who devise names for new businesses say that the best solutions are subjective and creative, rather than based on research or logic. They tap into people's associations with other meanings that convey the right impression or image. Your business name can also be fun. Remember that you are, in effect, launching your own business brand, and, like all brand-builders, you have to concentrate on gaining the widest possible awareness for your name.

If you know at the outset that your business is going to develop several arms or services, consider establishing an overall name and then labeling each separate activity under that umbrella name. For example, "The Periwinkle Group" could develop "Periwinkle Fishing Nets," "Periwinkle Waders," and "Periwinkle Hooks." This also makes your venture sound larger and more serious to potential customers. Do not choose separate names for different operations unless they are aimed at completely different markets.

When trying to come up with a business name, look at franchising magazines for inspiration, to see how the professionals do it; they are often working in very competitive areas with many companies vying for the same customers. Examine your competitors and list their names together with your comments. This is an important exercise and should not be overlooked.

There are other factors to consider in specialized circumstances. For instance, if you

FACT FILE

Once satisfied with your new business name, consider protecting it by registering it with the U.S. Patent and Trademark Office (see p. 186). This will prevent any other business from using the same name or one very similar, thereby cashing in on your goodwill (there are laws to prevent such tactics, but they are not always easy to apply). You can also register any logo that accompanies the name on your stationery, packaging, and so on.

are going to be an active exporter, check that your proposed name is not rude or puzzling in the languages spoken in your target countries. Where your customers are likely to find you through the Yellow Pages or a similar directory, and there is little differentiation between rival businesses (taxi services are a good example), consider using a business name that begins with A or even AA. Finally, your name must not include words that are restricted by law (see p. 165).

Before you make a final decision on your business name, try it out on as many people as you can and listen carefully to their replies. Their initial reaction is perhaps the most telling, as this will best equate to the reaction of a potential customer.

Understanding Business Basics

The fact that your venture is based at home makes little difference to its fundamental operation as a business. You will still need to get your pricing right, learn how to market the business effectively through advertising and promotion, and then drum up sufficient sales. You will also need to keep proper records for the tax authorities and your own financial control. This chapter introduces you to the organizations and people who can advise you in these various fields. It also shows you how to price your goods or services, promote your business, make sales, and keep simple accounts.

There are many organizations and people you can call on for advice to help you get the basics right as you start your business. Much of the advice offered is free, but the quality will vary, so it is wise to shop around. Find out as much as you can, but remember that advice can never be a substitute for making a decision. The following professionals and organizations can all be approached for advice, but the list is not exhaustive. For instance, you may need to speak to the fire safety officer, health and safety officer, environmental health officer – it all depends on your particular business.

Research every aspect of working from home as thoroughly as possible

■ **Accountants** Consult a qualified accountant when setting up to help you prepare your initial business plan. Once you start operating they can advise you on how to set up a bookkeeping system, and at the end of the tax year they can do your tax returns. Accountants vary greatly in their abilities and in the amount of time they are prepared to spend with small clients, so choose carefully.

■ **Banks** Managers and small business advisors in banks usually offer free business advice. Once started, remember to keep them abreast of any developments and plans.

CASE STUDY: Asking Others for Professional Advice

Charles, a former airline pilot, decided to set up a home-based internet business sourcing and supplying aircraft parts worldwide for vintage aircraft. As he was not sure how to price the parts, he got advice from former engineering colleagues before finalizing them. He then learned how to market his website to attract aircraft engineers to buy parts from him. Using both the phone and email, he contacted numerous people for advice on the best way to promote his business. He also placed regular but small classified ads in appropriate aviation magazines.

It took time to build up a reasonable number of customers, but the slow start of his business helped Charles to iron out various teething pains that he had with his computer system and to figure out the paperwork required to accompany certified aircraft parts.

STEPS TO TAKE WHEN LAUNCHING YOUR HOME BUSINESS

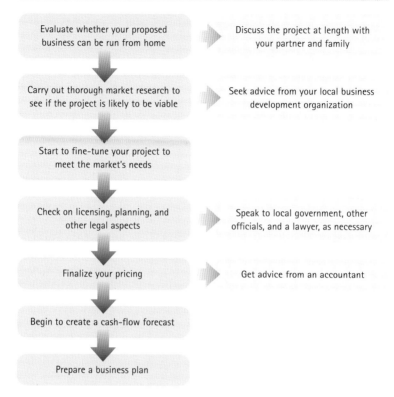

Evaluate whether your proposed business can be run from home

Discuss the project at length with your partner and family

Carry out thorough market research to see if the project is likely to be viable

Seek advice from your local business development organization

Start to fine-tune your project to meet the market's needs

Check on licensing, planning, and other legal aspects

Speak to local government, other officials, and a lawyer, as necessary

Finalize your pricing

Get advice from an accountant

Begin to create a cash-flow forecast

Prepare a business plan

■ **BUSINESS DEVELOPMENT ORGANIZATIONS** Most of these organizations will be able to answer your queries; if not, they can put you in touch with someone who can. Their advice is usually free.

■ **GOVERNMENT TAX OFFICES** Many of your straightforward tax queries can be answered by the appropriate tax office, most of whom have telephone helplines, free leaflets, and other useful information on their websites.

■ **LOCAL GOVERNMENT** They should be consulted on planning and licensing matters.

■ **LAWYERS** Hire a lawyer before you start up, and for other legal queries.

■ **TRADE ASSOCIATIONS** If there is a trade association, it may be worth joining for the benefit of their advice. Although they do not actually help you set up in business, they should be able to answer various key questions about your chosen business and how it is developing. Since your rivals may also be members of the associaton, you may need to be on your guard as to how much information you divulge about your venture.

■ **INSURANCE BROKERS** Your current home and car insurances are unlikely to cover your proposed business activities and may be invalidated if you do not inform your insurers of your new status. If you plan to employ anyone, even just on a part-time basis, you will require employer's liability cover. It would, therefore, be wise to consult a registered insurance broker before you start operating your business from home.

Pricing a Product or Service

The first business basic to consider is pricing. This is difficult to get right. A key element of working out your pricing is to understand your costs. Once you know these, you can use them in your pricing calculation. Two types of costs are relevant here.

▪ **Fixed Costs** Also known as overhead, these refer to business expenditure, which is basically fixed or constant, irrespective of the level of turnover. Most employee salaries and business insurances are examples of fixed costs. Home-based businesses generally have low fixed costs, which is a great advantage, but these costs must always be kept to a minimum as they can float upward and soon affect the profitability of a business. Businesses are usually better at controlling their variable costs than their fixed costs.

▪ **Variable Costs** Also known as direct costs, these comprise expenditure that varies directly in relation to the level of business, for instance, the cost of raw materials.

Pricing for Importers, Wholesalers, and Retailers

An easy way to price a product for importing, selling wholesale or retail, is as follows:

**Selling price per unit =
Net cost price + Markup
+ Sales tax (if applicable)**

For example, if you buy an article for $7.24 net (without sales tax added), and if the typical industry markup is 20 percent, the selling price would be calculated as follows:

$7.24 + 20% = $8.69

If you are sales tax-registered and the article is liable for sales tax, you would add sales tax on top of the total of $8.69.

The price you choose needs to meet your fixed and variable costs, and then make a surplus (your profit) on top. This is the minimum you need to earn from your sales to stay in business. It is from this profit that you can draw your wages.

Sending the Right Signals

Calculating a price solely on the basis of your costs is too simplistic; there are other factors you need to take into account. For example, your selling price can send an important signal to your customers. In the absence of other indicators, the price tells them whether you are offering an economy product or service, or whether you are at the top end of the market. Deciding where your own price point should lie demands a knowledge of your target market and the amount likely buyers will be prepared to pay. This requires prior experience of the industry or an accurate interpretation of your market research results. If you have existing competitors, they will have already created price norms in the market. Finally, if you have one major customer, they may simply dictate what price they will pay, in which case your calculations will tell you if that is sufficient for your business to be viable.

Understanding Markups and Margins

A markup is the amount added to the cost price to reach the selling price; a margin is the amount of profit you are making.

The calculation for a markup is:

$$\text{Markup (\%)} = \frac{(\text{Selling price} - \text{Cost price})}{\text{Cost price}} \times 100$$

The calculation for a margin is:

$$\text{Margin (\%)} = \frac{(\text{Selling price} - \text{Cost price})}{\text{Selling price}} \times 100$$

Markups and margins vary from industry to industry and in different parts of a supply chain. Learn the norms for your business; the only way to do this is to ask a trade association or contacts. Beware of a common error: sometimes people say their markup is 200 percent, meaning that they buy something for one price and sell it for double that price. In fact, this is a markup of only 100 percent.

ESTIMATES AND QUOTES

Service businesses usually provide customers with an estimate (or quote) which, if accepted, forms the basis of a contract between the two parties. An "estimate" is the approximate price for doing a job, but a buyer will normally ask for a "quote" in writing. A quote is a fixed price and, if agreed, is binding on both parties. Use your letterhead for the estimate or quote, and include your terms – for example, "Payment is due 30 days from the date of invoice." Provide sufficient detail to avoid misunderstandings, and add a clause that you will charge extra for any changes made by the customer. Your letter should also stipulate how long the quote is valid for.

DOS AND DON'TS OF PRICING

✓ Do put a realistic price on your products or services.

✓ Do include all costs in your pricing calculations.

✓ Do take into account the true value of your own time.

✓ Do compare actual costs incurred on a job with the invoiced price.

✓ Do react quickly but thoughtfully to a competitor changing their prices.

✗ Don't forget to increase prices in line with inflation.

✗ Don't make the price difficult to find in your sales literature.

✗ Don't price low just to get the work.

✗ Don't discount too much, too often.

✗ Don't think the customer is concerned only with the price.

WORKING OUT AN ESTIMATE OR QUOTE
It is important to be methodical and consistent when working out estimates and quotes for potential customers. Be realistic about your costs and always aim to make the maximum profit.

PRICING FOR MANUFACTURERS (INCLUDING CRAFTWORKERS)

If you are a manufacturer, a straightforward calculation to price a product is:

Selling price per unit =

(Cost of raw material + Direct labor + Overheads contribution) + Markup + Sales tax, where applicable

You can calculate the elements in this sum in the following way:

■ **COST OF RAW MATERIAL** This should be relatively easy to calculate per item, but always allow for wastage.

■ **DIRECT LABOR** This is the cost of employing staff to make the units. Staff costs should include about one-third as much again on top of the wage to allow for social security, paid vacations, and so on. If you are self-employed, do not price your own labor costs cheaply; if you do, and take on staff in the future, you will either have to raise prices or take a drop in profits to cover the extra cost.

Price your product to achieve the maximum profit possible

■ **MARKUP** To work this out, insert a known markup appropriate for your industry into the pricing equation (see p. 68) to obtain your selling price; you can then make slight adjustments to the final price as necessary. The markup needs to provide a small surplus (say five to 10 percent) to provide funds for future expansion, new product development, or simply to save for any future contingencies.

■ **SALES TAX** This is added only if your business is sales tax-registered and if the product itself is taxable (see pp. 179–80).

■ **OVERHEAD CONTRIBUTION** This considers the overhead (fixed costs) of the business, which obviously has to be supported by the production. To work out the overhead contribution per item, use the following calculation:

$$\text{Overhead contribution} = \frac{\text{Total overhead}}{\text{Total production}}$$

An important point to note is that this calculation assumes that everything that is produced is subsequently sold.

CASE STUDY: Working Out the Unit Price

ELLEN IS self-employed, making children's garments. The raw materials cost $10 per unit (allowing for wastage) and each item takes one hour to make, so in a 40-hour week she might make 35 such items (allowing for downtime, time spent on administration, and so on). The labor cost is $500 – equivalent to what it would cost to pay an employee to do the job, plus one-third extra for paid vacations, sick leave, and so on. So the direct labor cost would be:

$$\frac{\$500 + \$166.67}{35} = \$19.05 \text{ per unit}$$

Assume total overhead comes to $8,000 a year, and total annual production is 1,680 items (for 48 weeks' production, allowing for some vacation). The overhead contribution is:

$$\frac{\$8,000}{1,680} = \$4.76 \text{ per unit}$$

Finally, a markup is added of 10 percent. The selling price, therefore, is:

($10 + $19.05 + $4.76) + 10% = $37.19

In this case, there is no need to add sales tax. Ellen might choose to sell at more or less, depending on the competition and the market.

PRICING SERVICES

The pricing of services is usually based on hourly labor rates plus material costs. For consulting or freelance work, this is more usually called "fees plus expenses."

▪ CALCULATING HOURLY LABOR RATES

Hourly rate (+ sales tax, where applicable) =
$$\frac{\text{(total overhead including all wages)}}{\text{Total likely productive hours}} + \text{Markup}$$

First of all, find out the typical "going rate" for what you are planning to do. If you plan to employ anyone, allow an adequate hourly wage for them out of the amount you are planning to charge, making allowance for downtime and profit. Work out overhead and an appropriate markup. To calculate your productive hours, assume you (and any employees) will be productive (doing work for which you can actually charge) for, say, 75 percent of the working week. The actual figure may be lower. Being productive for 75 percent of the time means that in a typical 40-hour week you will be charging for only 30 hours, but having to pay your staff for 40. The remaining 10 hours are absorbed in getting sales, doing paperwork, traveling, buying materials, and so on. Do the calculation, and insert that figure into your cash-flow forecast (see pp. 96–9). If the forecast figure looks good, and your labor rate is

right for the trade, that is a good start. If not, see what you can realistically adjust.

▪ **MATERIALS** These are usually charged "at cost," but charging your customer the price you paid ignores the time you take to locate the materials, the cost of travel to get them, those held in stock, and so on. So most businesses define "at cost" as the retail price; they purchase the goods at trade or wholesale prices, giving themselves some margin.

CASE STUDY: Working Out an Hourly Rate

ANNE AND TOM are a mother and son team of interior designers. Their overhead is $10,000 per year and their basic working week is about 50 hours; they reckon they can do productive work for 40 hours. They take four weeks' vacation per year and, where possible, draw $50,000 a year each. The equation, assuming a 10 percent markup, would then be:

Hourly rate =
$$\frac{(\$10,000 + \$50,000 + \$50,000)}{2 \times (40 \text{ hours} \times 48 \text{ weeks})} + 10\%$$
$$= \$31.51 + \text{Sales tax}$$

They would probably round this figure up. The hourly rate is dependent on them achieving a full 40-hour productive week with no time lost. In practice, they also make a useful profit on the materials they use.

CASE STUDY: Looking at Different Options for Charging

CAROLINE IS A graphic designer who wants to freelance. Her plan is to work from her own home and to visit clients as necessary to get work and to discuss projects. She calculates the minimum hourly rate she must charge to provide an adequate "wage" and to cover any overhead. She needs to allow for time lost due to traveling, getting work, and administration.

Any materials used she will charge at cost. She may be able to quote her hourly rate for some jobs, while for others she may be given a budget to work to or asked to quote an overall price. Her difficulty with the last two situations would be estimating how long the job might take. She plans to keep a time log and, at the end of a fixed-price job, she will use it to calculate the actual hourly rate she achieved; this will help her with future estimates.

Different Methods of Advertising

The function of advertising is to arouse interest in potential customers and to encourage them to take the next step – contact you or place an order. With most advertising you are trying to target the person who can make the buying decision. It is therefore essential to choose the best medium for your message. Look back at your market research to help you to ascertain who your prospective customers are, where they live or work, what their needs are, and what sets them apart. This

Look at all the ways of promoting your business – advertising is not the only one

should help you work out which places and publications your advertising is more likely to be noticed by them.

There are many different methods of advertising (see right). Some forms are more expensive than others, or more effective, but cost and effect are not always clearly related. Before advertising in a particular newspaper, magazine, or directory, check to see if the publication in question carries ads placed by businesses that are similar to yours. If there are none, it may be the wrong medium for you.

Any advertising you do needs to be part of a campaign. People tend to forget most single ads as soon as they see them unless they happen to have a need for the product or service at the exact time they notice the ad. A successful campaign requires regular advertising. You don't need to take out large ads; in fact, a little and often will probably produce a better result.

CREATING AN AD

Designing ads demands time, thought, creativity, and experience. It is easy to get it wrong and produce an ad that costs money but produces little result. Look at previous issues of the publication in which you plan to advertise and ask yourself what catches your eye. It is tempting to design an ad that seems to address itself to all readers, but this scattershot approach is rarely effective. Instead, target a specific section of the readership (or audience) who will at least consider your product or service.

Think about the content of your ad. What is the message you are trying to convey? With a display ad, the illustration is the key. It can be a photograph or computer graphic, but it must look professional. Include people in any photos you use for the simple reason that we react more positively to people than we do to inanimate objects. Generally, your aim with an

COMMON ERRORS MADE WITH ADVERTISING

1. Assuming one big advertisement is all that is necessary.

2. Placing an advertisement in response to pressure from advertising salespeople.

3. Advertising in the wrong place (or at the wrong time).

4. Advertising without a clear idea as to your objective.

5. Using your business name for the advertisement's headline.

6. Designing an advertisement that projects mainly image, expecting a sales response.

7. Placing an advertisement too hastily, and not as part of an overall plan.

8. Omitting a clear call for action at the end of an advertisement.

9. Allowing too small an advertising budget for your needs.

10. Continuing to place advertisements without monitoring the results.

CHOOSING AN ADVERTISING METHOD

METHOD	COST	ADVANTAGES	DISADVANTAGES
DIRECT MAILSHOT LETTER	Low	■ Targeted audience ■ High response rate (2–5%)	■ Time-consuming to locate or produce a good mailing list
SMALL POSTER	Low	■ Large readership ■ Long life	■ Limited locations ■ Message must be short to make an immediate impact
MAILSHOT LEAFLET	Low	■ Can be part-targeted	■ Low response rate ■ Post office distribution is most effective but increases the cost
INTERNET WEBSITE	Low/Medium	■ Potentially huge audience ■ Full color, sound, and some animation possible	■ Difficult to stand out in the crowd
DIRECTORIES	Low/Medium	■ Ad life is one year ■ Allows comparison with competitors ■ May have wide circulation	■ Can only make changes annually
DIRECT MAILSHOT LEAFLET	Low/Medium	■ Targeted audience	■ Response rate is variable ■ Time-consuming (but less so than direct mailshot letter)
AD IN LOCAL PAPER	Medium	■ Local audience ■ Can repeat often ■ Supporting text in an article alongside is possible	■ Readership much larger than your target market
AD IN TRADE PUBLICATION	Medium/High	■ Targeted ■ Article often possible close by ■ Publication can have long life	■ If publication is relevant, none, except price
AD ON LOCAL RADIO	High	■ Wide audience	■ Ad time very brief so needs repeating frequently
AD IN NATIONAL MAGAZINE	High	■ National audience ■ Color may be available	■ Editorial unlikely ■ Need to book months ahead

ad is to get the reader to respond in some way, such as asking for more information by phone or email, or for a catalog. You are only trying to give them sufficient facts to achieve that end, nothing more. Remember that your ad must be honest and never misleading.

An effective style of display ad is one that looks and reads like a news item or feature article. In most cases, it will be necessary to have "Paid advertisement" printed at the top. If written skillfully, such an ad can be very effective.

■ **CLASSIFIED ADS** These need a catchy heading. You can even take out two or more different ads in the same issue – it is more effective than one long one. If you are placing a display classified ad, include a computer graphic if there is insufficient space for a good photo.

PLACING AN AD

If you decide to advertise in a publication, phone the advertising department and ask for their "advertising rates." Display ads are quoted in terms of an eighth, a quarter, a half, or a full page, and there will be a difference in cost between a mono (black and white) and a color ad. For the classified section, rates will usually be quoted as cost per word or line, or as cost per single column inch (sci), which is a space one column wide and one inch deep. Ask for a "rate card" to be sent to you, which will give all this information as well as details of the circulation of the publication.

MAGAZINE RESEARCH
Advertising placed in national magazines will reach a large audience. As the cost is high, research the most suitable publication well.

Always ask by which date your advertisement is needed; some publications have long lead times. When you place an ad, remember to send in a press release (see pp. 77–9), as an editorial mention can be an enormous help.

LEAFLETS AND BROCHURES

The purpose of a leaflet (also a pamphlet or brochure) is to convey a message in a lasting form. Leaflets can also carry a much longer, more detailed message than an ad, and be distributed to a targeted group of people or sent out in response to an inquiry. The method of distributing your leaflets is very dependent upon the type of business you are running and your potential customers. Leaflets can be put through mailboxes, mailed, handed out at an exhibition or other special event, or enclosed with a publication (where it is called an "insert").

You will probably need a professional designer to help you with the leaflet. Aspects to consider before you discuss the project with the designer include the following:

■ **SIZE** This will be determined by the amount of information you need to convey, the intended method of distribution (for example, does your leaflet fit inside an envelope?), and the amount you can afford.

■ **COLOR** A full-color leaflet is expensive, but it can be justified if your product or service is expensive or needs color to show its

Keep your advertisements simple and to the point

features, or to compete with a rival's full-color leaflet. If you need to produce only a small number of leaflets, say 50 or less, you could print them in full color using a computer and a high-quality color printer.

▪ **MATERIAL** Choose a weight of paper and finish (glossy or matte) that feels right.

▪ **CONTENT** A leaflet needs a catchy headline, an introductory sentence that explains what you are offering, and enough information to answer any likely queries, in particular the

price. Include good-quality illustrations as necessary, suitably captioned.

▪ **ACTION** You need to include a "call for action," which is a statement to encourage an immediate response. This is usually achieved by giving a time-limited special offer.

LOCAL RADIO

Commercial radio can be an effective advertising medium for a wide range of local consumer- and business-oriented products or

SAMPLE DISPLAY ADVERTISEMENT
This ad for a home-based cleaning company uses an eye-catching photograph and headline.

Call for action by offering an incentive with deadline

20% OFF ORDERS PLACED BY MAY 31ST

Good-quality, eye-catching photograph

Headline asks a pertinent question

NEED HELP WITH YOUR CLEANING?

We provide reliable and trained staff for office, factory, and domestic cleaning.

Design is simple, with no clutter to detract from the basic message

▪ ANY JOB CONSIDERED ▪

Short- or long-term contracts or one-time difficult jobs

Offer of free estimate makes potential customers feel that they can phone without commitment

▪ SATISFACTION GUARANTEED ▪
▪ EXCELLENT RATES ▪ FREE ESTIMATES ▪

For more information, contact John Smith

Use of contact name adds a human touch

Emphasis is given to the phone numbers to encourage a response

on office **303-345-6789**
mobile **087-654-3210**

J Smith & Sons
The Cleaning People

A mobile phone number indicates accessibility at all times

services, and a suitable place for home-based businesses to advertise. Start by speaking to the radio station's advertising manager. Costs are based on airtime, and you need to add about 10 percent to cover the production cost of making the commercial. Create as short an ad as your message requires. Most stations can help you produce the ad in their studios and offer free library music. Employ a professional to speak the voice-over.

HAVING YOUR OWN WEBSITE

An internet website is an important marketing tool for many businesses. It is vital to recognize that your website is an advertisement like any other, and should be designed with that in mind. If you have seen other business websites,

DOS AND DON'TS OF WEBSITES

✓ Do make it clear on your home page just what your business does.

✓ Do include some background information on your business.

✓ Do have a "return to home" button on each page.

✓ Do provide an opportunity for feedback by email or phone.

✓ Do give your full postal address to establish credibility.

✓ Do ensure your site is registered with all major search engines.

✓ Do provide useful links to related sites.

✗ Don't include too many photos on your opening page, as they slow it down.

✗ Don't have too many layers requiring a great deal of mouse-clicking.

✗ Don't insist on registration simply to get on to your site.

✗ Don't be anonymous – always provide contact names.

✗ Don't create your website then forget about it.

you will know that the quality and ease of use of different sites varies considerably. Visit a variety of sites and note features that appeal to you and that you find easy to use. Analyze how the sites are structured and the usefulness of the various links within them. As with the design of any advertisement, keep in mind your target market and their needs, in addition to your own e-commerce objectives.

Your opening home page should load quickly, without an initial "click here to enter the site" page. The home page should have your business title clearly visible and make a clear statement as to who you are and what you do, so that visitors know immediately if the site is relevant to them. Not only do you want to attract the right visitors, but also keep them interested enough to browse your other pages. A home page benefits from buttons that give clear options for moving around and locating further information. Ideally, this should not require scrolling down, which is universally disliked by browsers.

Promotion of your website is as important an activity as its creation. Merely creating a site is unlikely to generate sufficient visitors. Right from the start you should consider the keywords for the search engines to find. Look at rival sites to see which keywords they use. Also include common misspellings of your keywords. Ensure your new website is registered with all major search engines. Once it is up and running, be sure to promote the site through any other advertising you do, printing your website address on all your stationery and literature. The proactive marketing of your site will involve looking for other sites that relate to yours and suggesting a hypertext link directly to your site (possibly in exchange for a similar link from your site to theirs). Although time-consuming, this is potentially a very worthwhile process.

If you plan to sell on-line, this raises new issues. The first is how to have secure credit card or debit card transactions, which requires specialized knowledge to set up properly.

TIME SAVER

It may save you time and ultimately produce a more effective display ad if you employ a designer to help you. Look at ads the designer has produced in the past to form an idea of their work. Provide a detailed written brief and ask about likely charges.

Another issue is that your business needs to be structured to process these orders and handle the email traffic that the site should generate.

Finally, after putting a great deal of thought, effort, and money into the actual creation of your new website, you need to keep it up to date to maintain its effectiveness. Having out-of-date information on a site reflects badly on the business concerned.

MONITORING ADVERTISING RESULTS

Few businesses, whether large or small, make enough effort to monitor the results of their advertising, although this is crucial to testing and refining your advertising strategy. There are basically three direct ways and one indirect way in which you can monitor the success of an advertising campaign:

■ Ask any customer who phones or emails where they saw your ad.
■ In any ad incorporate a name or room number to your return address (a different one for each publication), so that you can detect the source of written replies.
■ Ask any customers you meet, for example, on your exhibition stand.
■ Observe changes in your sales. Athough this can be difficult to calculate as there will be other variables, it is still worth the effort.

ADVERTISING ON THE INTERNET
Now that internet cafés have made the internet accessible to almost everyone, it makes sense for even the smallest of businesses to have their own websites and capitalize on this latest form of advertising.

Producing Press Releases

If you can get a favorable editorial mention in a publication or a broadcast program that is relevant to your line of work, it can be an extremely cost-effective method of promoting your business. An editorial piece is more likely to be read and noted than an advertisement, and it will carry more authority.

The way to go about this is usually started with you producing a press release and sending it to the kind of publication that might be interested in your story. The editorial staff may then use the text from your press release to create a feature, usually backed up by a phone interview with you. If the matter is sufficiently newsworthy, they may send a journalist, and perhaps a photographer, to talk to you.

Just what makes a good story depends on the context. For instance, a trade publication will be interested in anything related to that industry, especially if the topic is new to them, while a newspaper will be looking for something of

more general interest, yet topical. A specialized consumer magazine's editorial interest, on the other hand, will lie somewhere between the other two types. If you read a few issues of each kind of publication, you will soon become familiar with the type of editorial features each one prefers to run.

There are some snags, however, in getting involved with the press. You cannot be sure that the publication will run your story, or the editor may choose to print your article days or weeks later, when it is much less helpful to you. In addition, they will probably write the piece in their own words, are quite likely to make mistakes (especially with prices or dates), and add their own bias, which may not be flattering. The whole process is completely outside of your control.

Sample Press Release

Keep any press release short, factual, and to the point, but ensure that it includes all the information a journalist is likely to need to write an article.

As press release ties in with a specific event, it indicates the earliest date for publication

Subject of press release is clearly indicated in heading

Start with the newsworthy event, then put it into context

Headed notepaper is used, with contact details

customer complaints *unlimited*

Boulder Canyon Drive

PRESS RELEASE
NOT FOR PUBLICATION OR BROADCAST BEFORE MAY 2

LAUNCH OF NEW CONSUMER COMPLAINTS BUSINESS

A new internet-based business went on-line today to help consumers with any complaints they may have.

This high-tech approach to consumer affairs is run by Suzy Smith, 42, a qualified lawyer and an expert in the field. She runs the business from a custom-built office near her picturesque home in the foothills. Her organization will give consumers the opportunity to have their complaints pursued. Suzy has created a network of associates (all with law or consumer affairs expertise) to deal with the inquiries, which are handled by email and fax to keep costs down and efficiency up.

Quotations and comments are included from relevant people

Suzy Smith said: "At present consumers who have a complaint do not necessarily know what steps they should take or who they should approach, or even if they may be due some compensation. However, most people are more concerned about getting an apology and the situation corrected than financial compensation. Our networked expertise amounts to almost 100 man years of work in this field, which people can readily tap into."

The director of the local enterprise organization, Robert Brown, said: "We are delighted to have been able to assist Suzy Smith with this venture. We helped her prepare her business plan and provided other advice. This is the 250th new business start-up that we have been involved with this year."

Indicates that photographs are included

Direct contact details

PHOTOGRAPH attached

FOR MORE INFORMATION
Contact   Suzy Smith
Tel   303-765-4321
Website   www. ... .com

Exhibitions, Seminars, and Promotions

For a home-based business, sales generally have to be made on a time-consuming, one-to-one basis. However, exhibitions and seminars give you the opportunity to meet potential customers *en masse*. There are also a number of promotional methods that are useful for securing future business from a large number of people.

EXHIBITIONS

At exhibitions your business has to show its wares alongside potential competitors on their own stands. Exhibitions are good for giving a home-based business regional, national, or international exposure, as well as providing useful contacts and feedback. But many new exhibitors are disappointed with their initial showings, which may be due to unrealistic expectations and inexperience.

First of all, you need to establish what you are likely to achieve from taking a stand at an exhibition, and decide which exhibition(s) you wish to appear at. Visit these shows and try to talk to anyone who will listen; small exhibitors are often willing to discuss the event with you, provided they are not busy on their stand. You will also need to make it clear who you are and why you want to speak to them so they know you are not a likely competitor.

Good stand positions are usually taken by long-term exhibitors or are very expensive, but you cannot afford to be in a poor location. Walk around and get a good feel for the show, so if you decide to take a stand the next time the event is held you will know which locations to avoid.

Making the most of an exhibition appearance requires an adequate budget and hard work before, during, and after the event. Because exhibiting can be time-consuming and costly, the decision to participate should not be taken lightly. During the show itself, remember to pace yourself and take time out to eat and drink, and sit down whenever you can. Avoid alcohol and turn in early at night. After the show, follow up any sales leads you have made.

SEMINARS

These are for presenting your product or service to a carefully chosen group of people whom you consider to be prospective customers. The key to a seminar's success is having the right people present; and once you have your captive audience you can give your sales pitch, but the presentation must always be interesting and entertaining.

You can either invite people to the event, which could be held at a convenient venue such as a local hotel, or you may be able to add your seminar on to some other event, such as a trade association or chamber of commerce meeting. Whether you are doing the presentation yourself or hiring a professional speaker, take the time to prepare high-quality visual aids, and have samples on display and

Promotional Techniques

Technique	Definition	Points to Consider
MAILSHOT	A personalized letter or a leaflet is sent to a customer introducing a special offer.	■ Useful for both consumer and business customers. ■ Cost is average compared to other methods, but depends on complexity of design. ■ Response rate variable and unpredictable.
SAMPLE	A sample of a product is sent to an individual.	■ Effective when sent to someone with major buying power in an organization, or to someone who influences buyers, such as the editor of a magazine. ■ Follow up with a phone call a week or so after sending.
FREE TRIAL	The customer tries out a product before buying or as an incentive to buy.	■ Most suitable for high-value, one-time purchases, which the customer tries for a set period of time, or for low-value, repeat-purchase items, such as consumables. ■ Can be very effective with a targeted market.
COMPETITIONS/ RAFFLES	A raffle is organized with prizes of the products to be promoted.	■ Requires legal advice to comply with regulations governing raffles, and local permission to sell the tickets. ■ Prize must be suitably attractive (or expensive) for people to enter the raffle.
IN-STORE DEMOS	A manufacturer or importer organizes a demonstration of a product in a store.	■ Store is usually carrying the product, so the demo often results in immediate sales. ■ Demo needs to be carried out with enthusiasm.
OPEN DAYS	An office, workshop, or studio is opened to the public.	■ A lot of organization is needed to make the day successful. ■ Need to put on special displays to interest visitors. ■ Event must be publicized well in advance. ■ Check you are covered by insurance for visitors.
VIDEO/CD	Information about a product is made available on a video or as video clips on a CD-ROM.	■ Ideal for conveying a complex message or to demonstrate how a product works. ■ A CD-ROM could have an interactive element and a frequently asked questions (FAQ) section. ■ Expensive to produce and to alter.
FASHION SHOW	Used in the fashion and accessory industry, a show is put on to display new products.	■ Requires considerable time, skill, and money to stage an impressive show with the right venue, experienced models, and good-quality sound and lighting. ■ A good means of influencing trade and public buyers.

ON THE CATWALK
Holding an in-store promotion, such as a fashion show, will introduce your product to a mass audience. Make sure that the event is fun for everyone concerned.

leaflets for people to take away. It is important to rehearse your presentation at least once at the venue so that you become used to the conditions and can time the presentations and iron out any technical glitches.

PROMOTIONS

Advertising, press releases, exhibitions, and seminars are not the only ways to let potential customers know that your business exists and what your products or services can do for them. There are many other promotional methods – some of the more popular ones are given in the table at left. It is important to note that the way in which you promote your business can depend on the circumstances and the timing; for the best results, focus on a particular objective rather than simply the desire to be better known.

Selling Techniques

With the possible exception of former sales staff, most people who start their own business have not had to sell to others before, and may feel daunted by the prospect. The good news is that there are many basic selling techniques that are easily learned and, when put into practice, should result in sales. You do not need to use a hard sell to succeed; in fact a gentle approach often works better. Even the most reluctant salesperson can feel elated making a sale, particularly when clinching the deal depended on their sales technique.

There is a saying that "customers buy benefits, not goods or services." This is an important concept to grasp. It is best illustrated by an example. Two soccer fans may buy a video recorder because they want the benefit of being able to replay their favorite games. If there were some better way to do that, they might not buy a video recorder. In other words, it is not really the recorder, with all its clever features, they want but the benefit it gives them.

With any selling, you must start out knowing your product or service inside out, and being aware of all its potential benefits to buyers.

FACE-TO-FACE SELLING

The first challenge is to get an appointment to see a potential customer. You can start by either writing a letter or by making a phone call.

Writing first and then telephoning about a week later allows you to introduce yourself and your business, while the phone call gives you the opportunity to request an appointment. Some prospective buyers will agree to meet you, others will refuse, while others may simply avoid speaking to you. Remember that the person you are contacting will be thinking "What's in this for me?", so keep your written and spoken messages relevant to *them*, rather than relevant to *you*.

MAKING A SALE

No matter how good your product or service, your selling technique is crucial to the success of your business. The sales meeting should follow a definite pattern.

■ **MEETING** Smile, make eye contact, and give a warm handshake. Hand over your business card and ask for the buyer's.

■ **GREETING** It is conventional to discuss noncontroversial subjects first for a few minutes, such as your journey or the weather. You may be offered a coffee or tea. These niceties all help to break the ice.

■ **OPENING STATEMENTS** You will probably get the chance to speak first, so deliver a short statement expressing what you can do and the likely benefits for the buyer. Do not talk for too long, as you need to know the buyer's reaction.

■ **NEGOTIATING** The buyer then details his or her needs and objections, and you try to convince them that you can meet those needs and that there are no grounds for objections.

■ **CLOSING THE SALE** In time you will sense when a buyer is ready to purchase. He or she may start to ask detailed questions or talk about methods of payment. Answer the

questions and then close the sale by taking out your order book and asking something like "How many do you want?" or "On what date should we start the work?"

■ **DOING THE PAPERWORK** Once the order has been agreed by both parties, ask the buyer to sign a duplicate copy of the order form, which should include the agreed price, terms, and timescales.

CONFIDENT OPENING
To make sure you engage the buyer's attention, it is important to establish eye contact and to smile warmly as you introduce yourself and shake hands.

Assuming you are given an appointment, then you need to be fully prepared. Learn as much as you can about the buyer (and his or her company, if a business buyer), then assemble your sales material. This is a key element of face-to-face selling and consists of samples, brochures, business cards, order forms, and possibly a calculator or laptop computer if you need to come up with quotes or estimates on the spot. Have your price list on hand and make sure you know your bottom price – the price below which you are not prepared to go.

SELLING BY TELEPHONE

The telephone can be a very useful selling tool, but to use it effectively requires skill and practice. The main advantages of selling by phone are that you can contact a large number of people in a relatively short period of time, and you can often get through directly to the decision-maker. The main disadvantages are that you cannot show your product or other sales material to the customer, and you cannot accurately gauge their reactions from their face or body language.

Preparation is essential. Know the name of the person you are calling and what you are trying to achieve with the call. Handle the conversation in very much the same way as you would any sales meeting. In your opening statement identify yourself and your business, and state clearly the purpose of your call. Rehearse this opening statement but do not recite it mechanically. Then concentrate on fact-finding and getting across your sales message. Do listen, though, and be prepared to answer questions and to enter into negotiations.

Since there is nothing in writing, always end the call by summarizing what has been agreed and later confirm it in writing, if necessary.

TELEPHONE SELLING
The more you sell by telephone, the easier it becomes. A relaxed but efficient manner engenders a positive response in potential customers. Always have your facts and figures close at hand to instill confidence.

SELLING BY MAIL ORDER

Assuming you have sufficient storage space, this method of selling is particularly suitable for a home-based business, as your customers can be located almost anywhere. The first step is finding those customers. Usual techniques are either to acquire a good-quality mailing list or to advertise (including on your website). Always carry sufficient stock to meet orders promptly, as customers expect a rapid turnaround. Handling phone orders takes time, but it should be made a pleasant experience for callers, so do not rush them. Payment should be by credit card, debit card, or check with order, as giving open credit can cause

problems, even if the sums of money are small. Packaging and distribution costs are high, and customers dislike paying much for "postage and handling," so the product prices need to absorb some of the distribution costs. Mail order succeeds mainly when the customer is unable to buy the products readily from local stores.

Keeping Simple Accounts

Business is all about money, and its proper management is paramount to the success of any venture. It involves the correct operation of your business bank account, and keeping accurate and up-to-date records, including a set of accounts. You should also carry out cash-flow forecasts at least every month to ensure you never run out of cash (see pp. 96–9).

YOUR BUSINESS BANK ACCOUNT

When you set up your business bank account, ensure you get monthly statements. These help you to check the balances in your accounts book. Once you have opened the business account, it is vital to keep track of the value of the checks you have written. If your check book has stubs, fill them in and then write on the next unused check stub the approximate amount left in the account. Thus you are always aware of the balance and are never in danger of inadvertently overdrawing the accounts. Watch out for direct debits and credits that will affect the balance.

Bank charges can add up to a substantial amount over the year and it is wise to take steps to keep the charges down by writing business checks only when you have to, using a credit card whenever you can, and minimizing the number of banking transactions you make. Ensure you know the exact charges that your account is incurring. Using the internet or phone to access your account offers a flexible, convenient way to keep track of your money and may give you lower charges, too.

If you handle cash, keep it separate from your personal money to avoid confusion and making the tax authorities suspicious.

KEEPING RECORDS AND ACCOUNTS

There are two reasons why you have to keep financial records: first, to meet the requirements of the tax authorities; and

---

BASIC ACCOUNTING TERMINOLOGY

CREDIT NOTE Although this may look like an invoice, it is, in fact, a statement of money owed in the form of credit.

DELIVERY NOTE A contents slip included with goods that are delivered or collected (usually on credit).

EXEMPT SUPPLIES* Business transactions that are not liable to sales tax.

INPUT TAX* This is the sales tax you pay on your business purchases and expenses, and which you can normally reclaim.

INVOICE The bill you receive when you buy something, or the bill you issue to your customers for selling goods or providing services.

OUTPUT TAX* This is the sales tax you charge customers when you make taxable supplies (see below).

RECEIPT A slip confirming payment. This is often not issued if payment is made by check, but is useful when payment is by cash.

REMITTANCE ADVICE A slip (often sent with a statement to a customer) that the customer then returns with their check to indicate who is paying.

STATEMENT A summary of invoices issued and payments received. Normally issued monthly to a customer who is buying on credit.

TAXABLE SUPPLIES* Business transactions that are liable to sales tax. Those not liable are called exempt supplies (see above).

TAX PERIOD* The period covered by a sales tax return; usually three months.

TAX POINT* This is the "time of supply" and is usually when goods were supplied or a service was completed.

SALES TAX RATE* If a total includes sales tax, multiplying the price by the sales tax rate will give the amount of sales tax.

* relevant only if you are registered for sales tax

second, to enable you to have a tight control over your business finances.

ORGANIZING INVOICES

Keep receipts and invoices for everything you buy in connection with your business. (Here, for simplicity, the word "invoice" will be used to mean receipt as well.) The purpose of keeping invoices is so that you have proof of purchase and can justify all of your expenses to your accountant and any tax official. As you receive invoices, they need to be filed in a useful and accessible way.

For those invoices paid by check, you could file them in a loose-leaf file, in check number sequence. Write the last three digits of the check number boldly in red ink on an outside corner of the invoice so that it can be easily cross-referred to your check book and accounts. You can use a card divider in the file to separate paid invoices from unpaid ones. This should prevent you from forgetting to pay any bills, especially if you always place unpaid invoices into the file as soon as you receive them.

BASIC RECORDS

Keep a record of your sales as proof for the tax officials, and for your own information. For a home-based business, this record is likely to be a duplicate copy of all the invoices you issue. In addition, you must retain your business bank statements, deposit books, check book stubs, orders and delivery notes, relevant correspondence, import and export documents, copies of any credit or debit notes, and a list of goods taken from the business for personal use or supplied to someone else in exchange for goods or services. If you transfer any money between your business and personal bank or credit union accounts, then you must also retain those statements. Record, too, all purchases or sales of assets used in your business. Ask your accountant in advance what records he or she will want to see at the end of your tax year. If you employ staff, you will also need to keep records relating to withholding.

BASIC BOOKKEEPING

You may be planning for your accountant to keep your books for you, but this is not ideal for two reasons. First, and most important, knowing your exact financial situation is the key to managing your business; if you do the books yourself, then you ought to know what is happening. Second, using an accountant to do your bookkeeping will be expensive.

There are many ways of keeping accounts, and any one is acceptable provided that you, your accountant, and a tax official can understand it. Knowing how the system works yourself is vital; some small businesses have failed partly because their bookkeeping system was so complex that the proprietor could not readily understand it. Unless you are familiar with bookkeeping, filling in an accounts book by hand will initially give you a better feel for your

GOOD BOOKKEEPING

1. Always do weekly (or monthly) balances, since these will soon reveal any errors you may have made.

2. A good time to do your books is just after you receive your bank statement.

3. From the bank statement, reconcile checks and deposit slips against the transactions listed, to reveal any checks not yet cashed or deposits not yet shown.

4. When balancing, if you are out by some amount, then first look for an entry of the same amount that might be in the wrong place or miscounted.

5. If not registered for sales tax, your figures should always include any sales tax you have been charged.

6. Remember that only expenditure that is wholly and exclusively for your business is normally tax-deductible and therefore worth recording.

7. Keep your bookkeeping up to date – it gets harder to do the longer you leave it.

SINGLE-ENTRY ACCOUNTS BOOK
The example illustrated here is for a cash business, and is a record of one week's transactions.

The week's transactions in cash, checks, postal orders, and credit cards are recorded here

This column records the week's business bank account transactions

This column shows the week's payments made by cash and check

Here, the "start of week" figure is 0 for the first-ever business week; otherwise, it is the previous week's "end of week" figure

Here, the "start of week" figure is 0 for the first-ever business week; otherwise, it is the previous week's "bank balance" figure

Write all daily sales here

This total should equal "Cashed checks" in the next column

Record money from other sources here

It may be easier to record these when your bank statement arrives

Ensure this figure is the same as "Total bankings" in the next column

If there is a discrepancy between the balance and the money counted, record it here

Complete this only when your bank statement arrives; the bottom line should equal the balance on the bank statement

Add checks minus bankings that have not yet appeared on the bank statement

Enter this total in the "Week's money balance" under "Cash payments"

Enter this total in the "Week's bank balance" under "Check payments"

WEEK COMMENCING ....

MONEY RECORD

MONEY IN HAND AT START OF WEEK	$	¢
	178	23

DAILY TAKINGS		
Monday	63	12
Tuesday	39	73
Wednesday	127	32
Thursday	98	40
Friday	122	43
Saturday	163	82
Sunday		
TOTAL TAKINGS	614	82

OTHER MONEY, LOANS, ETC		
Cash from bank	50	00
From private a/c	1,000	00
TOTAL	1,050	00

WEEK'S MONEY BALANCE		
Money at start of week plus daily takings plus other money, loans, etc	1,843	05
Less total bankings	1,571	71
Less cash payments	161	02
LEAVES: BALANCE	110	32

MONEY IN HAND AT END OF WEEK		
	110	22

DISCREPANCY +/–		10

BANK RECORD

BANK BALANCE AT START OF WEEK	$	¢
	841	27

DAILY BANKINGS		
Monday	158	23
Tuesday		
Wednesday	80	65
Thursday		
Friday	1,332	83
Saturday		
Sunday		
TOTAL BANKINGS	1,571	71

BANK DIRECT DEBITS, ETC		
Cashed checks (071)	50	00
Charges/interest/	34	75
lease/loan		
TOTAL	84	75

WEEK'S BANK BALANCE		
Bank balance at start of week plus daily bankings less bank direct debits plus bank credits	2,328	23
Less chk payments	1,920	21
LEAVES: BALANCE	408	02

BANK STATEMENT CHECK		
Balance (from above)	408	02
Add total checks	1,509	00
Less total bankings	1,332	83
LEAVES	584	19

PAYMENTS RECORD

	PAID BY CASH			PAID BY CHECK		
	REF	$	¢	REF	$	¢
Stock/Raw Materials						
A. Jones	133	22	20			
A. Ali & Co				072	87	23
L. Armstrong	134	12	32			
Brown & Son				073	107	24
J. Smith Ltd				076	156	90
Stock/Raw Materials subtotals		34	52		351	37
Advertising/promotion						
Business insurances						
Cleaning						
Withdrawals/Salaries/Pension (self)	140	80	00			
Electric/Gas/Heat (Elec)				074	23	79
Fees (e.g., accountant, lawyer)						
Car - Fuel				079	9	00
- Repairs/Service						
- Tax/Insurance						
Postage/Packages	136	1	12			
Rates						
Rent						
Repairs/Maintenance						
Staff wages J. Walker				075	22	60
I. Woodall	139	40	00			
Staff Withholding						
Stationery/Printing	137	3	50			
Sundries 135 56¢ 138 $1.32		1	88			
Telephone/Fax						
Traveling						
Any other expenses						
Refund customer (by mail)				077	13	45
CAPITAL EXPENDITURE						
Van (second-hand)				078	1,500	00
TOTAL CASH AND CHECK PAYMENTS		161	02		1,920	21

finances, especially in the critical first year of business. Then consider switching to keeping your accounts on computer.

Every business needs an accounts book to record the funds received and payments being made; and these records should relate to the bank statements, and invoices from sales and purchases. When you start, you will probably only need to keep a single-entry accounts book (sometimes called a "cash book"). You can buy a preprinted accounts book (similar to that shown at left), which comes with instructions. Alternatively, you could buy a blank "analysis book," which is merely ruled with lines and columns, has no headings or instructions (and therefore requires some knowledge of bookkeeping), but has the advantage of being more flexible. The headings used in a standard or a blank book need to relate to what is on tax forms; you can add your own subheadings relating to your own cash management systems if you wish. Cash businesses usually need to keep weekly records, and credit-based businesses monthly records.

Avoid letting your outgoings exceed your income — you will simply run out of cash

MORE COMPLEX BOOKKEEPING

As your business grows you may need to consider moving to more complex (and expensive) systems. As its name suggests, double-entry bookkeeping involves entering each transaction twice: once in the general ledger, and a second time in the appropriate ledger (such as a sales or purchase ledger). Usually the move to a double-entry multiledger system occurs not because your turnover has reached any particular level, but because you need more control of purchases and sales made on credit. The double-entry system enables you to keep track of credit transactions to come, as well as the current position. Not surprisingly, operating a multi-ledger system takes much more time and effort and its users usually computerize their accounts. The majority of computer accounts programs use a double-entry system; before you operate such a program, it is essential to understand the concepts behind it.

AT YEAR END

At the end of the year (your financial or tax year, rather than the calendar year), there are important, but relatively simple, additional tasks to carry out. For instance, if you hold any stock, raw material, or part-completed work, you need to do an inventory on the last day of your financial year. This involves counting all the different items you have and valuing them (normally at cost price). Another task is to list all your business creditors (people to whom you owe money) and debtors (people who owe you money) on that date.

From the accounts you keep and the additional figures you provide at the year's end, your accountant will produce a tax return, an annual profit and loss account, and a balance sheet. Together, these describe and sum up your business's financial position.

PREPARING A BUSINESS PLAN

Once you have decided which business to set up from home and how to go about it, you should prepare a business plan. This sets out in words and figures a proposed business venture and acts as a lead up to its launch. It is a summary of the research you have done so far, covering personnel, a description of your proposed project, and finance, and should be adhered to as you establish your business and also during the initial months of operation. The type of plan described in this chapter is also suitable for submitting to a bank if your enterprise is small yet requires some financial backing.

Although having a business plan does not in itself guarantee the success of your venture, it does help to focus your ideas. The purposes of a business plan are to:
■ transfer your thoughts to paper
■ help you to monitor the project
■ raise money, if necessary.
When you decide to set up a new business there are many aspects to consider, but by putting down the business idea in a structured plan you will be able to assess the project more objectively. Furthermore, to complete the plan you will have to answer a lot of questions and this will make you do the necessary research.

Plan ahead at every stage of starting up your business

Start by completing the business plan checklists on the following pages – use pencil to allow for any changes – or type out a similar document. If you need to raise money for your venture, you will have to submit a typed document to your bank and other potential financiers. The plan given here is suitable for the majority of small home enterprises, but where the total start-up funding exceeds a certain amount (your bank will inform you of what this is), a more detailed and lengthy plan is required. This is simply because the bank's level of scrutiny is greater, the larger the amount to be borrowed.

CASE STUDY: Anticipating Future Expenditure

CATHY HAD STUDIED design at art college and in her spare time made jewelry, which she sold to friends and to several local retailers. After a few years of doing a variety of sales jobs, during which time she saved some capital, she decided to turn her jewelry business into a full-time enterprise. Her plan was to start the business on a small scale from home, but eventually set up a direct sales organization,

where independent distributors would sell the jewelry. Cathy realized that there were many options open to her as the venture could be structured in a number of different ways, so she knew she had to write them down to resolve the questions. In writing her business plan, she discovered the level of additional research she needed to do and also what funds she would actually need; these turned out to be more than she had anticipated.

TWO HEADS ARE BETTER THAN ONE
Thorough research is vital when you are putting together your business plan. Make sure you involve all interested parties and enlist the help of a good accountant.

SUPPORTING DOCUMENTS
In addition to completing the checklists on the following pages, you should ask for your accountant's help to prepare a projected profit and loss account (sometimes abbreviated to a projected P&L). This is an important summary of the likely overhead that your business will face and the profit it should make. Larger projects will also require a projected balance sheet, which lists the projected assets and liabilities of the business. Ask your accountant to help you with this, too.

GETTING A SECOND OPINION
Even if you do not need to borrow money, you should still complete a business plan and show it to an accountant. This is a useful check to make sure that you have thought of everything and are not in danger of wasting your own

precious funds. In addition, if you know someone you can trust and who is already in business, you might ask them for their views on your plan.

Completing the Business Plan

Use the checklists on the following pages to help you prepare your business plan. The checklists are divided into five sections:
■ Part 1 – Personal Details (p. 90)
■ Part 2 – Project Description (pp. 91–3)
■ Part 3 – Start-up Costs (pp. 94–5)
■ Part 4 – Cash-flow Forecast (pp. 96–9)
■ Part 5 – Financial Summary (pp. 100–101).
Photocopy each checklist (permission granted by Dorling Kindersley) and then work carefully through each list, writing in your particular details. Not every question will be relevant to your project. Once completed, you have all the information you need for your business plan.

Part 1 – Personal Details*

You

Name: ....

Employment status: ....

Qualifications: ....

Relevant experience: ....
....

Dependant(s): ....

Reason(s) for starting a business: ....
....

Business Partner (where applicable)

Name: ....

Employment status: ....

Qualifications: ....

Relevant experience: ....
....

Dependant(s): ....

Reason(s) for starting a business: ....
....

Your address: ....
....

Home phone number: ....

Daytime phone number: ....

Mobile number: ....

Email address: ....

*Not necessary if you are showing this only to your family

PART 2 – PROJECT DESCRIPTION

General

Proposed business name (note 1): _____

Proposed legal form of business (note 2): _____

What will your business do (in some detail)? _____

Why is the business suitable for being home-based? _____

Which rooms/areas will the business require? _____

Market Research Results

Who will be your likely customers (note 3)? _____

What is the potential size of the market (note 4)? _____

Who is the competition? _____

What are the competition's strengths and weaknesses? _____

Why will customers use your business rather than a competitor's? _____

Pricing

What do your competitors charge? _____

What prices do you intend to charge? _____

What are your calculations and/or explanations for these charges? _____

Will you need to offer credit terms? _____

Advertising and Promotion
What do your competitors do?..

What are your options?..

What will be the cost of your advertising and promotion?...

How will you monitor your advertising and promotion?..

Employees
Will you need to employ anyone; part-time or full-time?...

What will be the function of employees?...

What will you pay employees?..

Do you have suitable facilities for employees?...

Does your home meet legal/insurance requirements?...

Suppliers
Who will be your main suppliers?...

What are their prices, lead times, and means of delivery (note 5)?...

What credit period are they prepared to offer?...

Legal Aspects
Are there any problems in working from your home (note 6)?...

Does your proposed business require any license or registration (note 7)?..

Will you be liable for business tax rates (notes 6 and 7)?...

Do you need to modify your home (requiring local planning permission)?..

Project Risk Assessment

What could be the main threats to your business? _____
_____
_____

What steps can be taken to minimize those threats? _____
_____
_____
_____

What contingency plans do you have? _____
_____

Insurances

What is the outcome of contacting your house insurers? _____
_____

What is the outcome of contacting your car insurers? _____
_____

Do you need any other business insurance? _____
_____

Timescales

What date do you aim to start the business? _____

What percentage of your day can you devote to the business? _____

What are the next three tasks you need to do? _____
_____
_____
_____

Notes

1. Note the legal requirements for business names (see p. 165).

2. The legal form (sole proprietor, partnership, or incorporated company) is covered on pp. 162–4.

3. Business customers or consumers? If business, state the type of business and where they are located. If consumers, state their age range, gender, income groups, and location.

4. It is unlikely you will supply the entire market, so be realistic about the share you will take.

5. You may have a problem if deliveries are made using a huge semi-tractor trailer.

6. Have you spoken to a lawyer?

7. Have you spoken to the relevant authorities?

Part 3 – Start-up Costs

Capital Expenditure (and Related Items)

Office Equipment	Details:	Costs:
Computer(s)		
Software		
Answering machine		
Fax		
Copier		
Phone(s)		
Mobile phone(s)		
Other equipment		

Office Furniture		
Desk(s)		
Chair(s)		
Shelving		
Cupboards		
Filing cabinet(s)		
Workbench		
Other furniture		
Lighting		

Machinery and Tools		
Specify:		

Vehicle(s) – for business use		
Specify:		
Vehicle tax		
Insurance		

Other Items (e.g. alterations to home): _____

Subtotal: $ _____

Administration Set-up Costs

Professional Fees	Details	Costs
Accountant		
Lawyer		

ADMINISTRATION SET-UP COSTS (CONTINUED)

Licenses ....

Subscriptions/Membership Fees ....

Business Insurances (not vehicles) ....

Stationery ....

Subtotal: $ ....

STOCK OR RAW MATERIALS

Suppliers	Details	Costs

Subtotal: $ ....

ADVERTISING AND PROMOTION COSTS

Item	Details	Costs
Advertising		
Leaflets		
Press releases		
Other promotions		

Subtotal: $ ....

ANY OTHER COSTS

Item	Details	Costs

Subtotal: $ ....

Completing a Cash Flow

Usually created with a computer spreadsheet, the cash-flow forecast is a key element of the business plan. It is just what it says: a prediction of the cash flowing in and out of the business, generally on a monthly basis. This forecast is normally done for 12 months, although a project with long lead times may need a 24- or 36-month forecast. In that case, the forecast for years two and three is usually done quarterly, as greater accuracy is unlikely.

Preparing the forecast requires estimates and assumptions, which should be explained in the business plan, together with hard facts derived from your research. The procedure for creating a forecast is given on pp. 98–9.

Rarely, if ever, is a cash-flow forecast right the first time. That does not diminish its importance, for the process of compiling the first cash-flow forecast forces you to face up to some harsh realities and make a number of important decisions. What makes a cash flow such an important tool for planning and controlling your finances is that you can update it regularly (at least monthly) and you can also experiment by inserting different figures to envisage different scenarios.

> *Be pessimistic with your cash-flow forecast and do not underestimate your overhead*

The following hints are intended to help you to complete your cash-flow forecast.

- **LINE 1 (SALES)** Here you estimate your likely sales (turnover) for the year ahead. If you are offering credit, you should show the payments in the month when you expect to receive the cash.
- **LINE 20 (REPAIRS AND MAINTENANCE)** Note that vehicle repairs are covered on line 17.
- **LINE 24 (STOCK/RAW MATERIALS)** Where relevant, there will be an initial stocking-up phase, and then this line should bear a relationship to the sales line, as you cannot make sales without stock.

FACT FILE

If it is very difficult to forecast your sales, do a break-even cash flow. Complete the whole cash flow, leaving the "sales" line until the end. Then insert what sales you have to make to break even – that is, ensuring the bottom line of the cash flow is positive or within your overdraft limit. You then know what level of sales you must achieve to survive.

If you are given credit by your suppliers, this can have a marked bearing on your cash flow.

- **LINE 30 (SALES TAX)** A small business may not need to register for sales tax unless its turnover exceeds, or is likely to exceed, the current threshold figure. In the example, the home-based craft shop has not registered for sales tax, so line 30 remains zero.
- **LINE 33 (NET CASH FLOW)** This is line 5 minus line 32. If the figure is positive it means that more cash was received than was spent during the month (good). If negative, more cash was spent than received (not so good).
- **LINE 34 (OPENING BALANCE)** This always starts at 0 for a new business, and each subsequent month equals the closing balance of the previous month.
- **LINE 35 (CLOSING BALANCE)** This is the forecast cash in the bank at the end of each month. If this line is negative, your bank account will be overdrawn. Either you need an overdraft, or you will need to cut down on expenses or boost sales income to get yourself "out of the red." The totals in this line represent neither a profit nor a loss. If you can keep the amount in this line positive (or at least within your overdraft limit), you will not run out of cash.

PART 4 – CASH-FLOW FORECAST

CASH IN	MAY	JUN	JUL	AUG	SEP	OCT	NOV	DEC	JAN	FEB	MAR	APR	TOTALS
1 SALES	1,500	2,000	4,000	6,000	4,000	3,000	5,500	10,000	1,500	2,500	4,000	4,500	48,500
2 BANK OR OTHER LOANS	0	4,000	0	0	0	0	0	0	0	0	0	0	4,000
3 OWNER'S CAPITAL	8,000	0	0	0	0	0	0	0	0	0	0	0	8,000
4 OTHER MONEY IN	0	0	0	0	0	0	0	0	0	0	0	0	0
5 TOTAL CASH IN	9,500	6,000	4,000	6,000	4,000	3,000	5,500	10,000	1,500	2,500	4,000	4,500	60,500
CASH OUT													
6 ADVERTISING AND PROMOTION	300	0	0	0	0	0	1,000	0	0	0	0	0	1,300
7 BANK CHARGES/INTEREST	0	50	50	100	50	50	50	72	50	50	50	50	622
8 BUSINESS INSURANCES	500	0	0	0	0	0	0	0	0	0	0	0	500
9 BUSINESS RENT	0	0	0	0	0	0	0	0	0	0	0	0	0
10 BUSINESS TAXES	0	400	400	400	400	400	400	400	400	400	400	0	4,000
11 CLEANING	0	0	0	0	0	0	0	0	0	0	0	0	0
12 DRAW/SALARIES/INSURANCE	0	500	500	750	750	750	1,500	1,000	1,000	1,250	1,250	1,250	10,500
13 ELECTRICITY/GAS/HEAT/WATER	0	150	0	0	150	0	0	150	0	0	150	0	600
14 FINANCE CHARGES	0	160	160	160	160	160	160	160	160	160	160	160	1760
15 LEGAL AND PROFESSIONAL	450	0	0	0	0	0	0	0	0	0	0	400	850
16 VEHICLE - FUEL	0	0	0	0	0	0	0	0	0	0	0	0	0
17 VEHICLE - OTHER EXPENSES	0	0	0	0	0	0	0	0	0	0	0	0	0
18 OTHER EXPENSES	0	0	0	0	0	0	0	0	0	0	0	0	0
19 POSTAGE/DELIVERY	0	0	0	0	0	0	0	0	0	0	0	0	0
20 REPAIRS AND MAINTENANCE	0	50	0	0	50	0	0	50	0	0	50	0	200
21 STAFF WAGES	0	0	0	0	0	0	0	0	0	0	0	0	0
22 STAFF WITHHOLDING	0	0	0	0	0	0	0	0	0	0	0	0	0
23 STATIONERY/PRINTING	50	10	10	10	10	10	10	10	10	10	10	10	160
24 STOCK/RAW MATERIALS	8,000	4,000	2,000	2,000	2,000	1,000	6,000	500	0	3,000	3,000	2,000	33,500
25 SUBSCRIPTIONS	0	0	0	0	0	0	0	0	0	0	0	0	0
26 SUNDRIES	80	50	30	20	20	20	40	30	20	20	20	20	370
27 TAX PAYMENTS	0	0	0	0	0	0	0	0	0	0	0	0	0
28 TELEPHONE/FAX	100	50	0	0	75	0	0	75	0	0	75	0	375
29 TRAVEL AND SUBSISTENCE	0	0	0	0	150	0	0	0	0	0	0	150	300
30 SALES TAX	0	0	0	0	0	0	0	0	0	0	0	0	0
31 CAPITAL EXPENDITURE	2,350	0	0	1,000	0	0	0	0	0	0	0	0	3,350
32 TOTAL CASH OUT	11,830	5,420	3,150	4,440	3,815	2,390	9,160	2,447	1,640	4,890	5,165	4,040	58,387
33 NET CASH FLOW	-2,330	580	850	1,560	185	610	-3,660	7,553	-140	-2,390	-1,165	460	
34 OPENING BALANCE	0	-2,330	-1,750	-900	660	845	1,455	-2,205	5,348	5,208	2,818	1,653	
35 CLOSING BALANCE	-2,330	-1,750	-900	660	845	1,455	-2,205	5,348	5,208	2,818	1,653	2,113	

HOW TO DO A CASH-FLOW FORECAST

These pages take you through the different stages of creating a cash-flow forecast on a computer spreadsheet as illustrated by the sample forecast on page 97. You start by filling in the estimated sales, which are likely to show seasonal variations and a gradual buildup. Next you estimate your outgoings. This should then reveal how much capital the business requires to get it started.

CASH IN											
1 SALES											
2 BANK OR OTHER LOANS											
3 OWNER'S CAPITAL											
4 OTHER MONEY IN											
5 TOTAL CASH IN											
CASH OUT											
6 ADVERTISING AND PROMOTION											
7 BANK CHARGES/INTEREST											
8 BUSINESS INSURANCES											
9 BUSINESS RENT											
BUSINESS TAXES											
CLEANING											

1 CREATE THE ROWS First open a blank spreadsheet on your computer. Next, create line (row) headings similar to the sample but adapted, if necessary, for your own venture.

CASH IN	MAY	JUN	JUL	AUG	SEP	OCT	NOV	DEC	JAN	FEB	MAR	APR	TOTALS
1 SALES													
2 BANK OR OTHER LOANS													
3 OWNER'S CAPITAL													
4 OTHER MONEY IN													
5 TOTAL CASH IN													
CASH OUT													

2 CREATE THE COLUMNS Working across the top line, write in the months as column headings, starting from the first month of business. Add a final column for the annual totals.

MONEY SAVER

As you become established, you may find it useful to break down the initial categories of your forecast. This will help you to see exactly how much you spend on specific items, such as stationery, and to assess more easily where savings can be made.

CASH IN	MAY	JUN	JUL	AUG	SE
1 SALES	1,500				
2 BANK OR OTHER LOANS					
3 OWNER'S CAPITAL	8,000				
4 OTHER MONEY IN	0				
5 TOTAL CASH IN	9,500				
CASH OUT					

3 ENTER THE CASH IN Now for the first month fill in the Sales (line 1) – unless you are doing a "break-even" cash flow, in which case complete this line at the very end. Skip line 2 at this stage, but fill in lines 3, 4, and 5 for the first month only.

CASH OUT					
6 ADVERTISING AND PROMOTION	300				
7 BANK CHARGES/INTEREST					
8 BUSINESS INSURANCES	500				
9 BUSINESS RENT	0				
10 BUSINESS RATES	0				
11 CLEANING	0				
12 DRAWINGS/SALARIES/NIC					
13 ELECTRICITY/GAS/HEAT/WATER	0				
14 FINANCE CHARGES					
15 LEGAL AND PROFESSIONAL	450				
16 MOTOR - FUEL	0				
17 MOTOR - OTHER EXPENSES	0				
18 OTHER EXPENSES	0				
19 POSTAGE/PARCELS	0				
20 REPAIRS AND MAINTENANCE	0				
21 STAFF WAGES	0				
22 STAFF PAYE/NIC	0				
23 STATIONERY/PRINTING	50				
24 STOCK/RAW MATERIALS	8,000				
25 SUBSCRIPTIONS	0				
26 SUNDRIES	80				
27 TAX PAYMENTS	0				
28 TELEPHONE/FAX	100				
29 TRAVEL AND SUBSISTENCE	0				
30 VAT	0				
31 CAPITAL EXPENDITURE	2,350				
32 TOTAL CASH OUT	11,830				

4 ENTER THE CASH OUT Fill in lines 6 to 32, skipping lines 7, 12, and 14 (also 30 if you are not sales tax-registered). Some of these expenses will occur in the first month only, although others, such as electricity or tax, may be due monthly or quarterly.

5 TOTAL CASH IN	9,500			

32 TOTAL CASH OUT	11,830			
33 NET CASH FLOW	-2,330			
34 OPENING BALANCE	0			
35 CLOSING BALANCE	-2,330			

5 WORK OUT THE CLOSING BALANCE
For the first column subtract line 32 from line 5 to get line 33; then add line 34 to get line 35.

10 BUSINESS RATES	0	400	400	400	400
11 CLEANING	0	0	0	0	0
12 DRAWINGS/SALARIES/NIC	0	500	500	750	750
13 ELECTRICITY/GAS/HEAT/WATER	0	150	0	0	150
14 FINANCE CHARGES	0	160	160	160	160

6 WORK OUT YOUR DRAWINGS
Insert in line 12 the minimum withdrawals on which you can survive for the month.

CASH IN	MAY	JUN	JUL	AUG	SEP	OCT	NOV	DEC	JAN	FEB	MAR	APR	TOTALS
1 SALES	1,500	2,000	4,000	6,000	4,000	3,000	5,500	10,000	1,500	2,500	4,000	4,500	48,500
2 BANK OR OTHER LOANS													
3 OWNER'S CAPITAL	8,000	0	0	0	0	0	0	0	0	0	0	0	8,000
4 OTHER MONEY IN	0	0	0	0	0	0	0	0	0	0	0	0	0
5 TOTAL CASH IN	9,500	2,000	4,000	6,000	4,000	3,000	5,500	10,000	1,500	2,500	4,000	4,500	58,500
CASH OUT													
6 ADVERTISING AND PROMOTION	300	0	0	0	0	0	1,000	0	0	0	0	0	1,300
12 DRAW/SALARIES/INSURANCE	0	500	500	750	750	750	1,500	1,000	1,000	1,250	1,250	1,250	10,500
13 ELECTRICITY/GAS/HEAT/WATER	0	150	0	0	150	0	0	150	0	0	150	0	600
14 FINANCE CHARGES													
15 LEGAL AND PROFESSIONAL	450	0	0	0	0	0	0	0	0	0	0	400	850
26 SUNDRIES	80	50	30	20	20	20	40	30	20	20	20	20	370
27 TAX PAYMENTS	0	0	0	0	0	0	0	0	0	0	0	0	0
28 TELEPHONE/FAX	300	50	0	0	75	0	0	75	0	0	75	0	375
29 TRAVEL AND SUBSISTENCE	0	0	0	0	150	0	0	0	0	0	150	0	300
30 SALES TAX	0	0	0	0	0	0	0	0	0	0	0	0	0
31 CAPITAL EXPENDITURE	2,350	0	0	1,000	0	0	0	0	0	0	0	0	3,350
32 TOTAL CASH OUT	11,830	6,210	2,940	4,180	3,605	2,180	8,950	2,215	1,430	4,680	4,955	3,830	56,005
33 NET CASH FLOW	-2,330	-3,210	1,060	1,820	395	820	-3,450	7,785	70	-2,180	-955	670	
34 OPENING BALANCE	0	-2,330	-5,540	-4,480	-2,660	-2,265	-1,445	-4,895	2,890	2,960	780	-175	
35 CLOSING BALANCE	-2,330	-5,540	-4,480	-2,660	-2,265	-1,445	-4,895	2,890	2,960	780	-175	495	

7 REPEAT STEPS 3–6 FOR EACH MONTH
You will almost certainly have a lot of negative figures in your bottom line (line 35), which indicates you need more start-up funding. If you have no negatives, you do not need a loan, and lines 2 and 14 will remain 0.

8 ESTIMATE THE MONEY YOU NEED
Assuming your line 35 figures are negative, try to estimate how much money you need for: capital expenditure (which would normally be funded by a loan, or lease); and the purchase of stock or raw materials (which would normally be funded by an overdraft). The cash flow should indicate a diminishing overdraft requirement as the months go on

CASH IN	MAY	JUN	JUL	AUG
1 SALES	1,500	2,000	4,000	6,000
2 BANK OR OTHER LOANS	0	4,000	0	0
3 OWNER'S CAPITAL	8,000	0	0	0
4 OTHER MONEY IN	0	0	0	0
5 TOTAL CASH IN	9,500	6,000	4,000	6,000
CASH OUT				
6 ADVERTISING AND PROMOTION	300	0	0	0
7 BANK CHARGES/INTEREST	0	50	50	100
8 BUSINESS INSURANCES	500	0	0	0
9 BUSINESS RENT	0	0	0	0

9 ADD LOAN REQUIREMENTS
Put any loan requirement figure into line 2 and add repayments on line 14. Check that the sum of line 2 together with any overdraft does not exceed your line 3 – banks usually prefer not to put more money into a project than that raised from other sources. Add figures in line 7 to cover normal bank charges plus interest on any overdraft (the latter is usually charged on a quarterly basis).

Use your cash-flow forecast to monitor your cash flow monthly or even weekly

Part 5 – Financial Summary

Current Personal Assets

Home ownership (note 1) ....

Savings ....

Stocks ....

Car(s) ....

Other major assets (note 2) ....

Forecast Domestic Costs (note 3)	**Details** (note 4)	**Costs**
Mortgage or rent		
Car loan payments		
Personal loan payments		
Pension payments		
Personal insurance		
Credit card payments		
Property tax		
Heat/electricity/water		
Phone(s)		
Direct debits		
Domestic loan repayments		
Estimate for food		
Estimate for clothes		
Estimate for other expenses		
Contingency fund (note 5)		

Subtotal: $ ....

Forecast Sales

Forecast total sales for first year (including/excluding sales tax?)   = $.............. (note 6)

Do you need to register for sales tax (note 7)? ....

On what basis are you calculating your first-year sales? ....

....

....

....

Forecast Business Costs (note 8)   Subtotals
Capital expenditure $ ....

    Administration set-up costs $ ....

    Stock or raw materials $ ....

    Advertising and promotion costs $ ....

    Any other costs $ ....

    Contingency fund (note 5) $ ....

                                              Total: $ ....

Personal funds available
    To meet forecast domestic expenditure $ ....

    For investment in the business (note 9) $ ....

Conclusion
    What is the amount of outside finance required? (note 10) $ ....

    What type of finance is required (note 11)? ....

....

....

Notes
1. This is the current market value minus any outstanding mortgage.
2. These are assets that can be readily sold to raise capital for the business.
3. This should be for the period it is estimated that the business will need to operate before it is profitable and generating some income. Think carefully about this as it will make a big difference if your estimate is six months but the business takes a year to become profitable.
4. For debts such as mortgage, car and personal loans, and credit card debts, give totals outstanding in this column.
5. Allow a contingency of 10 percent minimum, probably much more, depending on how sure you are with your figures.
6. This is the sales total (line 1) of your cash-flow forecast.
7. See p. 179 for more information on the need for registration for sales tax.
8. All these figures, other than the contingency, relate to your cash-flow forecast totals.
9. This is the owner's capital total (line 3) of your cash-flow forecast.
10. This is the bank or other loans total (line 2) of your cash-flow forecast plus a safe figure to cover the closing balance (line 35) should the latter be negative (i.e. overdrawn).
11. This should split the overall requirement into loans and overdraft.

Raising the Finance

Preparing your business plan will guide you toward how much money you need to raise to start your business. The main sources for a home-based business are, first, you; next, friends and relatives; third, banks, and, finally, for larger ventures, venture capitalists (see opposite), who might take an equity stake in the business. As well as financing major equipment, such as computer systems or vehicles, you can also take advantage of rent-to-own or leasing; and, if you need to make modifications to your home to accommodate your business, this could be financed by remortgaging your home. Get professional advice from your accountant before making any decisions.

FRIENDS AND RELATIVES

If any friend or relative agrees to help fund your business, it is essential that whatever is agreed is put down in writing. Unless it is a very small loan, the document should be drafted by a lawyer and give the following information:
- the amount of the loan
- when the loan is to be paid
- when the loan is to be repaid (be realistic)
- how the loan is to be repaid if the business runs into trouble (usually the repayment period is extended)
- what interest (if any) is to be paid
- to what extent the lender can interfere with the business
- who the money should be repaid to if the lender dies
- what should happen if the business stops operating – in the case of equity funding (that is, they buy some of the shares in your operating company), special professional advice is required, but that can have some advantages for you.

Spend time on your business plan even if you do not need any financial backing

BANKS

A bank will probably be your main source of outside funds, although be warned that they do not like to take risks and usually do not lend more than about half the total cost of the venture. Bank funding generally takes the form of loans and overdrafts.

- **LOANS** These are normally made to finance capital expenditure, such as computers, office furniture, or equipment. They can be at fixed or variable rates of interest, and are repaid monthly or quarterly over a pre-agreed "term" – usually two to five years.
- **OVERDRAFTS** Unlike loans, overdrafts are for short-term working capital. They can bridge the gap between buying stock and reselling it, providing a service and waiting to be paid, or buying raw materials and later selling a manufactured product. An overdraft, if granted, will be for up to an agreed amount. Never exceed this limit without prior permission from the bank manager, because the facility can be withdrawn at any time if it is thought that you are mishandling your financial affairs. An overdraft is usually the cheapest way to borrow money for your business, as you only pay interest on the daily balance "in the red." This interest is deducted automatically from your business bank account, usually each quarter.

Many businesses require a combination of loan and overdraft facilities when they start up. All banks publish and display their "base lending rate" but, as a home business, you will normally pay several percent more for your loan or overdraft. Ensure you know the rate that you are going to be charged and, remember that it is negotiable.

Many banks have their own format of business plan, which they may prefer you to use. These are sometimes paper-based or available on computer disk. Ask your bank what they would prefer to see.

ADVANTAGES AND DISADVANTAGES OF BUSINESS CREDIT

ADVANTAGES	DISADVANTAGES
You can get goods or services but not pay for them until some specified later date.	As a new business you may be refused business credit as you are an unknown credit risk.
Helps you through lean financial periods.	Business credit works both ways: your business customers will expect it from you, even if you are a new business.
Receiving business credit helps improve your cash flow dramatically.	Giving business credit will affect your cash flow adversely, which can be aggravated by customers being slow to pay or simply defaulting.
Reduces the need for short-term loans.	When offering business credit, you must operate an efficient billing and debt-recovery system.

Although you should not start by offering security against a business loan, a bank will normally request this in case the business fails. In any event you should not agree to security in excess of the value of loan you are requesting, and you should resist offering your home as security. If security is requested, always consult a lawyer before you agree to anything, and make sure you appreciate all the risks involved. This point is extremely important.

VENTURE CAPITALISTS
One of the fastest growing sources of private business funding today is individuals, often business people, who have already made their fortune and are now reinvesting it in other entrepreneurs' ventures. Known as venture capitalists, they are always on the lookout for new ideas and projects to back. But they are no softies! Just like banks, they expect a return, but they will probably be willing to help with advice and contacts, both invaluable to a fledgling home entrepreneur. Your venture will have to be reasonably substantial to interest them. Your accountant or lawyer may be able to help put you in touch with local business angels or support groups. As ever, obtain professional advice before accepting any equity funding from any source, particularly about the stake they wish to secure in your business.

USING BUSINESS CREDIT
If you need to purchase substantial amounts of goods or services, an excellent source of free finance is business credit. This is where a supplier allows you time, typically 30 days, before you have to pay. However, it is important to be realistic in your expectations of its use: there are disadvantages as well as advantages (see chart above). For example, as a new business you may be refused credit until you have satisfactorily paid for several invoices. But when your business is established you may be able to negotiate longer credit periods provided you have always paid on time.

Meanwhile, your business customers will expect credit from you, with larger companies sometimes insisting on 60 days or longer. This may be a problem for your cash flow, and it can be aggravated by one or more customers either being very slow to pay or simply defaulting on payment. In these circumstances, credit control is vital to your cash flow (and likely survival). Issue your invoices promptly and send out statements at the end of the month, as many companies only pay after receiving a statement.

ADAPTING
your home

Turning your home into a business headquarters as well as maintaining a domestic retreat requires a great deal of careful planning. This section outlines how to choose the most suitable space for your home office or workshop, from spare bedroom to garage and from attic conversion to basement. It reveals how to design and equip your new home work space to meet your needs most effectively, and offers pointers on creating a child-friendly office. The complex process of moving home and business together is also covered.

EVALUATING YOUR HOME

An estimated 20 million people in the U.S. work from home. Although many do not run their own businesses – either they are self-employed or work for an employer – the fastest-growing sector of business overall is based at home. This chapter examines how to create the optimum working environment, with the minimum disruption to family life, and also looks at various legal issues that may need to be considered when establishing your business at home.

If millions of people are able to set up their own venture at home, why not you? First, you need to determine whether your home can accommodate a business as well as its occupants. To do this, you must be clear about the type of venture you want to undertake. From that will stem the likely accommodation needs of the business.

Ask yourself whether your home is as suited to home working as you are

The chart at right gives a few examples of various business types and the kind of accommodation they require, but you will also need to consider the following:

■ **CREATING A DISTINCT WORKSPACE** Can you separate your working area from your home space? If not, work will bleed over into your home life to the detriment of both.

■ **KEEPING THE FAMILY AT BAY** Can you keep the rest of the household away while you are working? A major source of tension for the home worker is frequent interruptions, particularly from children.

■ **MAKING ROOM FOR YOUR OFFICE** Will you be able to create a comfortable working area without disrupting family life? Bear in mind that denying a room to the household can cause resentment, particularly among teenagers.

■ **HOLDING BUSINESS MEETINGS** If you anticipate having to hold business meetings at home, you will require a suitable private room or large table, away from the family, and possibly parking space.

■ **THE IMPACT OF POLLUTION** Will your business involve making noise, dirt, or fumes? If it does, you may have to seek planning permission, as well as the approval of neighbors.

CASE STUDY: Rethinking the Use of Rooms

DAVID WAS EAGER to pursue a publishing business from home. He and his wife concluded that a dedicated room would be needed to give him peace and quiet, as well as provide enough space to accommodate an assistant, when required. As there was no spare bedroom, they decided to turn the underused dining room into a home office with desks and a networked computer system. Since the business also needed storage space for pallets of magazines, they decided to use the garage. They agreed to work on this basis for up to two years to assess how well the venture performed. If it appeared successful, they would then consider building an office on top of the garage to provide a convenient home for the business and reduce the disruption to family life.

THE LIKELY ACCOMMODATION NEEDS OF THE BUSINESS

BUSINESS TYPE	EXAMPLE	WORK REQUIREMENTS	SPACE REQUIREMENTS
SERVICE COMPANY	Working at customers' homes and offices	Administration and preparation, some evening phone calls	Desktop, filing, storage: desk in bedroom or corner of kitchen table
	Based at home, using a phone and a computer	Selling, writing, administration, filing, phoning, emailing	Privacy, desk, filing: own room or partitioned corner of room
MAIL-ORDER VENTURE	Selling and distributing goods and services	Selling, administration, packaging, mailing	Office and storage space: own room or a corner plus garage
TRAINING BUSINESS	Teaching music, art, sports, exercise, computing	Preparing and delivering lessons	Ranges from corner of living room to dedicated equipped space
CRAFTS BUSINESS	Making and creating own-design works of art	Painting, woodwork, pottery, jewelry, clothes-making	Workspace away from living areas: garage, shed, attic, or basement
FOOD SERVICE BUSINESS	Preparing own recipes for general retail or own sale	Buying ingredients, cooking in quantity, wrapping, storing	Well-equipped kitchen, cold storage, administration facilities
HOSPITALITY BUSINESS	Running a bed-and-breakfast	Marketing, bookings, maintaining clean premises, cooking	Minimum of two large bedrooms, guest bathroom, dining room

Dealing with the Complications

As with most things in life that involve change, creating an effective workspace in your home is fraught with potential difficulties. It is best to be aware of these before making any final commitments. These complications fall into two categories: legal and neighbors.

LEGAL

Depending on the type of business you plan to set up, you may have to seek approval for it from various national and local government bodies, as well as organizations involved with the ownership and insurance of your home. The following issues need to be addressed:

■ **LOCAL PLANNING/ZONING REGULATIONS** Some districts do not allow businesses, no matter what they are, to be run from residential addresses. Check this with your local government's planning department.

■ **ALTERATIONS** If you need to carry out physical alterations to your property, such as creating a workspace in the attic or converting a garage to a workshop, you may need planning permission.

■ **FOOD REGULATIONS** Any business involving the handling, preparation, and selling of food will be subject to stringent controls covering equipment, cleaning, storage, and labeling. The local government's environmental health department will need to be consulted.

■ **WORKSPACE** You do not have to observe any particular regulations about the working environment as long as you are the only employee. But if you are likely to employ others, you may find you need to provide them with a minimum amount of working space and, if they will be using machinery, safeguards against injury.

■ **TENANTS** If you do not own your home, you should seek approval of the landlord – whether a company or a private individual – for starting a business. The odds are that your rental agreement will say that you are not allowed to run a for-profit venture from the premises without approval. That approval may not be granted if you are planning a business that will affect the condition of the house – through smoke and smell, for example – or the neighbors.

■ **MORTGAGE LENDERS AND INSURANCE** Read the small print of your mortgage agreement, and all home insurance policies. At the very least you may have to notify the agencies concerned before starting a business, and you may need to gain their formal approval for your plans. Existing home insurance policies will not cover any aspect of a business run from home. Again, at the least you may have to extend cover to costly office equipment.

This is not necessarily an exhaustive list of issues to address. You are going to need a lawyer anyway, so if you do not already have one, find a suitable firm, preferably through personal recommendation from others running local businesses. Read up on the likely legal issues relating to your specific business.

NEIGHBORS

Sometimes this issue can be the death of a promising home business! Do not assume that your new activities will go unnoticed, even if they are low-profile, or that, if you have good relations with your neighbors, the situation will continue once you start a business. Some people will not accept that you have the right to change your life if they think it might affect them, and they will become stubborn opponents. Against such entrenched attitudes it is hard to win a direct conflict. But remember, too, that there is no good reason why your neighbors should suffer just because you want to run a business from home.

The main potential areas for trouble between home entrepreneurs and their neighbors are:
■ noise
■ smell and smoke
■ external storage in the garden or driveway
■ visitors or employees taking up valuable parking spaces.

Use common sense to figure out if neighbors are likely to be affected by your business plans. For example, if you intend making wooden

---

MAINTAINING GOOD RELATIONS

Very many successful businesses operate happily from homes in the middle of town, in suburbs, and in the country. The secret is often to assume that there will be complications with authorities and neighbors, and to take careful steps in advance to mitigate them. Thinking through the situation from the point of view of others is the best defense against future problems. If you do not have a good relationship with your neighbors, it is likely to be difficult to get them to accept a business next door that causes disturbance and disruption. Equally, if you do have a good relationship with your neighbors, then friendly and informal consultation beforehand can often smooth the way. A good policy is to maintain a low profile.

toys in your garage during the evenings, beware of the noise that you will inevitably make and the interference caused to television reception by your electric tools.

Creating the Ideal Home Office

If you are serious about launching a business from a home base, you owe it to yourself to provide the best possible working conditions. Just because your HQ is also your home does not mean that you should have to tolerate an unpleasant or uncomfortable setup. Unless you envisage only a part-time venture to provide a supplemental income, trying to operate from the kitchen table will result only in frustration and inefficiency. Your business is unlikely to prosper under such conditions. The true extent of your commitment to a business venture will show in the decision you make over its location.

PRIORITY ONE

Maximize the amount of space you can devote to the business. Ideally, this should be a room (or part of a room) or an outbuilding that does not have to be cleared away for family or social gatherings. The location of your office is particularly important if you are likely to have business meetings at home; it does not present a particularly professional image to clients if they have to walk past the rest of the household getting on with their lives to reach you in the spare bedroom.

Other areas of the home that could be turned into a home office include:
▓ an underused dining room or playroom
▓ part of a living room
▓ a guest bedroom, with a fold-up wall bed
▓ a utility room
▓ dead space, such as a stairwell or landing.
Alternatively, and if you can afford it, create a new space out of an empty attic, basement, or garage. You can even build an extension, add

ROOM WITH A VIEW

It is always worth giving serious consideration to the location and layout of your home office. If you can, choose a room with a pleasant view and make the most of the natural light by positioning your desk by a window

another story onto an existing outbuilding, or create a custom-built structure in the yard.

Another option is to invest in one of the increasingly popular fold-up offices comprising a desk with computer rack and keyboard shelf, together with a pedestal drawer unit. When you have finished work for the day, clear away your papers (good for organization), fold up the unit, and push it into a corner, freeing up the room for domestic purposes.

However much you decide to spend on creating a home office, make sure you can reclaim the cost against tax over a period of several years. Check with an architect or real estate agent that you are adding to the value of the property rather than detracting from it.

PRIORITY TWO

Once you have your space, the conditions in which you are to work within it are important, too. For example, it would be impractical to expect yourself to spend eight hours a day working away in a drafty attic or cold basement. There are a number of key issues relating to comfort that should be considered.

■ **LIGHTING** The best light is natural light. A light, airy office with big windows is highly conducive to effective work. It will also minimize glare from your computer screen. If this is not possible, arrange a lighting system that evenly lights all the working surfaces to the same standard as natural daylight, to avoid eyestrain. If your work involves artwork and the use of colors, consider special lightbulbs that produce an effect close to natural sunlight.

■ **FRESH AIR** An overheated, stuffy room will quickly have your eyes drooping and your head sinking toward the desk, particularly in mid-afternoon, when energy levels are low. Ensure a good supply of fresh air. Research has shown that house plants help to improve air quality by absorbing toxins.

▓ **COLOR** Light pastel shades are most suitable for a working environment. They are less distracting than bold colors, and also help provide an atmosphere of space, calm, and control. Dark colors tend to create a sensation of confinement.

▓ **OUTLOOK** The best location for a home office is one with overlooking views. After all, what is the point of swapping a city-center concrete jungle for the domestic calm of the countryside if you cannot see the scenery? If you have to settle for a space without windows, place large photographs or portraits of the countryside on the walls, perhaps even a wall-sized photograph of a favorite view.

PRIORITY THREE

With your working environment settled, the last issue to consider is the arrangement of furniture, filing cabinets, computer equipment, and other components of the home office. This issue will most likely be decided according to your attitudes. Some people simply position the desk by a window so that they can see out, while, at the other extreme, some consult a feng shui expert to ensure that the layout accords with ancient ideas about harmony and positive thinking. Whatever your attitude, it is worth thinking practically about the layout of your workspace before you start spending money on a desk, chair, and other equipment. Here, too, it is worth considering the inevitable need for the networking of computers, printers, and scanners, together with the associated telecommunications equipment of phone, fax, and mobile-phone charger.

Give your home office a professional look, even if only you and your family will see it

Equipping Your Home Office

In what may be the first business transaction you make in your new life, you have to assign a realistic budget to equipping your home office with furniture and fixtures.

BUDGETING

Deciding how much you need to invest in your working environment will be dictated, first, by available finance and, second, need. Obviously, you will want to get the best value, and you also need to work out how you are going to pay for everything.

The first thing to do is to set an office equipment budget within your overall funding plan for the business, and then make sure you stick to it. There are many desirable distractions available on the home office market today, as a walk around any specialized store will show; but when first setting up in business at home you are unlikely to need everything you are tempted to buy.

The best purchasing deals are usually obtained through paying by cash and demanding a discount in return. Bank loans and credit cards are other methods of funding. Another option now increasingly available is to buy direct from manufacturers over the internet. Some of these even offer their own payment plans, but with all these deals, beware of high interest rates. As long as these items are for business use only, you will be able to offset their cost against your income for tax purposes by depreciating each item over its useful life, as determined by the Internal Revenue Service.

FURNITURE

The home office market is a multibillion-dollar industry worldwide, so there are many manufacturers competing for your business and offering a huge choice of products. Most large

furniture chains have their own home office
lines, while dedicated office furniture retailers
often carry products suitable for the home.

Before you make any big furniture-buying
decisions, remember that with a home-based
business you will probably be spending eight
hours a day, if not more, in your office, and you
will be sitting for around three-quarters of that
time. In addition, you will not be subject to the
usual distractions of office life – meetings,
casual chats, business lunches, and so on – and
so you will be even more dependent on the
specifications of your furniture for comfort and
the ability to concentrate.

Some home entrepreneurs take this process
so seriously that they call in specialized
designers to work out the optimum layout and
space utilization before placing any orders.
These space-planning advisers can be found in
most cities and also on the internet.

Start by making a list of your needs. For the
desk-based worker, the basics are, of course, a
desk, chair, filing cabinet, and probably a table
for a printer and scanner, as well as documents.
You will also need desk lamps, storage for
stationery, and desk trays. Then comes the
bookcase for reference works and perhaps a
wall chart or marker board.

This planning is complicated if you are
setting up a business with your spouse or
partner. Some people work well together and
can happily share a room with side-by-side or
facing desks. Others need a separate space and
will require the same equipment duplicated.

The most critical decision is not, surprisingly,
the type of desk, but the chair. A badly designed
chair can not only cause backache and sore legs,
but also adversely affect energy levels because of
a reduced blood supply to the brain.

When deciding on a chair, bear in mind that
you usually get what you pay for: a cheap chair
is unlikely to be truly comfortable and
supportive. Look for the following features:

▓ a five-legged base with double-casters, to
provide better stability and mobility

▓ gas-powered height adjustment over a range
of more than six inches

▓ an ergonomically shaped back, to support
the lower spine and shoulders

▓ adjustable armrests with padding, to support
the arms when using the keyboard

▓ firm upholstery that does not retain heat and
is not slippery.

Taking Account of Children

New home businesses are twice as likely to
be started by women. Recent research in
the U.S. shows that women are leaving
corporate jobs to become home entrepreneurs
at twice the rate of men. They tend to specialize
in the following types of business:

▓ publishing and other media

▓ graphic and internet design

▓ network marketing

▓ care services for the young and old

▓ crafts.

By 2005, it is estimated that 40 percent of all
home businesses in the U.S. will be owned and
run by women. It is a trend that is being
repeated all over the world, which is hardly
surprising – on two counts:

1 The corporate business world is still largely
male-oriented, and many women find it
more agreeable to run a business in their
own style from home.

OFFICE JUNIOR
Childcare may not always be available or desirable. Giving older children their own desk, stationery similar to yours, and perhaps even a play phone can help them to feel an important part of your working life.

■ Women still carry the main burden of bringing up children.

It is impractical to separate work from domestic responsibilities completely when you have young children, but there are ways of making your home office a safer place for them and a less disrupted workplace for you. The list on the right offers tips on how to make a child-friendly office and achieve such a balance.

The Ultimate Home Headquarters

Working from home is not just for the lone entrepreneur, whose vision is to build a business that will make him or her financially independent and support a reasonable lifestyle – although that is the main ambition of the majority of successful home enterprises.

MAKING A CHILD-FRIENDLY OFFICE

1 Make your office close to where your children play so that you are always on hand if there is a crisis.

2 Keep everything portable up on shelves away from small hands.

3 Keep babies out of harm's way in a playpen while you are working.

4 Attach locks to drawers and cupboards; simple magnetic ones will do.

5 Tape up, or otherwise protect, floppy disk drives on your computer.

6 Install software that prevents access to your work documents.

7 Make your mouse and screen accessible only by password.

8 Keep fixed hours so that children know when you are not to be disturbed.

9 Consider making your business an internet-based one to avoid direct client contact in person.

Modern business, with its ability to yield new markets capable of huge growth, is spawning a new breed of venturer whose aim is to build a multimillion-dollar business from home. But these are not just ordinary homes. Often designed and built specifically for the purpose, they are as much corporate headquarters as places to live. This may not feature in your game plan at the outset, but all of us need something to dream about.

The concept of building a substantial business, with dozens, perhaps thousands of employees, from a home base is still new. But as quality of life, as defined by freedom from stress and the ability to work in one's own style, becomes increasingly important, growing numbers of people are asking themselves why they should have to run their business from a corporate office as opposed to their home.

BIG BUSINESS FROM HOME

Obviously, enterprises with large numbers of employees based at a headquarters directly controlling a significant organization are not candidates for a home-based business – no matter how big the home! However, there is at least one organization accommodating 30 employees at its home-based headquarters, which is effectively an office block with living quarters built in.

The best candidates for a large, home-based business are probably the network marketing ventures, where a single entrepreneur can control a distributor network of thousands of self-employed people around the country, earning a multimillion-dollar income. Best established in the finance, health and beauty, home-care, leisure, and educational sectors, network marketing involves recruiting others to direct-sell the products on an incentive basis. For every dollar they make, you make a few pennies. Case studies in the U.S. show that you can build a $15-million business in five years.

ACCOMMODATING BIG BUSINESS

What type of home HQ do large ventures require? The office accommodation for network

LAP OF LUXURY
Taking advantage of modern communications technology, this entrepreneur can do much of his work from his luxury home, built as a result of his company's success.

TIME SAVER

Videoconferencing can be a useful tool for controlling a network of people from home, and is most effective for international business meetings. PCs often come with a mini-camera and special software to allow communication with similarly equipped machines via a phone line. There are also dedicated systems capable of transmitting high-quality pictures and sound.

marketing businesses can be as big or as little as you like, depending on the money available. The typical pattern is that entrepreneurs begin a business from their existing home in conventional style, converting a bedroom to an office or using a corner of the living room. Once they start achieving significant earnings, they custom-build a new home of sufficient size to accommodate substantial business premises as well as living accommodation.

Often a large, luxuriously equipped office, which would not disgrace a company's corporate HQ, will take a dominant spot in the new building, complete with an outer office for a personal assistant/secretary. Sometimes a couple will run different businesses from the same home, each with their own office and administrative support. But that is not the end of the business part of the establishment. There will also be a meeting room with presentation facilities and perhaps a formal dining room for business entertainment.

Remember to enjoy your success and be self-indulgent whenever you can

Living quarters tend to be equally luxurious in this type of setup, with seaside locations and swimming pools often a feature.

BUSINESS BACK-UP

How can large and successful ventures be supported from home? Communications technology is the simple answer. Modern email, phone, and fax systems allow daily contact to be maintained with large networks of people without the need to ever leave your chair (or chaise longue). PC-based cordless-phone systems give one person a variety of voice mailboxes, recorded messages for several phone lines, and conference call facilities.

CANDIDATES FOR SUCCESS

High-achieving home entrepreneurs fall into two basic types:

■ **THE DRIVEN** personable, sales-oriented individuals who find it easy to convince large numbers of people to follow their path. Outwardly confident, persuasive, and focused, these people are usually excellent recruiters to the cause and can rapidly build networks of distributors that span thousands of miles and even different countries.

■ **EXPERIENCED BUSINESSPEOPLE** who have sold a previous business or left high-earning corporate life and have significant resources to invest in a home-based venture. Typically, they will run portfolio lives comprising a range of business interests, from consulting to investing in other entrepreneurs' companies. They will manage their affairs according to the amount of work and investment they want to make.

CREATING A WORKPLACE

A business can be run from almost anywhere in the home, whether up in the attic, down in the basement, out in the workshop, or on the proverbial corner of the kitchen table. Nevertheless, it is important from the outset to find the best possible accommodation for your venture. If you do not, the odds are that you will regret it sooner rather than later. At best, your business will suffer from the inevitable inefficiencies that result from a cramped or temporary space; at worst, it will never realize its full potential. And neither will you. Looking at the main options available, this chapter will help you create a workplace that suits you and your business needs.

Although there are a number of different ways of incorporating business accommodation into the home, there are basically three main solutions to the challenge:

1. adapting the whole of an existing room or part of a room, such as a bedroom or dining room, into a home office
2. converting an attic into a home office
3. changing a garage or basement into a workshop or office.

But, before you contemplate any such project, there are some basic issues to consider, ranging from legal to operational. By definition, you are now contemplating a significant venture and will want to provide the most practical, comfortable, and efficient workspace possible, within the confines of space and budget. The following is a helpful checklist to run through before you get the architect in:

Design your home workspace at the start of your venture

- Running a business from home may require you to gain permission from your landlord, if you are in rented accommodation, or local government if you are a home owner. Consult a lawyer if you are in any doubt.
- Any structural work is likely to require planning permission; consult your local government planning department.
- Remember that dedicating a room or building to a business venture may result in that space being liable to business tax. There

---

CASE STUDY: Giving up the Master Bedroom

ANDY AND TINA decided to go into business from home, operating as distributors for a network marketing health-care product. They needed to work together in the same office and required a fair amount of storage space for their products. Their decision, to turn over their own bedroom to the venture, was made for three reasons: it was the largest room in the house, and they wanted to work at separate desks; it had the best storage space in the form of big closets; and it occupied a corner position, with large windows affording excellent natural light and a pleasant view. A year later, the couple had no cause to regret the decision they had made. The business had grown to the point where they now employed a full-time assistant, who worked in the same room.

CORNER OFFICE

*With a little imagination,
an underused corner in a
bedroom or living room
can be transformed into a
desirable working space.
The desk and shelves have
all been made to measure
to fit the awkward space.
At the end of the day, the
computer and keyboard
are pivoted over the desk
and the specially fitted
door to the office is shut to
hide the trappings of work.*

may also be capital gains tax implications
when you sell the property if you deduct a
proportion of house overhead costs against
business profits.

■ If customers for your projected venture will
need to visit you, you may want to consider
having a separate entrance for the business,
as well as meeting facilities.

■ Will your workspace be sufficiently apart
from the rest of the household to ensure
privacy and freedom from disruption?

■ Good lighting is vital, to reduce eyestrain.

■ You must be able to control the room
temperature and, ideally, the humidity.

■ The floor must be able to support the
additional weight of furniture and
equipment, such as heavy filing cabinets,
computers, and printers.

■ The space should be able to accommodate
comfortably the basic essentials of an office,
including filing and storage of stationery, as

well as an additional desk if you are likely to
employ an assistant.

■ Make sure that there will be enough outlets
and phone jacks.

From Spare Bedroom
to Home Office

Converting a spare bedroom into a viable
and comfortable home office is the easiest
option of all. A third of all home business
entrepreneurs have the luxury of a dedicated
room to devote to their venture. If you are in
the fortunate position of having more than one
bedroom to choose from, and you are likely to
conduct business meetings at home, select the
room nearest the front door. It looks
unprofessional to welcome a client into a
cluttered domestic scene and lead them past
noisy children's rooms to your "office."

If you have a choice, select the room with the largest windows, ideally in a corner of the house, so that you benefit from the maximum amount of natural light, which helps to reduce eyestrain. The table or desk at which you intend to work should be positioned by the window; and if you have a computer this should be placed at a 90-degree angle to the window, to minimize reflections.

The room may also have to serve as an occasional guest room, so consider installing a fold-up wall bed to free up floorspace.

You will probably need to install extra outlets. It does not matter how many the room already has, as there will not be enough once computers, printers, scanners, phones, faxes, and desk lights arrive, not to mention a radio or stereo if you listen to music while you work!

USING A GUEST BEDROOM AS A HOME OFFICE

Rarely used guest bedrooms can make ideal home offices. By installing a fold-up wall bed you will create extra space for your working area but still have sleeping accommodation should you have visitors.

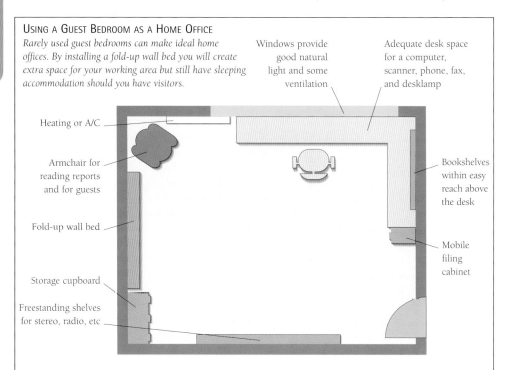

Windows provide good natural light and some ventilation

Adequate desk space for a computer, scanner, phone, fax, and desklamp

Heating or A/C

Armchair for reading reports and for guests

Fold-up wall bed

Storage cupboard

Freestanding shelves for stereo, radio, etc

Bookshelves within easy reach above the desk

Mobile filing cabinet

POINTS TO CHECK

■ **STORAGE** Figure out what you need to store, then decide on the type of storage. Items you use regularly should be placed close by; archived material can be stored away from the office, such as in the garage. Freestanding storage gives flexibility.

■ **LIGHTING** Good task lighting is essential, to prevent eyestrain. Position your desk by the window to make the most of the natural light, with your computer set at a 90-degree angle to minimize reflections.

■ **HEATING OR A/C** You will probably be seated at your desk for hours on end, so make sure the climate control is adequate.

■ **ELECTRICAL SOCKETS** You will always need more than you anticipate.

■ **TELEPHONE JACKS** All your phone lines – business, home, fax, internet – will need separate jacks in the home office.

If you are likely to have a large storage requirement or want to keep lots of books and magazines for reference, then consider installing a wall-mounted racking system.

From Attic to Home Office

The classic move for creating more space in a crowded house is to convert the attic. But it is a substantial project and deserves to be tackled as such. Putting down flooring, running in electricity and phone jacks, and working from an old table with a desklamp is no way to establish a professional home business.

Although converting an attic into a true home office is likely to be an expensive undertaking, the long-term benefit is that you will be adding value to your property, particularly if the space is big enough for future owners to use it as, for example, a children's playroom or guest room.

An attic can provide a blissful place from which to run a business. You are physically apart from the rest of the house, perhaps with good views, and have more peace of mind to concentrate than would be possible if you had to work from a downstairs room. But the attic must be comfortable and practical, with sufficient headroom to stand and enough space for at least one good-sized desk, if not two, to accommodate the inevitable computer, printer, fax, and other equipment.

POINTS TO CONSIDER WHEN PLANNING AN ATTIC OFFICE

1. Assess whether the existing access hatch or door is large enough for the necessary furniture and equipment to pass through.

2. Decide on the type of access, whether permanent built-in stairs or a temporary foldaway-type ladder.

3. Give the attic substantial flooring, not plywood, with insulation and soundproofing material underneath. Lay carpet on top.

4. Seriously consider installing roof windows, to make the most of the natural light and provide ventilation.

5. Line the sides of the roof with an appropriate board and insulation material, and decide on decoration and color schemes.

6. Research the most appropriate and effective form of heating.

7. Provide ample electricity power sockets and phone lines.

8. Get quotes for any structural work from recommended contractors.

Proper ventilation and insulation, which are essential for comfort and therefore efficient working, are major concerns in an attic, where it can be extremely cold and drafty in winter but stiflingly hot in summer.

CASE STUDY: Launching an Attic Business

TRICIA IS A management consultant. After the birth of her second child, she left her downtown job to start up her own venture from home, initially working part-time. As there was no spare room in the house, Tricia and her husband converted the attic into an office. They wanted to do it well so that the space could be used at a later date for other purposes, possibly as a children's playroom. They consulted an architect, who agreed on a budget, drew up the plans, and obtained planning permission. Five months after the birth of her child Tricia finally moved upstairs to her attic office and launched her business. She loves the convenience of working from home, and the fact that she is close to her children but does not have the inconvenience of regular interruptions.

Aᴛᴛɪᴄ Cᴏɴᴠᴇʀѕɪᴏɴ

A well-converted attic can make the perfect home office. This loft space is comfortable, light and airy, as well as secluded. A drawing board placed beneath the windows makes the most of the natural light.

If structural changes, such as inserting roof windows or a dormer window, are required, it is likely you will need planning permission. You should also seek the advice of an architect or structural engineer to establish if the attic floor can support the additional loading of furniture and equipment, not to mention you! Installing a permanent ladder or stairs can also have unforeseen consequences: for example, if your local government regards the conversion as an additional story to the property, you might be required to install fire-resistant doors on the floor underneath the attic.

Spend what it takes to get the best solution when converting an outbuilding

Converting a Garage into a Workshop

Any business involving non-office activities, such as manufacturing, crafts, workshop activities, or the actual storage and distribution of goods, is unlikely to be accommodated within the home. Even if you have enough space for such an enterprise and are willing to tolerate the disruption to domestic life, planning regulations usually prohibit any such work at home. Although people do start distribution businesses from the living or dining room, this is generally without the knowledge of the authorities and serves only as a stopgap until adequate premises can be found. But if the home is not an option, an outbuilding, probably a garage, certainly is.

ASSESSING SUITABILITY

Begin by examining existing outbuildings to assess their potential for such a business venture. Tool sheds are rarely adequate, so your attention is likely to focus on a garage. Even a small garage, as long as it is attached to the house or located close by, can accommodate a reasonable size of venture with careful space-planning and the proper facilities.

It is important to check that any essential supplies are available, such as water and gas, as well as electricity. A phone is probably not required given the flexibility offered by mobiles or digital roaming phones. As ever, you will have to find out whether the planning authorities will allow a for-profit business to be run from a garage, especially if it is part of a block of garages in a condo development.

PLANNING A GARAGE WORKSHOP

A garage will usually be an empty shell for you to convert into an efficient and comfortable workspace. Make sure the decor is pleasing and conducive to work.

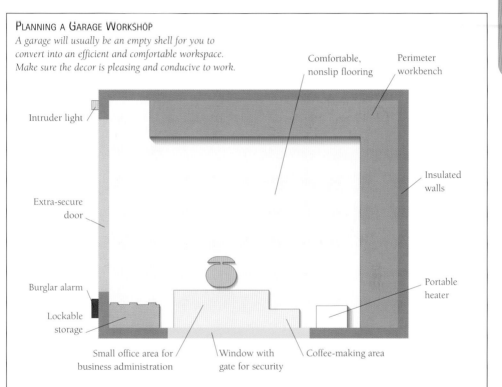

Comfortable, nonslip flooring

Perimeter workbench

Intruder light

Insulated walls

Extra-secure door

Portable heater

Burglar alarm

Lockable storage

Small office area for business administration

Window with gate for security

Coffee-making area

POINTS TO CHECK

▧ **ELECTRICITY** This may need to be added. Ensure you have sufficient outlets in suitable positions for electric tools.

▧ **LIGHTING** Make the most of any natural light, adding task lighting where appropriate.

▧ **FLOORING** Make sure the flooring is cushioned, particularly if most of your work is done while standing.

▧ **HEATING** This may need to be installed. Consider portable electric heaters. Insulated walls will help to retain heat.

▧ **SECURITY** Bolster security with window gates, a burglar alarm, an intruder light, and secure door. Use lockable storage for valuables.

▧ **COMFORT** Consider a small kitchen area for making drinks, and an office desk and chair for doing paperwork and taking breaks.

BICYCLE GARAGE

Repairing and servicing bicycles is an ideal business to conduct from a garage, with all the dirt and grease involved kept out of the home. In this garage, spare wheels are stored off the floor, creating more workspace.

comfortable and warm to do your best work – and a new venture will demand that you are at your best if it is to succeed. This may mean that the garage door will need changing, as traditional up-and-over garage doors are not particularly good at retaining heat. It might also be worth lining the garage walls with insulated board, which will not only keep the heat in but also help to prevent any noise from escaping and annoying your neighbors. You will also need the other basics of business accommodation: practical (if not comfortable) seating, good lighting, adequate storage and ventilation, as well as comfortable flooring if your work is carried out standing up.

Depending on the type and scale of your venture and, of course, the available space, you may want to consider building a second floor onto an existing garage so that you launch with a professional setup from the first day.

Ideally, the best external accommodation for a home-based manufacturing venture is probably a two-story building, comprising a double garage on the ground floor with office space above. That way the inevitable administration part of the business is not relegated to the kitchen table, and it is also kept separate from what may be a dirty or dusty manufacturing operation.

And you have to be sure that any displaced vehicle can be parked elsewhere safely without impinging on your neighbors' space.

The first essential supply is heating, assuming you will spend some time actually working in the premises. As with any other area used for business purposes, you have to be

---

CASE STUDY: Waiting for Planning Permission

JEREMY AND SOPHIE decided to start a soap-making business in the double garage beside their country house. They had enough space and no close neighbors to consider. Their first challenge was to get planning permission to change the use of the garage, which involved having plans drawn up for the minor structural alterations required, plus an

assessment by the local environmental health officer. It took four months before permission was given and they could install their equipment, by which time they were well behind schedule on their business launch plan. They concluded they might have been better off renting workshop space in the nearby town. Although not so convenient, production could have started sooner.

ADVANTAGES AND DISADVANTAGES OF USING A GARAGE AS A WORKSPACE

ADVANTAGES	DISADVANTAGES
No disruption to home life, but nearby	Loneliness; easy to overwork
No impact on home insurance	Potential business rates to pay
Can switch off from work once home	Loss of safe parking space for car
No dirt or noise in the house	Potential problems with neighbors
Could add value to garage property	May cost a great deal at the outset

Looking at the Technology Options

Having the right technology for your present business requirements, with the capacity to upgrade for your future needs, is an essential part of creating an efficient workplace.

The latest advances in technology have given the home-based business a real advantage compared with its corporate counterparts. In fact, for probably the first time, it is entirely possible for a home company to compete in specific markets on equal terms with corporate giants across the world – and beat them! Sitting in your home office, you can present yourself through the internet as a large-scale, professional organization, capable of delivering a wide range of products and services.

A popular image of today's well-equipped home entrepreneur is of a 20-something, computing whizzkid, surrounded by a wired world comprising workstation, laptop and palmtop computers, printers, scanners, faxes, phones, and videoconferencing kit. Such dedicated online entrepreneurs are becoming increasingly common around the world. But the majority of people running home-based businesses have a less committed relationship with technology. They use computing and telecommunications systems for efficiency, rather than as an end in itself. They are concerned with conventional business or, as it has become known, "old economy business," rather than specializing in technology products and markets.

Along with the phone, the computer has become an essential component of any modern business. It enables the home entrepreneur to manage sophisticated databases, organize work through planning systems, and produce professional documents – all of which used to require staff or, at best, part-time assistance. Above all, the computer gives access to an enormous number of potential customers and a vast range of information through the internet (see also pp. 32–41).

Although more than half of the homes in the U.S. now have a computer, it can still be difficult for people to appreciate the potential of modern software in helping them to run the most basic of businesses.

CHOOSING YOUR COMPUTER

When deciding which computer to buy, the challenge is to decide on a precise specification for a system before finding out the best source and the cheapest price. Most computers come

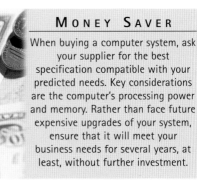

MONEY SAVER

When buying a computer system, ask your supplier for the best specification compatible with your predicted needs. Key considerations are the computer's processing power and memory. Rather than face future expensive upgrades of your system, ensure that it will meet your business needs for several years, at least, without further investment.

pre-loaded with software applications that include word processing, financial spreadsheet, calendar and contact management, and slide presentation programs. Most incorporate the software and modem that are required for internet connection. Many retailers, particularly mail-order and online suppliers, offer discounts on a combined purchase of computer, printer, and scanner; these are likely to be adequate for the majority of home-based business purposes.

There are three basic types of computer available on the market: PC (personal computer), Apple Macintosh, and laptop.

Always buy the best computer you can afford; your new venture is too important to put at risk

1 The PC is by far the most popular with more than an 80-percent market share in both business and personal markets, and with the widest range of applications software.

2 The Apple Macintosh tends to be preferred by designers and other creative professionals because of its graphics software, which is of a very high quality, its simplicity of use, and attractive appearance.

3 The laptop computer, which can be either a PC or Apple Mac, can be taken absolutely anywhere, and is increasingly used in conjunction with a mobile phone to enable business people on the move to access their email messages. Some laptops come with a docking station so that they can fit into a network system.

If you are not sure what type of computer to buy but you know that you need a reasonably sophisticated machine that will last you and your business for some years, it generally makes sense to look at higher-specification machines. These offer faster processing speeds, more memory capacity, and higher-quality screen images, together with the ability to multitask – that is, handle several jobs at once – thus improving efficiency. With computer capacity doubling every 18 to 24 months, your nice new machine will soon look outdated compared with the latest models, so it is best to buy the best, especially as prices continue to fall. The only exception to that rule is if you want to use a computer for only one or two basic functions, such as word processing.

QUESTIONS TO ASK YOURSELF WHEN CHOOSING A COMPUTER

1 Will you need to manage large databases of customer information?

2 Do you want a portable computer instead of, or as well as, a desktop computer?

3 Will you need any technical support to help you to operate and maintain the computer?

4 Will you need more than one computer?

5 Will you need high-quality color printing?

6 Will you be scanning high volumes of images for incorporating in documents?

7 Will other members of the family want access to your computer?

8 Will you require a specialized computer for uses such as graphic design or other forms of design?

CHOOSING YOUR PRINTER

Buying a printer is also a potentially complex area if you require a machine capable of more than basic black-and-white document production or high-volume printing. These days it is possible to buy office-quality color laser printers for comparatively little, to which can be added binders that allow you to produce professional bound documents. For the majority of home businesses, however, a simple and much less expensive inkjet printer will usually suffice.

COMPUTER DRAWING
Three-dimensional diagrams are drawn on the computer with a drawing tablet. Since computers and peripheral equipment continue to fall in price, such technology is now affordable for many home offices.

NETWORKING
An increasingly common scenario in households with a home business is a need for more than one computer; perhaps two people work together, or one machine is for business use, another for family use, with internet access for using email and games for children. In such circumstances it may make sense to link more than one computer, together with peripheral equipment, such as a printer and scanner. The advantages of doing this include:

▨ no need to remove continually and replace terminal connections to a printer
▨ ability to share files between computers
▨ facility for saving scanned images on any computer.

Keeping in Touch

Modern communications technology means that no one needs be out of contact with their business, clients, or suppliers, almost literally from one minute to the next. However, not everyone wants or needs such intensity of communication; for some businesses this degree of contact is inappropriate as well as undesirable, and a conventional phone and answering service is perfectly adequate for their needs. Here, though, we look at the current art of the possible.

Today the humble telephone is the doorway to a wide and ever-broadening range of communications services, both voice and data, although phone lines now carry predominantly data transmissions as internet usage continues to mushroom around the world. The most important issue, therefore, for the new home entrepreneur is to decide on the communications services that are relevant to his or her business.

Voice Communication

Telephones come in all shapes and sizes, from the conventional single handset to computer-controlled intelligent systems, which are capable of providing automatic responses, voicemail, intercom, and call rerouting services. And, of course, there is the ubiquitous mobile phone, which is also used increasingly to connect laptop computers to the internet for people forever on the move during the course of business.

Divert phone messages so that you are always in touch

- ▧ **Business Line** At the very least, a separate line for business calls is essential. It ensures you can continue to receive and make calls while the domestic phone is monopolized by the rest of the family. A separate line also makes accounting for business costs easier.
- ▧ **Mobile** Having a mobile phone is important if your business involves spending a great deal of time away from the home office, meeting customers and suppliers, or simply networking. It can also serve as a personal organizer with a contacts database and scheduling software.

TIME SAVER

It is important to manage your phone system rather than let it control your day. Select times to make and receive calls, such as 9–10 a.m. and 4–5 p.m. Leave the phone on voicemail for the rest of the day, with a short message asking callers to leave full details of their needs, so you are prepared when calling back. Use a speakerphone or headset to make your time on the phone as productive as possible.

- ▧ **Voicemail** The modern version of the answering machine enables you to leave up-to-date messages on your phone, such as "I'll be back at 12.30, please leave a message," and access them later through your normal phone, mobile, or computer.
- ▧ **Call Management System** Only for the seriously committed communicator, these new generation systems for home and office alike enable one person to have the telephonic equivalent of a receptionist. You can have different ringing tones to differentiate between regular callers, separate voicemail boxes for different businesses or "departments," and call routing to another number, and many other useful features.
- ▧ **The Internet** An increasing number of telecommunication companies offer voice communication over the internet via your computer. All you need do is to download appropriate software, then you can call any phone number in the world and talk at a cheaper rate than a conventional phone call, though the sound quality is variable. The same system also offers conference call facilities for three or more people.
- ▧ **Headset** Popular with office workers and those based at home, headsets allow hands-free communication so that you can use the computer or complete other tasks at the same time as you are talking. They are often used in conjunction with mobile phones.

Using the Written Word

Electronic communications are available in a bewildering variety of forms, but the main types appropriate for the home-based business are fax and email.

- ▧ **Fax** Not only can a fax transmit documents over a phone line, but it can also serve as a plain-paper copier. However, the trend now is moving toward multipurpose desktop fax machines that will handle color printing, scanning, and copying, as well as faxing.

░ **EMAIL** Normally accessed through your computer, email is now the most popular form of business communication worldwide. It allows you to transmit and receive instant messages, complex documents, and images at times that suit you. You can also access emails by dedicated email phones, as well as by digital mobile phones with software that enables them to connect to the internet.

WHICH PHONE CONNECTION?

For many home offices, a separate business line is enough. It can serve for both voice and fax, and perhaps for email, too, provided that it is not used too heavily. But, if email and the internet are crucial to your business plans, consider installing one of the multiline services on offer. Although they cost more, they provide faster internet access.

ISDN – Integrated Services Digital Network – connects you at more than twice the speed of normal analog lines. Not only does it reduce the time involved in connecting to the internet, but also in downloading files, including large graphics data. If your business is likely to require such levels of data transmission, explore the availability and cost of these digital services.

ISDN is already being overtaken by another form of digital media, called ADSL – Asymmetric Digital Subscriber Line. This offers speeds several times those of ISDN, together with permanent connection to the internet at a much cheaper rate than it would cost otherwise.

Many cable television systems also offer super-fast internet service.

As phone connections are such a complex and fast-changing issue, seek advice before making any commitment. Your local chamber of commerce or small business association, or independent research sources such as *Consumer Reports* magazine, should be able to help.

MOBILE COMMUNICATION
With the advances made in communications technology, keeping in touch with your home base, customers, and suppliers has never been easier, wherever you happen to be.

THE VIRTUAL HOME BUSINESS

Technology today offers the home entrepreneur remarkable opportunities, not just to develop and control a large enterprise but also to operate much more efficiently than has ever been possible. There are products and programs already available that make this happen, with yet another new generation of even more sophisticated software and systems coming up close behind. This day in the life of a home business entrepreneur gives a vision of how work and a personal life may be conducted in the future, although it could be a reality much sooner than you think.

Use technology to design your lifestyle exactly as you please

■ **LUNCHTIME** You are quickly eating a sandwich in the car in between visiting customers. You use your mobile communicator – combination phone and PC – to check the morning's email messages. You also need to update customer files, which takes five minutes, and to produce a new quote, which is produced out of the color printer built into the glove compartment in the dashboard. Finally, you visit the website of a supplier to ensure they can meet your deadline. All done, you check traffic conditions on the car's navigation system before heading off to see your next customer.

■ **HEADING HOME** It is time to go back home mid-afternoon for a little relaxation and a sauna before dinner, followed by a brief return to work. You dial in to the home automation system to heat up the sauna, turn on the oven to cook the ready-made meal you took out of the freezer before leaving home in the morning, and program the digital TV to download a movie ready for tonight's viewing.

■ **DINNER OVER** There is a little work to do before watching the movie. You sit down in front of the large, wall-mounted television screen, which also handles your computer, web browser, and videoconferencing facilities. First, you want to update the last presentation you made at a networking conference, so you change some of the background slides and record yourself making a fresh introduction, before transmitting it to the conference organizers for projection to the audience in the morning. You have a quick videoconference chat with your partner in Boston, who is working on a new technology project that you are hoping to market. After a final check of the stock market prices, it is time to pour a last glass of wine and relax while watching the movie.

Moving Home and Business Together

If you run a business from home and need to move, you will obviously have to move your business as well. Moving house is apparently one of life's more stressful events, so moving your business base at the same time will be particularly difficult. The key to surviving this potential ordeal is, first, to plan well ahead; second, to allow plenty of time for the actual move; and, finally, to bring in lots of helpers. It is a good idea to try to time the move to occur during a traditionally slack period of your working year.

YOUR NEW WORKSPACE

Decide where you want all your business equipment and materials to go in your new office. Check the room's dimensions and the location of heaters, doors, windows, power outlets, and phone jacks, then draw a sketch (to scale) showing furniture, tools, stock, as appropriate, in place. (See also workplace legalities on pp. 172–3.)

FACT OR FICTION?

Far-fetched as it may appear, this scenario is not science fiction. The technology is mostly available now. Increasingly, serious home entrepreneurs are specifying that their new homes incorporate "smart" wiring and computing systems to enable them to manage a complex, diversified business life from home office and car alike. These systems control the following:

▮ all the phone lines necessary for voice and data communication

▮ networked computers

▮ home automation systems for heating, kitchen appliances, and leisure facilities

▮ security systems, including video cameras

▮ video transmission channels, including videoconferencing

▮ sound and television systems in each room of the home

▮ remote controls for the above.

KEY TECHNOLOGY

The software and hardware that allow these systems to operate fall into three categories:

▮ internet PC computers, driving business-to-business e-commerce and other services, such as home shopping

▮ internet TV and video, with big-screen, high-definition home cinema standards, offering both entertainment and on-line learning through distant delivery

▮ internet wireless, which gives phone, email, and instant information through mobile data devices, currently known as mobile phones.

CASE STUDY: Working in the Future

BOB IS AN IT consultant specializing in optical computing. By choice he works from home, in a sophisticated office within a wired "smart" home that overlooks the ocean. His assignments originally took him all over the world, delivering high-value projects to corporate and government customers, as well as speaking at conferences. Now he prefers to deliver his service remotely, through email, videoconferencing, and a new virtual advisory product that uses sophisticated software to create a three-D image of himself answering real questions on clients' television screens. He is in the process of building a new "smart" home on a Caribbean island where he plans to live for half of the year, still delivering his service remotely. He is happy with life...

CREATING A PLAN

Once the move appears likely, start to plan. As time passes and the move date nears, you can refine the plan until it is highly polished and detailed. It should include the following tasks.

▮ **SORTING OUT OLD PAPERWORK** Once the decision to move has been made, start to sort out your paperwork and any stock you might have. Archive papers you need to retain (as prescribed by the tax authorities) and dispose of the rest. Burn old business correspondence and financial information. Be ruthless: throw out anything you do not need. Although this will take time, it will make the move easier and give you a fresh start in your new office.

▮ **PRINTING NEW STATIONERY** As soon as the house purchase is confirmed, check you have the correct address and your new phone number(s). Then initiate printing of new letterheads, business cards, and so on. This is an opportunity to redesign and improve your stationery. For existing leaflets, print small, self-adhesive labels with the new address. Update your address on any computer software you use and on your website.

■ NOTIFYING CUSTOMERS AND SUPPLIERS

You may choose to notify customers and suppliers before or after the move, depending on your business and the circumstances. Be aware that they may react negatively: suppliers will be anxious for you to pay any outstanding bills, and customers may think they are losing you. Judge their likely reactions carefully, and try to reassure everyone. You might consider reducing stock levels to a minimum. Ask key customers whether they would consider purchasing additional goods from you in advance, to tide them over during the move.

■ STAFFING

If your move involves losing staff, this will have major implications. First, staff morale will suffer when they are told of your impending move and the loss of their jobs; second, they may be entitled to a severance payment (see p. 175); and, finally,

Always plan for packing to take twice as long as you anticipate

their loss means you will have to find and train new staff. Try to keep up the morale of existing staff, as you will need their full support in the difficult lead-up to the move. Explain precisely why it is essential so they understand it is not any reflection on them.

Arrange thank-you parties in advance and ensure final paychecks are prepared and ready before the actual move date. It may be possible for staff to continue to work for you remotely for a couple of months to ease the transition for both parties.

■ MOVING COMPANIES

Some moving companies may move only personal belongings and nothing relating to a business; others may move the business furniture but not any equipment or stock; and others may impose extra charges or conditions. Remember that their insurance may not cover business items. It may be that some equipment is either too precious or vulnerable for you to trust to anyone else.

For the sake of security and confidentiality, make an inventory of everything to be moved and then decide if you will move it all yourself or split the task between yourself and a moving company. This needs to be done before the firm's estimator visits, so an accurate quote can be given. You could try to get the moving company to take the business furniture, including (empty) filing cabinets, as they are bulky and heavy, and move the rest – equipment and any stock – yourself. Ask the moving company to split their invoice into two sections so that you can set the business part against tax. Check what your own in-transit insurance covers you for; moving valuable items in your car is unlikely to be included.

DO-IT-YOURSELF MOVE

Moving your own office equipment, or at least some of the lighter items, is not only cheaper but also allows you to keep a close eye on valuable or confidential material.

■ **PREPARING A BUDGET** This need not be complicated, just a list of likely moving costs.
■ **NOTIFYING TAX AUTHORITIES** Once you move, you must notify the tax authorities without delay (see p. 181).

THE MOVE

■ **PACKING** Assuming you are going to have to pack some or all of your business things, buy sturdy moving boxes in advance. These are available flat-packed and in all sizes, but anything larger than about 12 x 9 x 9 in will be too heavy to carry easily once they are filled. Smaller cartons are also easier to pack into a van or car trunk. Filing cabinets usually need to be empty for reasons of weight. There are special cardboard archive boxes that take filing cabinet suspension files. Computers and photocopiers should be transported in their original packaging. If unavailable, ask your local computer shop if they can provide you with some suitable packaging; you do not want a hardware problem on setting up your computers at your new location.
■ **TIMING** Try to make your business move on a different day from the domestic one, to reduce the inevitable problems, unless you have very few business items to transport.
■ **HELPERS** For the day of the move, muster as many willing hands as you can. Make up a proper roster and build in a contingency plan. Remember to thank everyone.
■ **SAFETY** The actual move may involve unusual risks, especially if young children are involved, if you or others are in a rush, or if there is heavy stock or equipment. If you plan to transport any stock or equipment on a car seat, secure it with seat belts. Better still, rent a moving van.

PLANNING A JOINT MOVE
This simple planner shows the various stages involved in moving your home and business. Although this takes place in August, the preparations start in May.

	STATUS OF HOME PURCHASE AND MOVE	ACTION		
MAY	■ Survey carried out ■ Price negotiated	■ Start sorting out old paperwork ■ Create inventory ■ Tell staff about the move ■ Contact moving companies	and ask for quotes ■ Check dimensions of new home office ■ Prepare a budget	
JUNE	■ House purchase confirmed	■ Refine moving plans ■ Book moving van		
JULY	■ Contracts exchanged	■ Confirm new address/ telephone numbers ■ Print new stationery ■ Notify customers and suppliers	■ Organize staff and helpers to assist with move	
AUGUST	■ Purchase completed ■ Keys handed over	■ Load rented van with stock the day before the move ■ Notify your bank and the tax authorities		

GETTING
the balance
right

*Working at home requires a great
deal of self-discipline. This section
contains a self-assessment exercise
that enables you to discover how well
you separate work from home life. It
offers a 10-point plan for keeping
your business running smoothly while
also looking after your health and
spending the amount of time you
would like with your family. It
provides tips on dealing with loneliness
and staying motivated, and offers
guidelines on how to deal with
succession issues in a family business.*

MANAGING DOMESTIC ISSUES

For an employee, home usually represents a retreat, a place in which to relax and unwind; but for those working from home for the first time the situation alters significantly and major problems can arise. Most of these can be avoided, however, with some forethought, discussion with other family members, the creation of a distinct working zone, and fixed working times. The successful management of the work/home divide can also be influenced by personality. If you are a workaholic, you will probably still manage to work whatever the conditions. At the other extreme, if you are easily led astray, a home environment may offer too many distractions.

There are many domestic benefits to working from home, particularly if you have preschool or school-age children. You are likely to see much more of them than if you were out working all day. It is also a huge advantage having a parent based at home to help care for children when they are sick.

CASE STUDY: Finding the Right House for Work and Family

MARTHA AND HER partner had three young children and planned to move to be closer to her partner's work. They drew up a list of the facilities that they would need and, since Martha wanted to start a home-based business, additional space for an office was essential. They also needed to be in walking distance of a school, playgroup, and post office. Athough they knew it would take time to find a suitable house, they felt the search would be worthwhile. Martha planned to work fixed hours, and so the couple decided that once they had found the right house they would look for a babysitter for their two preschool children, so that Martha could work uninterrupted.

Working from home can also be a very comfortable experience. Commuting is no longer necessary, so you do not need to get up so early, and your working environment can be as pleasant as you wish to make it. Tea, coffee, and snacks are always on hand, although this might be a disadvantage if you are trying to lose weight. You may even find the time to watch a key event on television.

There are also domestic financial benefits: two cars may no longer be necessary; your home insurance may be lower; and you can offset some of your office running costs against the business.

CREATING A PHYSICAL SEPARATION

It makes a lot of difference to the smooth running of your domestic and business life if your office or workshop is in a custom-built office or a self-contained space, such as a spare bedroom. This kind of physical separation can make both aspects of your life much easier to manage, benefiting you as well as your family.

Wherever you work, think of your home, or a specific part of it, as your place of business during working hours. So, when you settle down to work in the morning, view it as going to a "normal" job.

The Need for Self-discipline

As an employee working in an organization, discipline is usually imposed by your employer, managers, and colleagues. In other words, you have to conform. But when you are working for yourself in a home environment, those same controls do not exist. Although most people would see that as a blessing, it does mean that you need to set your own standards of self-discipline.

FACT FILE

A home-based business may require an employee, either full- or part-time. This raises a host of issues, including providing adequate working space, a bathroom, parking, privacy, insurance coverage, access while you are away, and the impact of having another person in the house. It is probably only practical to employ staff if your home is spacious or you are working from a suitable outbuilding.

10-POINT SELF-DISCIPLINE PLAN

1 SET YOUR WORKING HOURS Decide from the outset what your working hours are going to be. Discuss them with other members of your family and fix a large sign displaying them on your office door so that everyone is clear on the issue. You can reinforce this by saying to the family each morning that you are "going to the office" or "starting work." If you usually take a lunch break, include that on the sign, too. You may find that you have either given yourself too many hours or too few to get through your

ALL HANDS ON DECK
A comfortable workspace that is conducive to work is an important aspect of working from home.

HOW WELL DO YOU SEPARATE YOUR WORK LIFE FROM YOUR HOME LIFE?

Study each of the following questions and decide which of the three answers best describes your situation. Score 4 points each time you answer A, 2 points for each answer B;,and zero points for each answer C. Add up your scores, and then check the score assessments in the results panel at the bottom. The questions are not in any order of importance.

Do you have an attic, outbuilding, or garage conversion to work in?
- **A** Yes. ☐
- **B** No, but I have a separate room in the house. ☐
- **C** No, I need to use part of a domestic room. ☐

Do you have the house to yourself all day?
- **A** Yes, I tend to be on my own for most of the day. ☐
- **B** No, I'm on my own for only part of the day. ☐
- **C** No, there are other family members in the house. ☐

Do you avoid seeing your family during working hours?
- **A** Yes, when I'm working I prefer to be on my own. ☐
- **B** No, I don't mind seeing them sometimes. ☐
- **C** No, I like to stop work and have a chat with them. ☐

Do you have a policy not to be interrupted while you are working?
- **A** Yes (or I'm on my own during the working day). ☐
- **B** No, but I'm usually left in peace. ☐
- **C** No, and I am interrupted frequently. ☐

Is your home free of pets?
- **A** Yes, I don't have any pets. ☐
- **B** No, but someone else looks after them. ☐
- **C** No, I have to take care of them during the day. ☐

Do you have a separate phone in your work area?
- **A** Yes, and it has its own number. ☐
- **B** Yes, but it's on the domestic phone line. ☐
- **C** No, it's the same phone used for domestic calls. ☐

Do you avoid doing tasks unrelated to business during working hours?
- **A** Yes, I try not to mix work and other tasks. ☐
- **B** I sometimes have to do other tasks, too. ☐
- **C** No, I usually do other tasks as well. ☐

Do you have a fixed policy on domestic work/ yard work/home improvements, and so on?
- **A** Yes, my partner knows the business is more important just now. ☐
- **B** No, but there is not too much for me to do. ☐
- **C** No, I still have a lot of commitments. ☐

Do you discourage relatives and friends from visiting during the day?
- **A** Yes, they visit out of working hours. ☐
- **B** No, but they let me know beforehand. ☐
- **C** No, many arrive unannounced. ☐

Do you avoid domestic diversions?
- **A** Yes, while working I keep focused on my work. ☐
- **B** Yes, most of the time. ☐
- **C** No, I tend to be easily diverted. ☐

RESULTS

0–10 points
You need to carry out a fundamental rethink if you are to separate work from home life.

12–20 points
Look at the questions and your answers again, as there is some doubt about your ability to separate your work from your home life.

22–30 points
Look at those questions where you had a low score and discuss the issues with your family as it may indicate problem areas.

32–40 points
It seems that you are succeeding in separating your work from your home life. Well done!

work. Modify the hours as necessary, but do make sure others know what your timetable is. Setting yourself fixed working hours has a number of important benefits. First, it gives you something to aim for – that is, by 8:30 or 9 a.m. you have to be at work. Second, your customers know when to contact you. Third, your family understands not to interrupt you during your normal working hours, except in an emergency; and, finally, you know when to stop work in the evening.

2 DRESS FOR WORK To help you get into the right frame of mind for work, dress as befits your line of business; obviously, for nonoffice work you need to wear the appropriate overalls and so on. If, as an employee, you have been used to wearing very casual clothing, this is the time to upgrade and dress better – after all, you are now the boss! Wearing dressy clothes might seem a bit contrived, but it does really help you feel that you are at work rather than relaxing at home. The added benefit is that if a business contact appears on your doorstep without warning, you will not be caught out looking sloppy or unprofessional.

3 ESTABLISH WORK PRIORITIES On any given working day you may be unable to get through all the tasks you have given yourself, for whatever reason. Without the framework of an organization to guide you, it can be difficult to figure out which tasks can wait until the next day. One strategy for setting your priorities is to write down everything you have to do at the very beginning of each day. Make this work list the first thing you do each morning. Review the list and number each task in order of priority. Then follow the list rigidly; that is, do task "2" after task "1," and so on. In that way the most important jobs are always dealt with first. (See also pp. 45–6.)

Keep up to date with your paperwork to ensure a smooth-running business

4 PACE YOURSELF As the old adage goes, "time is money," so you need to work at a pace that is commensurate with the likely return. If you work too slowly, your earnings will be low. You will probably know instinctively if you are working fast or slow, as customers are likely to praise your speed or criticize your slowness. Your earnings should be similar to others in your business, which you can find out from an industry association. If you are doing repetitive work, time how long you take to do it and then try to do it faster. Think of it as a fun challenge, and reward yourself if you do well (see also Fact File below).

5 COMPLETE YOUR PAPERWORK Doing the paperwork inevitably associated with any business is never a very exciting task, but it is absolutely necessary. If you fail to keep the administration of your business up-to-date, you may be investigated by the tax authorities. The IRS and sales tax authorities are particularly strict about the paperwork that needs to be done, and the need to get sales tax returns in on time. If you are incorporated, the various returns must be made promptly. With all businesses, keeping your accounts up-to-date is a key task. If you are having a

FACT FILE

For the home-based entrepreneur there are no such things as a letter of commendation from the boss if you do well, or a promotion. You can, however, reward yourself and increase your motivation. If you achieve a particular target, give yourself a chocolate bar or something more substantial that you have always wanted. A picture or description of the reward on the noticeboard may focus your efforts.

problem staying on top of your paperwork, especially the accounts, set aside a specific time to do them, such as every Sunday evening, and keep to that system. (See also pp. 48–51)

6 **MINIMIZE INTERRUPTIONS** As an employee, interruptions are inevitable, but at least they are usually work-related. Operating from home makes you more vulnerable to interruptions from family, neighbors, friends, and relatives. Older generations, in particular, often fail to understand that you are working and not on vacation. Instead of pretending to be out when they stop by, it might be a better strategy to appear in your working clothes and let them know politely that you are working. They will eventually learn not to interrupt you. A more difficult problem may be caused by your own family, especially if you have young children who cannot read your working hours sign. This

Be polite but firm in discouraging social visits during your working day

GET SMART
Completing your paperwork promptly – filing tax returns, invoicing, and so on – will help you to control your business affairs. If you are busy at work, you may have to do some paperwork out of business hours.

is where having your office or workshop separate from the domestic part of the house can be an enormous advantage. You may consider having an intercom to allow family members to contact you without them having to enter your workplace.

7 **AGREE ON DOMESTIC RESPONSIBILITIES** You and your partner (where applicable) need to have a clear understanding as to what you can and cannot do around the home during your working hours. Home improvement and yard work need to take second place to your enterprise, at least until the business becomes established, which will take many months, perhaps even a couple of years. It

also means that you should not take on new pets or hobbies.

■ **RELINQUISH OUTSIDE DUTIES** You may have a role in the local community, such as a PTA officer, or you may do charity work. You might also be involved in a sport. When you start your business you need to minimize all such outside responsibilities, as you need to focus your entire energies on your own business. Working from home makes you vulnerable to requests for help, but you should be strong-minded and turn them down, at least at the outset.

■ **AVOID DIVERSIONS** Life is full of pleasant activities that you would probably rather do instead of working. Although some diversions are obviously of a domestic nature, others may appear to have some work relevance. However, you do need to keep very focused as to which activities earn income and which do not. Your daily work list (see point 3 on p. 137) should help you to avoid these distractions.

■ **ASSESS YOUR OWN PERFORMANCE** At the end of each major job, or at least annually for more repetitive type work, you should assess your performance to see where you can make improvements. This should be done objectively and it is best written down to help you focus your thoughts.

AVOIDING DIFFICULT TASKS

When you work for an organization, you will sometimes be faced with unpleasant or difficult jobs. Although you may procrastinate, the pressures of the organization will ultimately require you to do these jobs. But when you are your own boss based at home there is no one overseeing your work and insisting that such tasks are completed. If you do not like making sales calls, you may convince yourself that the priority is for the office to be cleaned or for some new software to be loaded onto the computer. These may certainly be useful things to do, but you are stopping yourself from fulfilling the key task of getting out there and

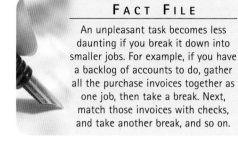

FACT FILE

An unpleasant task becomes less daunting if you break it down into smaller jobs. For example, if you have a backlog of accounts to do, gather all the purchase invoices together as one job, then take a break. Next, match those invoices with checks, and take another break, and so on.

making some sales, which is what the business survives on. This is where self-discipline comes in. It also helps if you have a partner familiar with your business to remind you gently that you need to face up to whatever it is that you are avoiding. These unpleasant tasks tend not to go away – they just become more urgent – but they are often not as bad as you imagine them to be.

Allowing Your Children to Help You at Work

If you do not have children living at home with you, you can skip this section. For those of you who do, read on. For older children who might work in the business full-time after leaving school or university, refer also to the next chapter (see pp. 142–9).

When you are under pressure it may be very tempting to ask your children to help out, which could be a good strategy indeed, but only if the children wish to be involved; they should not be made to feel that they have to. On the other hand, you may have a child who is pestering you to allow them to assist you.

WHAT CHILDREN CAN DO

Older children may have grown up watching your venture start and develop. In that case, they will probably know a surprising amount about the business, even if they have not been helping in it. They are also likely to share your professional values. These are enormous advantages when it comes to them assisting you as they will be able to help for short periods of time without much additional training. From moving stock around (make sure that it is not too heavy) to helping with the paperwork, packaging orders, and stuffing envelopes, there is often much they can do. Where appropriate, children can even help you to serve customers, but see under "The Customer's View" at right.

Depending on your business, there may be legal constraints on how a child can help; they would not be able to serve in a bar or operate machinery, for example. If you are in any doubt, get legal advice.

THE CHILD'S VIEW

There is no doubt that some children like to help their parents with their work at various times during the evenings, weekends, or vacations. However, schoolwork and other activities may prevent some children from helping at all, while others will not have much interest in being involved. Some will, in fact, resent the intrusion of the business into their domestic life, particularly if customers visit the house and they, as children, are asked to clean up or make themselves scarce.

If you have teenage children, you may need to install a separate phone line, especially if they

TEACHER AND PUPIL
Involving an older child in your business during school vacations can be very rewarding for both parties. As long as you structure your working day and are able to teach your child and answer their questions, they will pick up all kinds of valuable commercial information, as well as grow in confidence and self-esteem.

use the internet. If a child is likely to answer a business call, make sure you teach them to speak clearly and courteously and to take a message. Have a phone message pad beside the phone – with a pen chained to the pad!

If you enlist the help of an older child on a regular basis, then you need to include that child in the decision-making processes of the business. In other words, you need to begin to treat them as an adult and to discuss business issues with them. They also need to become privy to the innermost workings of the venture, such as its sales, profits, problem areas, your customer base, and goals.

THE CUSTOMER'S VIEW

All businesses need to project a professional image so that customers feel confident that any promises made will be fulfilled. In a business context, children, especially young ones, are best neither seen nor heard. Customers will probably not be at all impressed if a young child answers the phone, opens the door to them at your home, greets them on an exhibition stand, or serves them in a café or store, no matter how smart or polite the child. It will also appear unprofessional if a child can be heard in the background during a business phone conversation.

TO PAY OR NOT TO PAY

Whether you should pay your children for helping you in the business is an important issue, especially for them. It all depends on the work done and the length of time it takes to do it; certainly, regular employment or long-term

SURVIVAL STRATEGIES FOR WORKING WITH CHILDREN

1 Restrict a child's duties to reflect their age and abilities.

2 Remember that young children need sufficient rest and play.

3 Remember that older children need time for homework and study.

4 Praise a child's efforts; it will improve their self-confidence enormously.

5 Try not to talk about business in the evenings and on weekends.

6 Celebrate any business successes together as a family.

work on a major project would seem to warrant some kind of reward. Teenagers, in particular, are interested in earning money and many have paid part-time jobs. In the long run, paying children will motivate them and create a happy working environment.

The rate of pay for children should be at least what you would pay a nonfamily employee. It should be calculated on an hourly basis and paid either weekly or monthly, without delay or deductions (other than tax). It may be a good idea to put in writing what the child's pay will be, the hours you expect them to work, and when they will be paid, so that there are no unfortunate misunderstandings. Make sure that you check the tax situation with your accountant.

HANDLING FAMILY BUSINESS ISSUES

It is one thing to have a home-based business where you work on your own, but it is something entirely different if your partner is involved in the business. The situation becomes even more complex if your children form a part of it, too. There is nothing unusual about family-run businesses, but living and working under the same roof can be stressful. However, open discussion and a mutual understanding of the position can alleviate any problems. Working with your family has the potential to create a very strong business team and one that can also be hugely satisfying for all those involved.

The first family business situation to consider is when a couple works together without any children. The second is when a child, or children, joins one parent, or both, in the business. (In this chapter, "child" means offspring, regardless of age.)

Consider the alternatives to working with family

Couples Working Together

It is very common for couples to work together. Sometimes the situation is brought about by necessity, sometimes by choice; but all too often insufficient thought is given to how the personal relationship might be affected by it. Indeed, the same couple may have thought long and hard about living together or having children, but they will often accept working together without much consideration at all.

Being in business with a partner is not right for everyone. To see whether it is likely to cause problems for you and your partner, look at the self-assessment checklist on p. 144. You might also discuss possible areas of friction with your partner so that you can try to avoid them. You need to be quite clear as to who will do what in the business and the hours each of you might work; these may be different depending on

CASE STUDY: Adjusting to Changed Circumstances

JOHN AND LIZ ran a business together from home, importing medical equipment. When the business first started, John spent most of his time on the road, visiting customers and taking orders. Liz, on the other hand, did all the paperwork in the home office, while taking care of their children. Once the children had grown up and moved away, Liz felt increasingly isolated and became depressed. The couple then decided to share their duties: Liz started visiting some customers and taking orders while John spent more time at home. Although there was a period of readjustment, particularly for John, the change in responsibilities had unexpected benefits, as Liz turned out to be exceptionally good at selling while John found time to indulge his hobby of home improvement.

your individual domestic responsibilities. The results of the checklist and the subsequent discussions should help you decide if working together is a good idea for both of you.

THE BENEFITS

There are many major potential benefits for couples who work together. In addition to having another pair of hands to physically do the work, there is also someone else to discuss business matters with and help make good decisions. Simply talking through an issue with your partner can make the right course of action clearer in your own mind. Often a partner can see a solution that you overlook because you are too close to the problem. Furthermore, each partner will bring his or her own skills and abilities to the business, which should enhance its chances of succeeding. It is also a useful safety valve to be able to talk about any problems with a sympathetic partner. In fact, the business can be a very strong partnership, able to weather the bad times as well as enjoy the good times.

SURVIVAL STRATEGIES FOR WORKING WITH YOUR PARTNER

1 Acknowledge your partner's abilities and talents on a regular basis.

2 Make sure that you have your own areas of responsibility relating to your particular strengths.

3 Avoid expressing criticism of your partner's mistakes.

4 Make sure that you praise your partner's efforts.

5 Respect the role that your partner has in the business and the work that they do.

6 Take time to celebrate your business successes together.

7 Recognize that you and your partner will both, at times, need "space."

ASSESSING YOUR BUSINESS COMPATIBILITY WITH YOUR PARTNER

Both partners need to do this self-assessment questionnaire on their own. Look at each of the following questions and then decide which of the answers best describes your situation. The questions are not in any order of importance. Score 4 points for each answer A, 2 points for each answer B, and zero points for each answer C. Add up your scores, then look at the score assessments in the results panel at the bottom and discuss each question and answer openly with your partner.

Have you both always wanted to run your own business?
- **A** Yes, we have. ☐
- **B** No, but we both do now. ☐
- **C** One of us feels less strongly about this. ☐

Do you both want to start the same type of business?
- **A** Yes, undoubtedly. ☐
- **B** We have slightly different views on this. ☐
- **C** One of us would rather start a different type of business. ☐

Are you both prepared to give up a lot to launch your business?
- **A** I think we are both prepared to sacrifice a lot. ☐
- **B** I'm not sure we both want to sacrifice to the same extent. ☐
- **C** I think one of us would rather not give up anything. ☐

Do you both rate starting a business as more important than a career?
- **A** Yes, I think so. ☐
- **B** We both feel that we want to try out something different. ☐
- **C** I'm not sure. ☐

Who makes the major decisions in your relationship?
- **A** We make decisions together. ☐
- **B** We usually accept each other's decisions. ☐
- **C** We tend to have disagreements on major issues. ☐

When you disagree, can you put it behind you quickly?
- **A** Yes, we can resolve most disagreements by discussion. ☐
- **B** Sometimes we do, sometimes we don't. ☐
- **C** I'm not sure. ☐

Do you have business skills that complement your partner's?
- **A** Yes, we are both good at doing different things. ☐
- **B** We are quite similar. ☐
- **C** I don't know. ☐

Do you both accept similar risks?
- **A** Yes, we both tend to take similar risks. ☐
- **B** We sometimes have different risk thresholds. ☐
- **C** I don't know. ☐

Do you spend a lot of time together?
- **A** Yes, we like to be together. ☐
- **B** We don't spend much time together. ☐
- **C** We presently live different lives. ☐

Do you both have the same long-term goals for the business?
- **A** Yes, I think we do. ☐
- **B** I think we share some goals, but not all of them. ☐
- **C** No, we don't (or we don't have any long-term goals). ☐

RESULTS

0–10 points
Are you really sure that working together is a good idea?

12–20 points
You need to look at the questions and your answers again, as there is some doubt as to your compatibility in a work situation.

22–30 points
Look at questions where you had a low score. Compare with your partner's score and discuss the issues, as they may indicate areas of friction.

32–40 points
You appear to be compatible workwise with your partner. Go for it!

THE DOWNSIDES

Inevitably, there are potential downsides of working with your partner. First, as a household, you will have all your financial eggs in one basket, which is a risk you must be prepared to take. However, if one of you also has an outside job during the early stages of your business or during difficult times, that will provide some kind of financial cushion. Second, working together may impose a strain on your personal relationship. One thing is certain: it is very likely to change your relationship, whether you want it to or not.

Bear in mind that your child may not want to join the family business

Parents and Children Working Together

Many parents like to feel that their business will one day be taken over by one or more of their children when they are old enough to do so. This strategy has many benefits to both generations. Children who have been brought up in a working family business will, undoubtedly, be helping as soon as they are old enough to carry something without dropping it. But not all offspring will wish to enter the business. While some will see it as a natural step in their lives, others will not. Only a quarter of family businesses survive to the second generation.

One issue to consider is whether your child should join the business straight from school, from college, or after they have been out in the world and acquired some business experience. There is no correct answer, but most people would advise that acquiring outside experience usually benefits everyone.

If you have existing employees, you need to consider how they would feel if one of your children comes into the business. This will not be so difficult if they already know the child and if he or she has worked in the business

during the school vacations. It is important that you are not seen to be giving the child extra benefits or treating them more favorably, which an employee might, quite reasonably, resent. Your children need to realize that they have not suddenly been transformed into a "boss" and they should treat existing staff with the respect they deserve. In turn, they are more likely to be treated with respect.

HIRING AND FIRING CHILDREN

Before you take on any of your children to work full-time in your business, you (and your partner, where relevant) need to consider fully the following issues: first, does your child really want to work in the business? Maybe they think you will be brokenhearted if they tell you they would rather do something else, so you do need to find out their true wishes. Second, are they actually competent to work in the business? The simple test is, would you employ

SURVIVAL STRATEGIES FOR WORKING WITH YOUR CHILDREN

1. Remember that your children are now independent adults.

2. Recognize the contribution that your children make to the business.

3. Offer similar pay and conditions as you would to any other employee.

4. Ensure family members all have a proper job description.

5. Have regular, formal family business meetings.

6. Invite a non-family business adviser to your meetings.

7. Make sure you do not hire your children simply because they need a job.

8. Attend seminars that cover family business issues.

KEEPING IT IN THE FAMILY
If you wish your children to join you in the family business, it is important to keep them fully aware of how the operation is running. Share your dreams with them and encourage them to help out in their spare time.

them if he or she were not your child? It is probably very difficult for you to be objective in your assessment of your child's abilities (or lack of them), so it might be a good idea to discuss this aspect with an outside adviser, such as your accountant. Next, there is the question of what job the child will actually have. Assuming that the business is currently functioning satisfactorily without their input, it means creating a new post or relinquishing yours. If you are not retiring, this raises the key issue of whether the business can actually afford an extra wage. Will the addition of the child increase your sales or cause you to increase your overheads without commensurate benefit?

Before you hire your son or daughter, it may be worth pausing to consider how you might fire them should the unfortunate need arise.

Just how would you get rid of them without creating a rift in the family? There are no easy answers, but do consider the issue at the outset.

On the positive side, your children are often far more dedicated than the average employee. They will probably be prepared to work long hours, their values will be similar to yours, and they will be completely trustworthy. If they have been brought up within a family business environment, they are likely to understand the minutiae of the operation particularly well.

Planning Ahead and Succession

Once your business is established, there will come a time when it is useful for you to create a long-term plan. The process may take many months, even years, while you ponder the different options. As it becomes clear in which direction you should be heading, start to structure your thoughts to form the basis of the plan. Its format can be similar to your original business plan, but the objectives are now very different – the viability of the business is not an issue and you are not trying to raise finance. What you are trying to do is to create a five- or 10-year plan with a clear objective. You need to allow for the unexpected as circumstances invariably change. For instance, you may be convinced that one of your children will take over the business when you retire, but that child might marry, move away, and decide that it is no longer in his or her interests to run the business. When you feel that you have a plan,

Produce a succession plan right away

show a draft of it to your accountant and discuss it at length with your family before you proceed any further.

Your plan may be to sell the business, to cease operation, or to hand it on to the next generation. These different options all need long-term planning.

SELLING A BUSINESS

While you are running a business, you minimize your tax by offsetting operating costs against profits to reduce the net profit figure. However, the selling price of a business is a multiple of its profitability, so it is useful to maximize your profits for the last few years before a possible

CHOOSING FUTURE OPTIONS FOR YOUR FAMILY BUSINESS

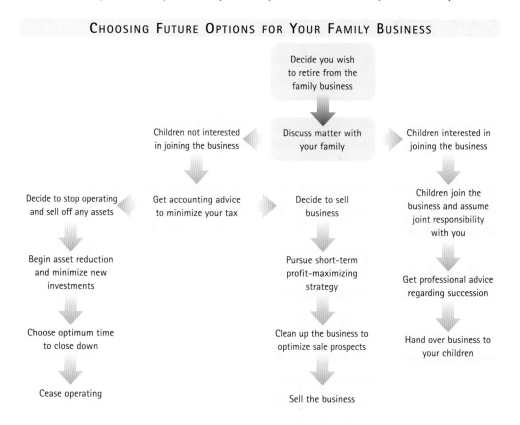

Decide you wish to retire from the family business

↓

Children not interested in joining the business ◀ Discuss matter with your family ▶ Children interested in joining the business

↓ ↓ ↓

Decide to stop operating and sell off any assets ◀ Get accounting advice to minimize your tax ▶ Decide to sell business

Children join the business and assume joint responsibility with you

↓ ↓ ↓

Begin asset reduction and minimize new investments

Pursue short-term profit-maximizing strategy

Get professional advice regarding succession

↓ ↓ ↓

Choose optimum time to close down

Clean up the business to optimize sale prospects

Hand over business to your children

↓ ↓

Cease operating

Sell the business

sale, and especially in the final year. To do this, first restrict all expenses, and second, as you approach the final year end, invoice all possible sales. Ask your accountant for other specific suggestions.

If your business and home are inextricably linked – for instance, if you run a local store attached to your house – selling the business will also mean selling your home. The sale value of both will be as much related to the property market as to your profitability.

CEASE OPERATING

The optimum time to cease operating depends on the nature of the business, the tax position of the proprietors, and many other factors.

Good accounting advice is vital to recover the most money (after tax) from your business. Seek this advice at least a year or more before your planned closing date.

FAMILY BUSINESS SUCCESSION

You may decide to hand over the business to one or more of your children. As with selling a business, the issue of home and business being linked is one factor. Unless your circumstances are very straightforward – for instance, if you have only one child and he or she is capable of taking over the business and is willing to do so – you will need specialized professional advice.

It may seem premature, but if you envisage handing over the business to your children, the

HAVING FREE TIME
Whatever you decide to do with your business on retirement – sell it, pass it on to your children, or cease trading – you will have time to do things that were impossible when you were the boss.

legal form of your business may be affected at the very outset. It is much simpler to hand over an incorporated company than if you set up as a sole proprietor or partnership.

■ **SOLE PROPRIETOR/PARTNERSHIP** With an unincorporated business it is not legally possible to separate the management of the business from its ownership, as they are one and the same. This means that the only way a child can enter the business fully will be as a partner, and they will therefore become jointly and severally liable with their parents for any debts and liabilities of the business. The child could be an employee, but if they carry out the management functions of a partner they may be deemed in law to be a partner. An alternative may be to start business as a sole proprietor or partnership when it is just you and maybe your partner in the business, and then change to an incorporated company at the appropriate time.

■ **CORPORATIONS** With a corporation it can be a relatively straightforward process to include the next generation. The reason for this is that the ownership of the company (by shareholding) is separate from the management (which is carried out by the directors). If there is only one child, shares can be transferred at the appropriate time, although there may be tax implications. If there are two children who wish to take over the business jointly, shares can be transferred equally. The problem occurs when there is a child (or children) who wants to take over the business, and others

who do not. Such a situation requires not only specialized advice but also sensitive handling, as there is great scope for family rifts, the more so the greater the value of the business in question.

PLANNING RETIREMENT

Another complex issue is what wage or compensation, if any, the business should give you after you retire. This is a potential minefield. One strategy might be to take out a personal pension while you are still running the business, with some of the business profits going into the pension fund. This means that on retirement you will have an external pension without the business being burdened with continued payments to your pension fund on your retirement. The added advantage of this approach is that your pension is not tied to the fate of the business, which might cease operation at any point in the future.

There are many other factors to consider, which will require some detailed research. Get professional advice appropriate to your particular circumstances.

Some useful succession strategies include:

■ transferring shares only to children who are working in the business
■ transferring shares equally where there is more than one child in the business
■ creating a family council to meet occasionally to discuss the future
■ using an outside adviser at these family council meetings
■ compensating nonworking children.

Maintaining Your Health and Sanity

Being physically and mentally fit is important if you are to function effectively at work; but for the home entrepreneur, especially one who works alone, it is absolutely vital. Although it may be tempting to work very long hours, particularly at the outset when you are trying to establish your venture, both you and your business will inevitably suffer. This chapter highlights the importance of managing stress effectively and keeping in shape, and also suggests ways to cope with loneliness and stay motivated.

It is important not to underestimate how much your physical and mental health affects your work performance. Keeping in shape and adopting a sensible approach to work will give you more energy to achieve your business goals and increase your output.

Dealing with Stress

Running your own home-based business can be very stressful. While some stress is good, making you more alert mentally and physically for a short period of time, too much is bad, as the adrenaline surge causes a chemical imbalance in the body, which results in physical symptoms such as headaches, insomnia, and stomach ulcers. If you ignore such symptoms for long enough, you will probably become seriously ill, and your business will be in real trouble. It is crucial, therefore, to devise some strategies both to reduce your everyday stress levels at work and to combat the negative effects of stress on your mind and body by incorporating some forms of relaxation techniques and exercise into your weekly routine.

Managing Your Workload

If you feel that your business is making impossible demands on you – you are working seven days a week and still do not have enough time to do everything, you are always under pressure to meet the next deadline, or you feel as though you lurch from one crisis to the next

CASE STUDY: Making Changes to Your Business

John ran a small marketing company representing a number of craftworkers. His role was to get orders from retailers, instruct the craftworkers to supply direct, and then bill the retailers. After a few years John realized that the business was less fun than it had been. This was partly because he was too busy to take a break and partly because he was spending more and more time chasing slow payers. He became depressed and found it difficult to sleep, so he decided to make some changes. First, he hired some part-time help, and then he stopped all credit to poor payers. Although this meant losing a few accounts, he felt that it was worth it. He also found that having an assistant allowed him to take more time off and to have vacations with his family.

– then something is fundamentally wrong with the way you are operating your business, and you need to look at ways of managing your workload more effectively. Consider implementing any of the following solutions:

1 IMPROVE YOUR TIME MANAGEMENT The way in which you manage your time may be inadequate. If you are inefficient with your time, tasks will take you much longer than they should and you will end up working evenings and weekends just to keep up (see also pp. 45–6). Analyze your use of time.

How much time do you spend on doing tasks that do not really matter? At the beginning of each day and each week, sit down and make a list of all the tasks you need to complete. Now categorize them according to whether they are urgent or important, or neither. Strike off the list those tasks that are neither urgent nor important. Prioritize the rest as follows: do immediately all the small tasks that are urgent; then plan specific times during the week or day for the larger urgent tasks; finally, allocate time in your planner during future weeks for the important tasks that are not yet urgent.

Is your estimation of time faulty? Do you always think a task will take less time than it does? If so, you are an overachiever, and you are pressuring yourself unnecessarily. Try to be more realistic about what you can achieve in a day. Plan your time more accurately according to your experience rather than your hope. Physically block in amounts of time in your planner for each task, so that you do not double-book yourself.

RELAXATION TECHNIQUES

By practicing some form of relaxation on a regular basis you will not only reduce your overall stress levels but you will also be able to relax at will; for example, before attempting a particularly difficult negotiation. There are many forms of relaxation techniques to choose from. Here are just a few that can be carried out at home by yourself.

■ **AROMATHERAPY** This relaxation therapy uses essential oils for massage or in the bath. It is especially beneficial for the treatment of stress-related disorders, such as insomnia. The oils, each with different benefits, are available from health-food stores.

■ **MEDITATION** This ancient relaxation technique involves clearing the mind of thoughts to create a sense of inner calm and tranquillity. Regular practice of meditation is said to improve memory and concentration, as well as relieving the symptoms of stress. Find a quiet place to sit, close your eyes, and relax your body. Concentrate on your breathing, establishing a slow and steady rhythm. Recite a mantra – a meaningless word you have chosen – until you wish to end the meditation. Practice this for 20 minutes a day.

■ **SELF-HYPNOSIS** This technique is ideal for helping you to handle anxiety-inducing situations with greater ease. Relax and concentrate on your breathing. Then count evenly from one to 10. Now visualize yourself succeeding in the situation that makes you anxious. Count in your mind to three, and open your eyes.

■ **YOGA** Practicing yoga exercises, or *asanas*, improves the flexibility and suppleness of your body at the same time as sharpening your intellect and increasing a sense of inner awareness and calm.

AROMATHERAPY OILS
Basil and neroli oil are recommended for the relief of anxiety and tension. Add 10 drops of each to the bath just before it is completely filled.

Do you pace yourself badly, setting off each day at lightning speed, only to run out of steam by lunchtime? This way of working is counterproductive, resulting in a degree of poor-quality work, which you will have to do again later, wasting precious time. Resolve to pace yourself better, working methodically rather than frantically for optimum productivity. Remember that it was the tortoise rather than the hare who won the race. To make sure you stay fresh, take regular mini-breaks from your work: walk to the local store to buy a newspaper; make yourself a cup of coffee; have lunch away from your workstation.

2 **RESTORE ORDER** Is your work space cluttered and messy? Such an environment is stressful in itself and causes you more stress when you cannot find something you need. Try to reintroduce order to your desk and room. Sort through the clutter: throw away anything you do not need; act upon whatever requires action; and file or store anything that is important. Invest in appropriate storage facilities and use them.

3 **HIRE STAFF** If you always seem to have too much work to do and too little time in which to do it, but you feel that your time management is satisfactory, then you should perhaps consider employing someone to help you on a regular basis. They could work on a part-time basis to begin with, which is not such a great commitment and

would ease the financial burden. The three key questions you need to ask yourself are: Is the workload likely to remain the same or diminish? Can the business afford to pay someone? Where would a new employee actually work? If space in your home is tight, a new employee may be able to do the work in their own home. The same applies to outsourcing work, such as secretarial duties and financial administration.

4 **NEGOTIATE DEADLINES** If a customer says they really must have something delivered by a certain date, and this imposes an unreasonable strain on you, then ask them exactly why the work needs to be done so quickly. Often there is no good reason at all, and a later date can be agreed quite

TIME SAVER

Before you recruit anyone to work for you full- or part-time, write down what specialized skills the new employee should have or acquire, and then consider how best for them to learn these skills. A few minutes spent planning could save a lot of time later, especially if the new employee subsequently makes a mistake due to a lack of training.

entrepreneurs work more than 50 hours a week, which is unsurprising when you consider how few barriers there are between home and work. Fear is often the driving force behind many successful entrepreneurs, who hardly dare to let up, even when their businesses are well established and undeniably successful.

Yet, if you do not take real breaks and vacations away from home, the odds are that, unless you are exceptionally energetic, the quality of your work will suffer. This, of course, produces a vicious circle of declining effectiveness that could damage and even destroy your business. The one exception to this general rule is during the first year of your new venture. New entrepreneurs will often work right through those 12 pressured months without a vacation, to ensure that they get off to the best possible start while their motivation and inspiration are at their peak.

HOW TO SCHEDULE IN VACATIONS

If you run a one-person business or you work with your partner, then taking time off can be problematic as customers increasingly expect you to be available almost 365 days a year. The situation is much easier if you employ someone to hold the fort while you are away. A part-timer could fulfill that role, looking after the day-to-day business while you are away on vacation or if you are ever sick.

If you do not have an employee, then there are several aspects to consider. First, you should have your vacation breaks during quieter periods of your work year. However, if you have children of school age, these quieter periods may not coincide with their school vacations. Next, you need to decide if you should simply take a break and not tell anyone. This may be possible for some businesses, but with others you might need to inform major customers so that they can phase their requirements to avoid your vacation period.

It is interesting to note that home-based entrepreneurs all report that it takes them several days into a vacation before they feel

FAMILY VACATION

Becoming your own boss is likely to have been prompted by a desire for a better quality of life. It is, therefore, important to take time off for family vacations away from home and where work does not come into play.

amicably, which would allow you to do the job at a reasonable speed. Some customers impose unreasonable deadlines simply to flex their muscles; do not accept such nonsense. You may well be better off without their business, as such clients are often poor payers, difficult, and picky.

TAKING REGULAR BREAKS

Taking time off is a big challenge for many people who run their own small businesses from home. Studies show that on average home

To ensure that you exercise regularly it is important to identify an activity that you like or feel you could enjoy with training. Answer the questions below to identify an activity that you find appealing, that complements your particular physical attributes, and that you can do on a regular basis. If your choice of exercise also generates contact with other people, it will help you to deal with any problems of loneliness arising from working at home.

Do you participate in an existing team sport such as football or hockey?
- ☐ YES *Ensure you keep it up, by committing time in your planner.*
- ☐ NO *Consider trying one, perhaps through friends or contacts who play.*

Are you good at racket sports such as tennis or squash?
- ☐ YES *Join a local club and go along regularly.*
- ☐ NO *Try a beginner's course at a nearby sports center.*

Have you always wanted to try golf?
- ☐ YES *Find a friend who plays and try a round at his or her club.*
- ☐ NO *Don't bother! Golf either grabs you from the outset or leaves you cold.*

Would you consider fitness training through one of the popular exercise routines?
- ☐ YES *There will probably be a local class, so track it down.*
- ☐ NO *Get a book and try some of the moves at home.*

Do you feel that you might enjoy running?
- ☐ YES *Go along to the local running club and get some encouragement.*
- ☐ NO *Try some gentle jogging around your area to get a feel for it.*

Would you use an exercise machine at home?
- ☐ YES *See if there are any second-hand ones advertised locally.*
- ☐ NO *Visit your local sports center to sample their machines and consider joining.*

relaxed, so to really unwind you need at least a week away, preferably two. To get the most out of your vacation, you should not take your mobile phone or laptop computer with you. But if you have someone looking after the fort, it is reasonable to give him or her a contact number in case of an emergency.

If you really cannot get away for a week, then a long weekend break is better than no break at all. Just make sure that you leave home. Switch your mobile phone off and leave your telephone answering machine on.

Keeping Physically Fit

The fitter you are, the more effective you are likely to be at your home business. The improved blood supply that results from regular aerobic exercise, in which the pulse rate and breathing are increased for a sustained period, stimulates your brain to be more creative and to work at a faster pace for longer. Running, cycling, playing tennis, and exercise routines are all forms of aerobic exercise. Non-aerobic exercise, which involves short bursts of energy for specific areas of the body, is also valuable. Weight training, yoga, tai chi, and straightforward walking are all forms of non-aerobic exercise. This kind of exercise, which is noncompetitive, enables you to stretch and strengthen the muscles exercised, making you more supple. It also relaxes you, providing an effective antidote to stress (see p. 151).

Ideally, you should try to include both aerobic and non-aerobic exercise in your weekly routine. Yet many people who start home businesses, particularly office-based ones, rapidly lapse into a sedentary mode of work and lifestyle, failing to pursue any form of exercise at all. In doing so, they run the risk of becoming desk potatoes, sapping all their reserves of natural energy. How, then, is it possible to reconcile the issue of keeping fit with keeping focused on your business?

SCHEDULING AEROBIC EXERCISE

Ideally, you should make time to actually leave the house and conduct your own aerobic exercise program. This could be jogging around the park before you start work, taking an exercise class at the local gym during a lunch break, going for a half-hour swim at the end of the day, or cycling to the store or post office every day instead of using the car.

If you feel you do not have the time to exercise away from the house on a regular

JOGGING AROUND THE PARK

Going jogging once a day will help you develop a healthy heart, increase your lung capacity, and improve your stamina. Sustaining physical fitness also keeps your mind alert, improving your overall effectiveness.

FACT FILE

Swimming can be aerobic or non-aerobic depending on how fast you swim. It is an excellent all-around exercise, which builds up the efficiency of your heart, lungs, and muscles, increases your physical stamina, improves your suppleness, and relaxes your whole body.

basis, consider installing an exercise machine in or next to your office or workshop. Experts say that a 20-minute workout on a rowing, cycling, skiing, or running machine is as beneficial as going out for a run (apart from the lack of fresh air). It will give you a break and allow your mind to work away on a current issue. The only drawback is the need to have a shower or towel down afterward!

INCORPORATING NON-AEROBIC EXERCISE

If you cannot bring yourself to break a sweat in the interest of fitness, then try incorporating regular non-aerobic exercises into your routine. Gentle toning and stretching exercises, whether pursued at the gym or in your own home, will help to reduce the inevitable stiffness that settles in with constant repetitive tasks, keeping you supple and releasing tension.

Such exercise can even be practiced at your desk if time is tight. The 10-minute set below is based on in-seat relaxation programs devised by airlines for long-haul passengers. Try them at least once each morning and afternoon, and every hour if you are particularly prone to stiffness or whenever you need a screen break.

■ **FACE** Tense, then relax your forehead and scalp. Grimace, then relax. Shut your eyes tightly, then relax. Repeat the entire sequence 10 times.

■ **NECK** Rotate your head gently to each side, as far as it will go without straining. Now move your head back to the center and lift it up and down. Repeat the whole sequence five times.

■ **SHOULDERS** Shrug your shoulders up to your ears while breathing in fully. Exhale quickly and drop the shoulders back down. Repeat five times.

■ **ARMS** Lift your arms above your head, clasp the outside of one elbow with the other hand and stretch. Repeat the routine five times on each side.

■ **FINGERS** Hold the middle two fingers of one hand still while trying to spread the outer two away. Then take the first two fingers and separate them from the other two. Repeat 10 times for each hand.

■ **BACK** Sit up straight and arch the small of your back away from the chair. Even better, lie face down and do a push-up while keeping your pelvis still. Repeat five times.

■ **BUTTOCKS** Clench tightly one at a time and hold for a count of 10. Repeat five times.

■ **LEGS** Tense your legs as if you were about to stand up, then relax. Stretch out the legs, pointing the toes, then relax. Repeat the sequence five times.

■ **TOES** Curl the toes under as tightly as you can for 10 seconds. Relax, then repeat the sequence five times.

Coping with Loneliness

Most human beings are social animals and need interaction with other people to provide mental stimulus. Yet running your own business can be a lonely experience, especially if you are a one-person venture, and even more so if your line of work rarely takes you away from home. Many of the social needs of employees are met through work relationships and meeting colleagues and their partners after hours. But that is no longer the case when you start your own business, so it is important to make new contacts. Of course, this will be all the more difficult as you will probably have little spare time or energy during the first months of a new business. Family and old friends are most important during this particularly vulnerable phase, so you should always make time to keep in touch with them.

NETWORKING WITH PEOPLE

A network of people is good for business and your social life. There are a number of different ways to network. These include:

■ **KEEPING UP WITH OLD WORK COLLEAGUES** If you are working in the same industry as you were as an employee, keeping in touch with your old colleagues has the added benefit of allowing you to keep up with the trade gossip, which may indicate sources of work, new developments, as well as which companies to avoid approaching for work.

Keep in touch with what is happening in the general business world

■ **ORGANIZING A GET-TOGETHER WITH YOUR CUSTOMERS AND/OR SUPPLIERS** Informal lunch or evening sessions allow everyone to put faces to voices and build on the personal relationships that are such an important part of business. Such occasions are ideal for brainstorming new ideas and discussing opportunities in a relaxed and more open way than is usually possible.

■ **JOINING A PROFESSIONAL ASSOCIATION** The value of such associations to you will depend entirely on the kind of work you do and the quality of the association concerned. Some associations are excellent and relevant, while others are perhaps less so. Membership can be expensive, so you need to assess the association carefully before joining. Ask existing members if they find it worthwhile. If your work is of a local nature, joining your local chamber of commerce may be a better move.

STAYING IN TOUCH
The telephone is a very effective tool for networking with people, enabling you to keep in touch with friends and colleagues, and preventing you from feeling isolated. Make short phone breaks a part of your daily routine.

■ **CONTACTING TELECOMMUTING ORGANIZATIONS** These relatively new groups may be appropriate for your business and useful as an alternative or adjunct to joining a professional association (see p. 184). Most of them produce publications, both in print and on-line, offering advice, contacts, and business ideas.

■ **PLAYING A SPORT** Leaving the house and playing a sport, such as tennis or softball, is doubly beneficial: it ensures that you meet people and hopefully forge new friendships, and it also helps you to keep in shape. However, you do need to commit the time regularly, booking slots in your planner and keeping them sacrosanct.

■ **TAKING PART IN ON-LINE CHAT ROOMS OR NEWSGROUPS** If you can find them (and can spare the time), virtual conversations appropriate to your work can be fun and informative. Try using coffee or lunch breaks to dip into a sample of on-line networks and test their suitability as substitutes for the sort of conversations you used to have when you were an employee. There are also a growing number of on-line business networks that can be used as chat rooms, where you can post questions about issues and have them answered by people with the relevant experience.

■ **STARTING OR PARTICIPATING IN A LOCAL TELECOMMUTERS' GROUP** Increasingly, community groups are forming to provide a contact network for people working from home, whether they are running their own businesses or not. A wide range of issues, from motivation to technology, is usually discussed in these groups, which can provide a powerful support net during difficult times.

■ **TALKING ON THE PHONE** It is easy to tell which people work on their own at home from their phone bills, which are always larger than normal. A part of their daily social interaction is talking at length to customers, suppliers, and friends. While this is valuable in terms of preserving your sanity, it is important not to let the gossip prevent you from getting through your work.

■ **WRITING EMAILS** Although emails seem to be an increasingly popular method of communication, especially over long-distances, they do not have that all-important human touch. The advent of video links through computers will be a huge step forward for many working at home, reinstating human contact.

Staying Motivated

You will start your business with boundless energy and enthusiasm, but as time rolls on some of that excitement will become dulled by the relentless round of work, billing, chasing late payers, dealing with difficult customers, and so on. Survival, and indeed your happiness, require a multipronged strategy:

1 CELEBRATE SMALL ACHIEVEMENTS Think of the key goals you need to achieve each day, and list them. Then work toward those targets. When you achieve them – whether it is a new sale, clearing out an old file, or installing a new program on your computer – reward yourself. This might vary from giving yourself a cookie with your coffee to taking the afternoon off to go horseback riding or to visit an art gallery. What matters is that you have set yourself a target and achieved it. By marking the moment with a treat, you will enjoy yourself and improve your self-confidence and motivation.

2 CHANGE TASKS Running any small business requires you to do a whole host of different tasks, some of which may be rather laborious or boring. To keep up your motivation and effectiveness, you need to be able to judge when you are becoming stale at doing a particular job. Then, rather than wasting time and losing impetus staring out of the window or working at a slow pace, you should stop and start a different job or take a break. It is important to keep fresh!

3 PLAN VARIETY Build variety into your working day so that each one is slightly different. This might be achieved by radically changing your work pattern. If you are working with your partner or an employee, you could do some of their work in exchange for their doing some of yours. They will probably appreciate the variety, too. A more radical solution is to diversify your business. This should be motivated not simply by potential financial gain but also by the fun and change it might bring.

4 GET ENOUGH SLEEP If you are running short of sleep, a whole range of unpleasant symptoms can occur. The first is that you tend to become short-tempered. Then your enthusiasm wanes as your exhaustion level rises. Next, you begin to make mistakes and, finally, your health deteriorates: as your immune system becomes compromised, it is less effective, so you catch colds and other infections more readily. You may be able to cope fine for a few days on less sleep than usual. For example, if you have a big order to fulfill or some major crisis occurs, then the adrenaline will pump through your body, ensuring you meet the deadline or fix the problem. However, your effectiveness afterward will be lowered and you will need more sleep than usual for a few nights.

GETTING READY FOR SLEEP

Spending eight hours in bed may not equate to a good night's sleep if you are lying awake worrying or thinking about the day's work.

If sleeplessness is a problem, then you need to actively work at getting a good night's sleep by winding down for an hour beforehand. Then, if you wake during the night, you need to consciously avoid thinking about work. Instead, try concentrating on another image such as a large, white sheet or a piece of paper. Every time a work matter flits into your mind, consciously push it off the sheet. Alternatively, picture a favorite vacation scene and imagine all the smells and sounds of the area. As you do this, relax your whole body, tightening and releasing the muscles in each part of your body, starting at your toes and working upward. This simple technique works for most people with a little practice.

Ten Excuses for Not Working

There are a legion of distractions or excuses you can find for not working when you are no longer interested in what you are doing or motivated by the same goals as you were when you set out. These are just 10 of the more common excuses given for stopping work. If you regularly use any such excuses to stop working, then perhaps you should reappraise your whole approach to being a home entrepreneur.

1. Need to walk the dog.
2. Must complete a home improvement job.
3. Need to do an exercise class at the gym.
4. Must check the mail.
5. Need to make another cup of coffee.
6. Must watch the news on television.
7. Must check my emails.
8. The plants need watering.
9. The grass needs mowing.
10. The newspapers need to be read.

Changing Tack

If you find that you are becoming more and more dissatisfied with your home-based business, and are constantly coming up with excuses for not settling down to do your work, it is probably time to re-evaluate your goals and maybe consider a complete change of direction.

You may decide that you simply want to work fewer hours so that you can spend more time pursuing other activities, such as a hobby or sport, or to study part-time. There is no reason why you should not do this as long as you can still earn a reasonable income. If work simply is no longer your main priority, relax and accept the fact that you are unlikely ever to become a business mogul.

Alternatively, if working part-time is not an option, consider switching from one type of business to another that is closer to your own interests and desires. Perhaps you are a talented artist, photographer, or musician, or have a particular academic strength. Why not turn your favorite hobby or expertise into a business by offering private lessons from home? Perhaps you have some capital and love sailing. Why not buy a sailing boat and charter it to individuals and groups. If you are very knowledgable about your local area, why not organize sightseeing tours and offer your knowledge to others. Or you might like to offer a service investigating family trees. There really is no limit to the number of hobbies that can be adapted to become a profitable business.

Sightseeing Tours

Conducting or organizing sightseeing tours for groups of tourists or students is an ideal way of combining in-depth knowledge of, say, the history or architecture of a particular city with earning a living working from home.

USEFUL
information

*T*his section covers important
aspects of the law and taxes as they
apply to a home business, providing a
straightforward, basic grounding in
the numerous and complex regulations
that are likely to affect you. The
Glossary explains key business terms,
while the Useful Contacts and
Suggested Reading sections point you
toward other sources of information.

Legal Matters

There are an increasing number of laws and regulations with which businesses, including those run from home, must comply in the U.S., and in each state. This chapter provides general guidance, but should not be regarded as a complete or authoritative statement of the law. For more information, consult an attorney or the relevant authorities.

Choosing Your Business Status

An early decision you need to make is what legal form your business should take. If you are going to be a one-person business, you could be a "sole proprietor" (that is, "self-employed")

or a "corporation." If several people are involved on an equal basis, you need to be a "partnership" or a "corporation." When you start up, inform the Internal Revenue Service promptly (see p. 177).

Sole Proprietor

This is probably the most common legal status for starting a business. You can do business

---

Drawing Up a Partnership Agreement

These are suggestions of clauses to consider in a partnership agreement. You may not need all those listed here, and you may wish to include others; this is a starting point.

■ **Description of the Proposed Business** This should not limit future developments.

■ **Location** Initial location of the business.

■ **Date of Commencement** Some agreements also state the duration for which the agreement is to last, though this can be extended by arrangement between partners.

■ **Capital** The initial capital each partner will provide at the commencement. If, due to personal circumstances, the partners contribute different amounts of capital, then they might choose either to: apportion the profits in the same ratio as the amounts invested; or allow time, say six or 12 months, for the partners to equalize their investments to allow the profits to be shared equally. In both cases voting rights and personal drawings (wages) should be equal.

■ **Role of Each Partner** Definition of the role, adding that the partners will not undertake other employment or self-employment during the period of the agreement. Where one partner is a "silent partner," this would obviously need to be taken into account.

■ **Decisions** The particular circumstances where decisions need to be unanimous to guard against reckless acts by individual partners. For example: agreeing or terminating contracts; offering or terminating employment; entering into or terminating property lease arrangements; lending, borrowing, or removing any property or assets of the business.

■ **Voting** The voting rights and who might arbitrate should there be disagreement.

■ **Operation of the Bank Account** For example, how many signatures are required on checks (often, only one signature for amounts less than some specified figure).

■ **Division of Profits and Losses** This includes the nomination of an accountant.

■ **Level of Drawings and Expenses** There could be an upper limit per annum on the level of expenses.

under your own name or a business name. You can also employ staff. Should the business fail owing money, then you are personally liable, and your creditors can seize your personal possessions through the courts to recover their losses. Many businesses start as sole proprietors, but as they grow they usually change to a corporation status for three reasons:
▨ It provides limited liability protection of their personal possessions.
▨ It is easier for them to raise larger sums of money for expansion.
▨ It permits other people to take a stake in the business.

PARTNERSHIP

If two or more people work together and none is an employee of the other(s), the law regards the arrangement as a "partnership." A partnership can take on employees. Unless there is an agreement to the contrary, profits in a partnership have to be shared equally between partners. Likewise, each partner will be regarded by law as "jointly and severally liable" for any debts that the business may run up. What this means in practice is that if the first partner buys a car, for example, using a business check that subsequently bounces, the car dealer can pursue the second partner for the entire amount.

It is therefore essential to start off with a good written partnership agreement. Start by drafting your own agreement, get advice from an accountant, and then see an attorney who can draw up the final document. There are many complex issues involved and you will need professional advice.

▨ **VACATIONS** The length of vacation that can be taken. Also, who needs to agree to proposed vacation dates, and any restrictions as to duration or to not taking vacations during prescribed busy times of the year.

▨ **ILLNESS OR INCAPACITY** The procedure in the event of illness or incapacity of a partner.

▨ **ADMISSION OF A NEW PARTNER** The procedures for admitting a new partner. This might also include a clause that allows the expulsion of one partner under certain specified circumstances.

▨ **RETIREMENT OF AN EXISTING PARTNER** Usually the retiring partner is entitled to an equal share of the business assets, excluding goodwill, as valued by the firm's accountants at the date of retirement. Payment to the retiring partner must be made in installments that are fair to the outgoing partner and yet affordable by the business. The tax implications for both parties need consideration, too. Goodwill should probably be excluded, as: any goodwill the business has built up has already been enjoyed by the outgoing partner by way of shared profits; the departure of the partner might alter any goodwill significantly; and it is a very difficult aspect to quantify.

▨ **DEATH OF A PARTNER** Usually an agreement will state that the partnership will continue and the estate of the deceased partner will be entitled to a proportion of the business assets, excluding goodwill, with phased payments made to the estate.

▨ **TAX CONSIDERATIONS** A clause for tax reasons where the partners (and their executors) elect to have the profits of the business assessed to income tax on a continuation basis as if no change in the partnership had taken place.

▨ **DISSOLUTION** The dissolution of the partnership by mutual agreement and what should happen to the assets.

▨ **UNFAIR COMPETITION** It may be wise to incorporate an unfair competition clause if you are concerned that a partner may leave the business at some time in the future and set up in competition with you. The wording of this clause can be tricky and must not attempt to prevent a person from earning a livelihood.

A "silent partner" is someone who invests in a business, but does not work in it. His or her role within the partnership should be spelled out clearly in the agreement, but they are usually "jointly and severally liable" in the same way as a full partner.

But be warned: There is really no such thing as a "silent" partner. All partners, whether or not they are involved in the day-to-day operation of the business, are jointly and severally liable for partnership debts and obligations, to the full extent of each partner's assets. In fact, wealthier, so-called silent partners are better targets in a lawsuit because they have more assets, and may know little or nothing of the circumstances of the claim, or the possible defenses.

However, if you insist on the partnership form of business entity, there is a way to protect investors who have no control of the business, but want to share in the profits. That form is the limited partnership.

A limited partnership consists of one or more general partners, and one or more limited partners. General partners operate the business and are fully liable for debts incurred, but limited partners play no part in operating the business, and are only liable for business debts to the extent of, and in proportion to, their investment in the business. Beyond that amount, creditors may not reach the assets of a limited partner, but this protection vanishes if the limited partner has gone beyond playing a passive role in operating the business.

Choose your partners carefully. They could lead to your personal bankruptcy just as easily as helping you to make your fortune. Partners, even within the same family, commonly fall out. It may be better for them to be your employees rather than partners. Finally, remember to take out "key-man insurance" (see p. 169).

CORPORATION

A corporation is regulated by the laws of the state where it is incorporated, which is usually the state in which its principal office or place of business is located. Ask your attorney and accountant whether there are advantages to incorporating in another state.

You can incorporate a corporation yourself, or through an agent, and there are services that can prepare and file incorporation documents for you. However, incorporation has important tax, legal, and business implications, as to which these agents and services do not provide advice. Let your attorney and accountant help

SHOULD YOU FORM A CORPORATION?

ADVANTAGES OF A CORPORATION	DISADVANTAGES OF A CORPORATION
■ Limited liability of shareholders: should the corporation fail, in most cases all you would lose is your share capital (unless you have signed personal guarantees or are guilty of a crime)	■ Directors' wages are subject to tax
	■ Higher annual accounting charges
	■ Possibly higher mandatory insurance premiums
■ Easier to raise larger sums of money	■ Public disclosure of some key data
■ Easier format to cope with investors who do not want to work in the business	■ Cannot offset losses against your previous income tax
■ Greater credibility with some customers	■ Cannot easily move personal funds in and out of your business bank account
■ Possibility of advantageous tax rates (although this can vary)	■ Onerous legal responsibilities on all directors

navigate the many, and sometimes confusing, laws and regulations.

Each state has different requirements for corporate meetings and books, the number of officers and directors, their rights and responsibilities, and so on. Each state also differs on corporate franchise taxes, sales or use, and property taxes, if any. Also, sales, use, and property taxes can vary from one county or municipality to another. The secretary of state of the state of incorporation can provide free or low-cost brochures that are highly recommended reading.

A corporation that has an office or does business in another state may be required to register and to pay annual fees. Failure to comply may prohibit the corporation from suing a customer in the "foreign" state on an unpaid balance, or from asserting the claim as a defense if the corporation is sued in that state.

Internal Revenue Service regulations allow for two types of corporations, with different requirements and tax consequences. In general, a corporation must pay tax on its income, and when part or all of its income is distributed to its owners, they too must pay tax on their income.

There is also a Subchapter S corporation, which is treated for tax purposes as a partnership, allowing the income to pass through the corporation without being subject to taxation. Using Subchapter S avoids double taxation of corporate income, but limits the number of shareholders and classes of stock.

When you ask your accountant whether a corporation is best for your needs, also ask which type of corporation is best for you.

There are special requirements for public corporations, which offer stock to the public. Selling stock may help raise needed capital, but it is highly regulated by the U.S. Securities & Exchange Commission or, in some cases, state authorities. It is possible to buy a "shelf corporation" that is already registered with the appropriate authorities, but the complexities of public corporations are beyond the scope of this book.

If you dream of having your business on Wall Street, obtain a brief overview of public corporations by reading *Q&A: Small Business and the SEC; A Guide to Help You Understand How to Raise Capital and Comply with the Federal Securities Laws*. This booklet was prepared in cooperation with the SEC Office of the Chief Counsel for Advocacy, and is published by the Office of Small Business, Division of Corporation Finance. It is available in many libraries, and from the Securities & Exchange Commission.

Choosing Your Business Name

As a sole proprietor you can do business under your own last name (with or without first names or initials) – for example, Smith, William Smith, W. Smith, Wm Smith, or William David Smith. You can also trade under a business name, such as William David Smith dba Smith's Gifts (DBA stands for "doing business as"). A partnership can operate under the names of all the partners or under a business name. A corporation registers its name at the time of incorporation. If a business name is to be used, it must be filed with the clerk of the county where the business is located.

WORDING

There are some names that you cannot use for your business. The name you select should not be offensive, and the use of certain words may be barred or restricted under applicable state law.

Before using a business name, check your local phone book and relevant trade journals to ensure you do not inadvertently choose a name that is the same or very similar to an existing business. You should also make a search of your state's trademark register.

There is no registration of business names, although no two names of corporations can be exactly the same. If planning a website, check there is no such domain name already registered.

LETTERHEADS AND INVOICES

Your letters and invoices should state the name, address (including Zip code), and telephone number. If your business has a license that must be displayed, such as for a home-improvement contractor, include the license number.

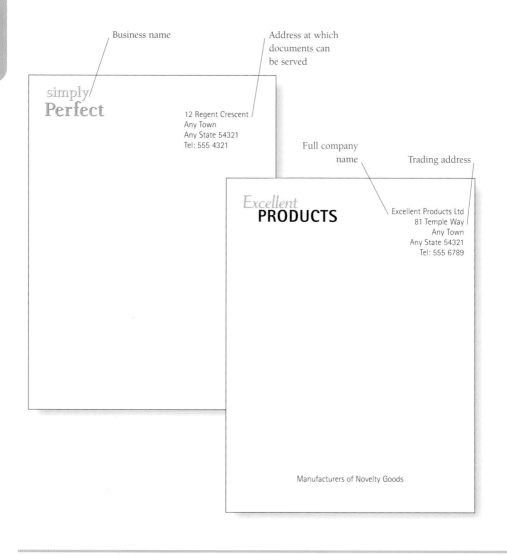

Business name

Address at which documents can be served

simply
Perfect

12 Regent Crescent
Any Town
Any State 54321
Tel: 555 4321

Full company name

Trading address

Excellent
PRODUCTS

Excellent Products Ltd
81 Temple Way
Any Town
Any State 54321
Tel: 555 6789

Manufacturers of Novelty Goods

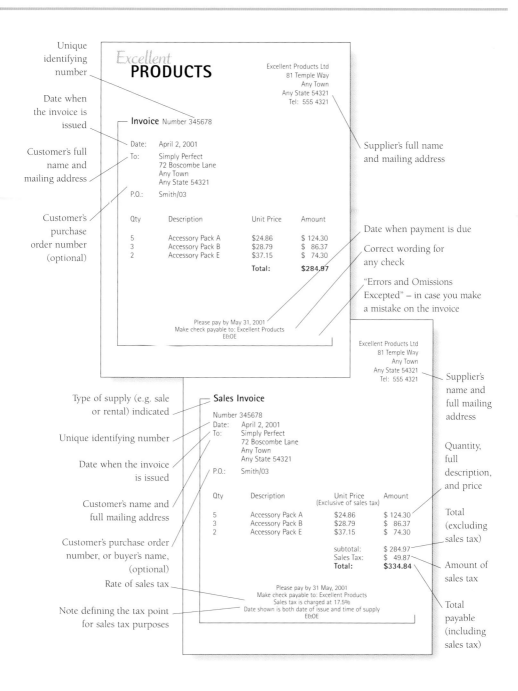

Unique identifying number

Date when the invoice is issued

Customer's full name and mailing address

Customer's purchase order number (optional)

Excellent
PRODUCTS

Excellent Products Ltd
81 Temple Way
Any Town
Any State 54321
Tel: 555 4321

Invoice Number 345678

Date: April 2, 2001
To: Simply Perfect
72 Boscombe Lane
Any Town
Any State 54321
P.O.: Smith/03

Qty	Description	Unit Price	Amount
5	Accessory Pack A	$24.86	$ 124.30
3	Accessory Pack B	$28.79	$ 86.37
2	Accessory Pack E	$37.15	$ 74.30
		Total:	**$284.97**

Please pay by May 31, 2001
Make check payable to: Excellent Products
E&OE

Supplier's full name and mailing address

Date when payment is due

Correct wording for any check

"Errors and Omissions Excepted" – in case you make a mistake on the invoice

Excellent Products Ltd
81 Temple Way
Any Town
Any State 54321
Tel: 555 4321

Type of supply (e.g. sale or rental) indicated

Unique identifying number

Date when the invoice is issued

Customer's name and full mailing address

Customer's purchase order number, or buyer's name, (optional)

Rate of sales tax

Note defining the tax point for sales tax purposes

Sales Invoice

Number 345678
Date: April 2, 2001
To: Simply Perfect
72 Boscombe Lane
Any Town
Any State 54321
P.O.: Smith/03

Qty	Description	Unit Price (Exclusive of sales tax)	Amount
5	Accessory Pack A	$24.86	$ 124.30
3	Accessory Pack B	$28.79	$ 86.37
2	Accessory Pack E	$37.15	$ 74.30
		subtotal:	$ 284.97
		Sales Tax:	$ 49.87
		Total:	**$334.84**

Please pay by 31 May, 2001
Make check payable to: Excellent Products
Sales tax is charged at 17.5%
Date shown is both date of issue and time of supply
E&OE

Supplier's name and full mailing address

Quantity, full description, and price

Total (excluding sales tax)

Amount of sales tax

Total payable (including sales tax)

Licenses and Registration

You can start most businesses right away as there is usually no need for registration or licensing, but there are important exceptions, in most cases governed by state or local laws. Some examples are: selling tobacco or alcohol; providing driving instruction; operating an employment agency; child care; scrap-metal dealing or processing; providing public entertainment; owning a nightclub; providing massage; dealing in second-hand goods; operating as a street vendor; driving a taxi or private rental car; operating certain goods and passenger vehicles; cleaning windows; hairstyling; selling door to door; running residential care and nursing homes; betting and gaming; most activities relating to pets or animals; providing credit services (and debt collecting, hiring, leasing, and so on). Also, if you are going to sell or handle food, speak to the state and local health department at a very early stage of the project, and before you start operating.

The list above is not exhaustive, and failure to obtain a license or register may be a criminal offense, or may prevent you for collecting unpaid accounts. Contact your county clerk and local authorities to find out if your project needs a license or other approval.

Business Insurance

If you have a vehicle, employ anyone, or have plant and machinery, it is a legal requirement to have insurance coverage for these risks. It is prudent to be adequately insured for other risks, and for specialized risks associated with your business, so you should discuss your proposed venture with an insurance broker. Take out as much insurance as you need, and review the position at least once a year to take into account changes in your business.

When Starting Up

The following are insurances that you might want to consider before you start business, as you acquire a vehicle, premises, and so on:

▪ **Vehicles**
Most states require auto insurance, but if you intend to use your car in the business, check that your insurance covers you and any other driver for the commercial purpose you propose. Car insurance is normally for social, domestic, and pleasure purposes only unless specified otherwise, and generally there will be an additional premium for using your car in connection with your business.

▪ **Workers' compensation and disability insurance**
Each state has its own laws requiring employers to provide workers' compensation and limited disability insurance for all employees. Remember that a partnership or corporation "employs" its owners as employees, and their wages are subject to mandatory insurance as well. Also remember that sole proprietors are not employees, and must provide their own insurance for on-and off-the-job accidents and illnesses.

The insurance premiums are based on the risks involved in the particular industry within that state, and the premiums can sometimes be reduced by rigorous safety training and other measures. Ask your insurance agent if you are eligible for these reductions.

Workers' compensation provides coverage without fault, and is the employee's exclusive remedy against the employer for the negligence of the employer or a co-worker. However, if the employer did not maintain workers' compensation insurance, the employee may sue the employer. Also, in many states, failing to carry required workers' compensation is a crime, subjecting violators to fines, penalties, and even imprisonment.

▪ **Engineering**
If the business has plant or machinery that must have a periodic statutory inspection,

then it is usual to arrange for this to be done by a specialized engineering insurer.

▓ PUBLIC LIABILITY

This provides you with protection against claims for which you may be legally liable brought by anyone other than employees for bodily injury or loss, or damage to property, arising in the course of your business. It also covers the legal costs that may be incurred when defending against such claims.

▓ PRODUCT LIABILITY

This provides protection for legal liability of claims arising from injury, loss, or damage due to products you have sold, supplied, repaired, serviced, or tested. It can be expensive but is usually unavoidable.

▓ PROFESSIONAL INDEMNITY

This is for consultants (legal, technical, management, marketing, financial, and so on). The insurance protects you against your legal liability to compensate third parties who have sustained some injury, loss, or damage due to your own professional negligence or that of your employees.

▓ GOODS IN TRANSIT

As a rule, auto insurance policies do not cover goods being carried in the vehicle, so if you intend to carry goods you may need this additional insurance coverage.

▓ PREMISES

If you plan to work from home or store business goods at your home, your normal domestic policy is unlikely to cover your business risks. Furthermore, working from home or storing goods may invalidate your existing policy; discuss this with your insurer. If buying commercial premises for storage or if it is a condition of the lease that you should insure the premises, then you should make sure that you are covered against fire and other perils (burst pipes, storms, malicious damage). Check, too, that any plate-glass windows are covered. Your insurance broker will advise you if you need to be covered for "property owners' liability," as this risk may already be covered by the public liability policy.

▓ STOCK, FIXTURES AND FITTINGS, PLANT, AND MACHINERY

Be careful not to underestimate the value of these. Note that, if your cover is for "replacement value," it provides for the full replacement cost, while "indemnity value" is the current market value less depreciation (which can be significant). Insurance should cover losses due to theft, vandalism, fire, flood, and so on. Accidental damage or "all-risks" cover can be arranged, but is expensive.

▓ MONEY

If your business involves handling cash in significant amounts, then insurance coverage against theft would be prudent. Policies normally cover loss of money on the premises and also money in transit to or from the bank. If covered for cash in transit, be sure to comply with any stipulations by the insurers.

▓ "KEY MAN" INSURANCE

This is a life insurance policy payable to the other partners in the event of a partner dying. The insurance enables the surviving partners to purchase the deceased partner's share of the business from the estate and to continue operation.

ONCE ESTABLISHED

As your business becomes established, you may want to consider the following types of policy:

▓ EMPLOYMENT PROTECTION

When you are employing people, particularly a large number, the complex employment legislation which covers employees' rights, unfair dismissal, and so on can cripple a small company both financially and in terms of management time if a personnel problem occurs. This insurance covers not only legal fees but can also cover personnel advisory services that you may need.

▓ FIDELITY GUARANTEE AND INTERNAL THEFT

This provides protection against dishonesty or theft by members of your own staff.

▓ CONSEQUENTIAL LOSS

If your premises are put out of commission due to fire or any other insured peril, then this insurance will restore the financial position of the company as if the calamity had not occurred. Such insurance can be expensive, but failure to have it may close down a business should such a disaster occur.

▨ **PERSONAL HEALTH AND DISABILITY**

It is wise to consider personal health and disability insurance cover for yourself to provide you with an income should you be unable to work. Similarly, if the company is very dependent upon one or two other key people, it may be wise to insure them against death, accident, or sickness, for the business may suffer financially in the event of their prolonged absence from work.

A final caution – should you ever need to make an insurance claim, the insurers will scrutinize your policy to see if you have not declared some material matter or not complied with one of their stipulations, as this would give them a reason to not pay out. So make a full declaration, read the small print of the policy, and comply with any stipulations the insurers make.

Business Legislation

The following areas of law and regulation are particularly relevant to sales and marketing businesses, but may also apply more widely.

An important feature of our federal system of government is that many aspects of interstate commerce are regulated by federal law, which is often the minimum guarantee of protection. Unless federal law preempts them from doing so, states and localities may add further, and sometimes different, refinements. For that reason, the laws of each state and each locality may differ significantly, and may differ from federal law.

It is important to remember that "interstate commerce" has proven to be a difficult concept to define, and the courts continue to struggle with the concept. In general, any business that uses interstate methods of transporting goods

or ideas, such as the postal service, the telephone, or the internet, should expect to be held to federal standards, although state and local laws will also apply.

ADVERTISING AND SALES PROMOTION

Much of the regulation of advertising and promotion is self-regulation, with industry groups largely policing themselves. These groups are usually very influential because their membership is composed of the largest and most prominent companies in the particular industry, and the group's ethical standards become the industry's code.

There are few regulations governing advertising and sales promotion as such in United States. Although federal and state laws do not regulate advertising, they do prohibit the use of false and misleading statements to sell goods.

On a national basis, the Federal Trade Commission administers laws and regulations that prohibit the use of fraudulent, deceptive, and unfair business practices in all manner of trade involving interstate commerce, and state and local laws often supplement the federal rules and regulations.

Enforcement actions can be brought by both federal, and by state or local, authorities for violations of different laws involving the same deceptive scheme. In general, these laws prohibit false advertising, and regulate the use of comparative statements in marketing materials.

ARBITRATION VERSUS LITIGATION

Business agreements should be reviewed carefully as to whether they specify where any claims or disputes must be brought. Also, an increasing number of business agreements require arbitration, or other methods of alternative dispute resolution, rather than litigation. Resolving disputes outside the court system is much faster and less expensive, and is becoming a preferred way to handle many business claims.

AVOIDING BIAS COMPLAINTS

Federal laws bar employment, credit, housing, and other forms of discrimination or harassment based on race, color, religion, sex, national origin, age (over 40), or disability. Some state and local laws prohibit bias for other reasons, such as sexual orientation and marital status. Offenders can be fined, and can be sued for monetary and compensatory damages. To learn how to comply with these laws, contact the U.S. Equal Employment Opportunity Commission, and your state and local civil rights authorities.

BUSINESS AND INTERNET DOMAIN NAMES

The use of business names is regulated by state law. In general, sole proprietors may operate under their own last names, with or without the use of first names or initials, such as W.D. Smith dba ("doing business as") Smith's Gifts. Partnerships may operate under the names of all the partners or under a business name. Corporations may operate under the name of incorporation or under a business name. Business names are generally filed in each county in which the company does business.

Some state laws prohibit the use of certain words or terms in business names, especially names that would be deceptive or misleading.

State laws prohibit two corporations from using the same name, or a confusing variation of the same name. Before selecting a business name, check local telephone and relevant business directories to avoid using a name that is the same as or very similar to that of an existing business.

The advent of the internet has created an entirely new problem in the use of domain names, and an entirely new set of regulators. Disputes over the use of domain names involve mandatory arbitration by panelists chosen by one of several international organizations authorized by the Internet Corporation for Assigned Names and Numbers, commonly known as ICANN.

These international arbitrators are not bound by U.S. law or custom, or by state or common-law rules of evidence. The fact that a name is legally registered in a particular state, or a trademark (see below) is registered in the United States, does not guarantee that an arbitrator will not bar the domain name registrant from using that name. The arbitrator can assign the domain name to another business, especially one that has used the name, or a part or variation of the name, under trademark or for a long time. This area of the law is particularly unsettled at present

CLEAR PRINT AND PLAIN ENGLISH

Many state laws require the use of large, clear print, in some cases bold-faced, in certain contracts and insurance policies. Many state laws encourage, and in some cases require, the use of "plain English," rather than legal or industry terminology, in contracts, especially those involving consumers.

COMMERCIAL DEBTS

Commercial purchases are regulated by state laws, most of which follow the Uniform Commercial Code. Buyers should promptly inspect the goods, as to quantity, quality, and fitness. Unless they are unconscionable, invoice terms, including discounts and interest, will be upheld. Buyers should also promptly inspect statements of goods sold and delivered, because they may be held liable for accounts stated, to which there has been no protest.

COMPETITION

The Federal Trade Commission and some state regulatory agencies also prohibit anti-competitive agreements, whether written or unwritten, between two or more businesses or trade groups, as well as abusing a dominant position in the market by a business. Examples of such anti-competitive agreements include the fixing of purchase or sales prices, the sharing of markets, or the application of different trading conditions to equivalent transactions.

The agencies have the authority to block mergers and acquisitions, and to force companies to sell divisions, leave markets, or split themselves into several different companies, in order to encourage competition and to punish anti-competitive actions.

CONSUMER CREDIT

The Federal Trade Commission administers the Fair Credit Reporting Act, which gives consumers the right to inspect and challenge information in credit reports that can adversely affect their credit ratings. The act also allows consumers to opt out of marketing lists prepared by credit reporting agencies that are used to solicit customers for credit cards, insurance policies, and other financial products.

The Federal Trade Commission also administers the Truth in Lending Act which, with Regulation Z, requires businesses that offer credit terms in any form to disclose the credit terms and conditions, especially the annual percentage rate of the cost of credit.

The Truth in Lending Act and Regulation Z, which are enforceable under state as well as federal law, prohibit the attempt to disguise a credit transaction through the use of terms such as "budget plan" or "easy monthly payments," and require the disclosure of the true nature of the transaction.

Some state laws also regulate, to varying degrees, the provision or denial of credit, the use of credit reports, the use of marketing lists, and so on. Interest rates for credit terms and conditions, including credit cards, are set by state law. Federal and state laws prohibit the use of discriminatory criteria, such as race or religion, to determine creditworthiness.

CONSUMER PROTECTION

The Federal Trade Commission, as well as state and local agencies, regulate many aspects of consumer protection. Federal and state regulations prohibit deceptive business practices in the sale of franchises, network marketing and business opportunity plans, and work-from-home programs. Similar regulations prohibit the use of unfounded claims to promote the sale of diet, health, and fitness products.

Federal regulations prohibit the fraudulent use of "Made in the U.S.A." labels on products, and prohibit deceptive product labeling.

Both federal and state authorities are gearing up to stop the growing problem of identity theft, and the fraudulent use of the identification and credit profile of unsuspecting victims.

The Federal Trade Commission publishes several booklets to educate businesses about the applicable rules, and to encourage compliance, including: *A Business Guide to the Federal Trade Commission's Mail Order Rule*, *A Businessperson's Guide to Federal Warranty Law*, *Complying with the 900-Number Rule: A Business Guide for Pay-per-Call Services*, *Complying with the Telemarketing Sales Rule*, *Guides Against Bait Advertising*, *Guides Against Deceptive Advertising of Guaranties*, *Guides Against Deceptive Pricing*, *Guides Concerning Use of Endorsements and Testimonials in Advertising*, *Guides Concerning the Use of the Word "Free" and Similar Representations*, *Guides for the Use of Environmental Marketing Claims*, and *How to Advertise Consumer Credit: Complying with the Law*.

COOLING-OFF PERIODS

Some state laws give consumers greater protection, such as an extended right of cancellation, for items sold door-to-door. Similar laws extend cancellation rights in certain financial products, such as mortgages.

COPYRIGHTS

The concept of copyright relates to original literary and other creative works, including advertisements, and marketing brochures and materials, in all types of media and means of dissemination, including the internet. Often no registration is required other than the use under common law, but legal protection requires being able to prove who created the work, and when. Protection is automatic and immediate, but it is advisable to use the copyright symbol (c) together with the date the work the work was first created. Registration with the U.S. Copyright Office is strongly advised.

DATA PRIVACY

See Consumer Protection (above). Many states are enacting or considering laws to grant individuals greater control over the use and dissemination of their private data, especially credit and medical information. This area may become subject to greater federal and state regulation, especially with the increasing ability to identify and create databases of genetic or heritable medical conditions.

ENVIRONMENTAL PROTECTION

Federal, state, and local laws and rules regulate the safety of our air, water, and environment, and the safe handling and disposal of both hazardous and non-hazardous substances and waste. In addition to being aware of federal laws administered by the U.S. Environmental Protection Agency, you should familiarize yourself with applicable local rules by contacting your state or local environmental control or conservation department.

If your business uses or produces toxic substances, or produces waste or pollutants, contact your industry or trade association for the most current information, and the best ways to comply with the law.

FALSE AND DECEPTIVE PRODUCT LABELING

See Consumer Protection (above).

FINANCIAL SERVICES

The sale of financial services is highly regulated by federal or state authorities, or both. In general, the sale of insurance products requires a state license, and the sale of investment products requires licensing by a federally authorized organization, such as the National Association of Security Dealers. Selling other investment-related products, such as real estate and mortgages, generally require state licenses.

FOOD SAFETY

There are stringent rules, generally set by local authorities, regarding most aspects of food preparation, handling, and marketing. These rules address premises, equipment, refrigeration and storage, cleaning, food handling, work methods and training, labeling, vermin control, and other aspects of the business. In addition to frequent, random, mandatory inspections, many areas require licensing and training certification.

FRANCHISE AND NETWORK MARKETING

See Consumer Protection (above). Many states are enacting or considering laws to provide greater protection for purchasers of franchises and multilevel marketing plans.

MAIL ORDER AND TELEMARKETING

See Consumer Protection, above. Federal Trade Commission rules prohibit using abusive or deceptive telemarketing methods, such as misrepresenting, or failing to disclose, costs, conditions, refund or cancellation policies, the odds of winning a prize or premium, or credit card laundering. Sellers by mail or telephone order must ship within the time specified, or within 30 days.

OPTING OFF DIRECT MARKETING LISTS

See Consumer Protection (above).

PATENTS

The U.S. Patent and Trademark Office grants patents to unique inventions that advance the state of the art. A patent application requires proof that the invention is unique, that the applicant invented it, and how and when it was invented. The office's publications explain the application process, the benefits, and the fees.

PRICE MARKING

State laws require goods offered for sale to be clearly marked as to price, but these laws differ markedly as to the specifics, and as to how they are interpreted. Some states require each item to be clearly marked as to the price of that unit. Other states merely require the per-unit price be displayed reasonably near the item. Local ordinances may offer consumers greater protection.

TRADEMARKS

Trademarks and business logos must be unique, and may not be deceptive or misleading. They should be registered with the U.S. Patent and Trademark Office.

WARRANTIES

Federal law does not require a warranty, other than that warranty advertising not be false, misleading, or deceptive. In general, warranty terms are regulated by state law, most of which follow the Uniform Commercial Code, especially in business to business sales. Consumers are often given greater protection, including requirements that goods correspond with the description, are of satisfactory quality, and are fit for the purpose. Consumer services must be performed with reasonable care and skill, within a reasonable time, and for a reasonable charge. Like their rights, consumers' remedies vary from state to state.

WEIGHTS AND MEASURES

The regulation of weights and measures in the sale of food, beverages, household supplies, etc., is generally regulated by state law and administered by local authorities. Enforcement is typically through the use of spot- and random testing, especially during holidays and other peak buying periods.

Workplace Legalities

There are a number of legal requirements and guidelines to be aware of when you consider working from home.

WORKING FROM HOME

If you own your home, it may be an infringement of local planning regulations or bylaws to work there, and it may also breach a condition of your ownership of the house. If you have a mortgage, the mortgage lender may not like it. Conducting business from a privately rented or publicly subsidized house will almost certainly breach your tenancy agreement. If you are a public housing tenant, ask a friend to make discreet inquiries at the local government offices to let you know where you stand. In most cases, if your neighbors object to your business activities, you could have a problem, so it is essential to get proper legal advice. In addition, ask your accountant about capital gains tax and business rates implications. If you are working from home, inform your insurers – there are special policies for home-based businesses.

PLANNING PERMISSION

If you need to carry out physical alterations to your property, such as create a workspace in the attic, convert a garage into a workshop, or build a new outbuilding to house your business, then you will almost certainly require planning permission. If structural alterations are involved, this will also need formal approval. It is important that your house remains primarily a domestic residence and that any business-related aspect is secondary. In addition, you will usually need planning permission for any signage, which is unlikely to be approved in a residential area.

ZONING REGULATIONS

Most communities have zoning or planning regulations that specify where people may live, and where they may engage in certain business and commercial activities. These regulations tend to be strictly enforced. If you work from home, you probably live in an area zoned for residential use. Your neighbors do not want you to engage in prohibited activities, and they may act as "watchdogs," policing their neighborhood to keep it safe, and to protect property values in the area.

In general, professional practices (accounting, law, and medicine), consulting, and marketing businesses may be conducted from home. However, this may not be the case if you have extensive client or employee traffic, or send or receive many deliveries, especially of merchandise. If you market products or equipment by mail, telephone, or over the internet, consider having the distributor shipping directly to your customers.

Carefully review your deed or lease, as well as local zoning or planning regulations, to be sure that you may conduct your business from your home. If your business is prohibited, challenging, or trying to change or be exempted from, the regulation can be long, expensive, and time-consuming, with several hearings and possible court proceedings.

Even if a previous business or property owner engaged in this activity without a problem, your new business operation may invite your neighbors' scrutiny. Also, a new neighbor who just bought property in an expensive residential area may notice that your existing business violates a deed or lease restriction, or an ordinance. Zoning violations can be raised no matter how long you have been engaged in the prohibited activity, and no matter how difficult (even impossible) it will be for you to comply. People have been forced to move or cease doing business, after years of blissful noncompliance.

FIRE SAFETY

If you employ anyone, you need to ensure they have a means of escape in the event of fire, and to provide a means of fighting a fire (such as a suitable fire extinguisher). If you employ more than a certain number of people or you plan to operate a bed and breakfast or guest house, you will usually need a fire certificate. Contact your local fire department for more information.

BUSINESSES SELLING FOOD

If your proposed business involves the making or selling of food, consult your local health department to ascertain what regulations are currently in force. Converting non-food premises for food may be very costly. If you plan to sell alcohol, check on local licensing laws and opening hours.

Hiring, Supervising, and Firing Employees

Federal, state, and local laws prohibit discrimination in hiring, paying, promoting/demoting, disciplining, and terminating employees. Most federal employment laws only apply to businesses with 15 or more employees, but state and local laws can apply even if you have only one employee.

The federal Fair Labor Standards Act requires paying the federal minimum wage, $5.15 per hour, with time-and-a-half after 40 hours per week. It prohibits certain types of work in an employee's home, restricts the hours of children under 16, and forbids employing anyone under 16 in certain dangerous types of work.

The federal Family and Medical Leave Act requires employers with 50 or more employees to provide up to 12 weeks of unpaid leave for the birth or adoption of a child, or the serious illness of an employee or an employee's family member.

Few home-based businesses are subject to these federal laws, which are administered by the U.S. Department of Labor. To learn more, visit the department's "elaws" website.

Occupational and safety regulations are administered by the U.S. Department of Labor, as well as by state authorities. However, local regulations and licensing rules may apply to particularly hazardous activities, such as dangerous equipment or machinery, toxic chemicals and products, and the like.

State and local laws may apply to businesses with fewer employees than are covered under federal law, or may give employees greater rights and protections. For example, many state and local laws restrict employing children under 18 in certain activities, especially if they attend school, no matter how few people your business employs.

There is no requirement that employees be represented by a union, but if your employees want to join a union, consult your attorney to avoid violating the employees' right to be represented by a union.

If your employees join a union, state laws differ as to whether they must all join, or whether they must pay dues whether or not they join. State laws, and industry rules and practices, also apply to disciplining or terminating workers, and displacing workers by closing local operations and moving to another location. Consult your attorney if these situations apply to or affect your home-based business.

Employees who lose their jobs without fault are entitled to unemployment insurance, which is governed by state law. Disputes as to the circumstances of the termination, or whether the former employee is available and looking for work, are decided by the state's department of labor or employment security.

Workers, including corporate officers, who incur a job-related injury or occupational disease are entitled to workers' compensation. Workers injured off the job are entitled to disability benefits. As far as home-based businesses are concerned, both programs are governed by state law, which also applies to the obligation, if any, to keep the job open if the worker returns from disability.

If your work involves trade secrets, you may require employees to sign confidentiality agreements, promising to not disclose trade secrets to competitors, or to use them themselves. You may also have employees agree to not compete with you after their employment is terminated. Such agreements, which are governed by state law, must be drafted carefully, to avoid preventing former employees from earning a living.

State law also governs whether an employee has a right to a job, or if the employment is at will. However, you are not able to fire an employee for discriminatory reasons, or for requiring that you comply with employment and certain other laws.

Be sure to check state law as to allowed pay deductions, and the form and frequency of payment. Make no deductions not required by law, except by agreement with the employee or by court order.

Immigrant Employees

Federal law prohibits employers from hiring people, even as independent contractors, who are not authorized to work in the U.S. Federal and state laws also prohibit employers from discriminating against employees or job applicants because they look "foreign" or have foreign-sounding names; they may in fact be citizens or immigrants authorized to work here.

Do not ask about employment status during the job interview. Instead, after a job has been offered and accepted, ask the prospective employee to complete Section 1 of the I-9 form, available from the U.S. Immigration and Naturalization Service, on or before the first day of work.

After the prospective employee shows documentation of being authorized to work, complete Section II of the form, and keep the form on file. You must keep records for either three years after hiring or one year after termination, whichever is the later.

Proper documents include a U.S. passport, employment authorization card, certificate of naturalization, or documents proving identity and the right to work, such as a Social Security card and a state-issued driver's license. You may keep copies for your records, but if you do so, do so for every employee.

Employers who knowingly hire unauthorized workers or ignore I-9 requirements can be fined up to $1,000 for each employee. Continuing violations can incur penalties of up to $10,000 per worker.

FINANCIAL MATTERS

This chapter is an introduction to income tax, Social Security contributions, corporation tax, capital gains tax, and sales tax. The information is for general guidance only and should not be regarded as a complete or authoritative statement on taxation. For more information, consult an accountant or the Internal Revenue Service (IRS).

When you start business, you must notify several tax authorities without delay. If you are a sole proprietor or starting a partnership, you can now do this using just one form.

EMPLOYER IDENTIFICATION NUMBER (EIN)

Sole proprietors who hire employees or independent contractors, and partnerships and corporations, must have an Employer Identification Number (EIN), which is issued by the U.S. Internal Revenue Service. This is in addition to the Social Security Number required for each individual who owns all or part of a business. Contact the IRS for application form SS-4, to open a business tax account and be assigned an EIN.

SALES AND USE TAXES

Unlike many European countries, there is no national sales tax, or built-in "value added tax." Sales and use taxes, when they are imposed, are set by states, counties, or municipalities.

Sales taxes apply at the point of purchase by the eventual consumer, not at each point along the business cycle. If you buy goods for resale, or buy food to prepare for taxable service (such as a catering service), your purchases should be exempt from sales tax. Contact your state or local tax authority for a resale certificate and number, which you will need to show your suppliers that your purchases are tax-exempt.

Tax rates and exemptions, and the particular goods or services to which they apply, vary from one locality to another. If you sell by mail, telephone order or, in some cases, the internet, you may have to collect sales tax based on the rate that applies to the purchaser's tax jurisdiction. The right of states to tax internet sales is a point of much discussion on the national political scene, and the status is unsettled. Consult with your accountant about collecting and remitting sales taxes.

SOCIAL SECURITY

Social Security is the national system for retirement and disability income. The system provides income for retirement and permanent disability, as well as for surviving spouses and minor children.

Each person has a unique Social Security Number assigned for life by the Social Security Administration. If you change your name, as a result of marriage, for example, contact the Social Security Administration so the records for "Mary Smith" are transferred to "Mary Smith Brown."

The current combined Social Security and Medicare tax rate is 7.65 percent. The rate applies to the first dollar earned per year, and the maximum amount to which the rates apply changes from year to year.

This rate is deducted from the employee's pay by the employer, who remits payment on a quarterly basis. The employer, when filing, pays the same amount. For example, the employer would deduct $76.50 from the weekly pay of an employee earning $1,000 per week. When filing the quarterly return, the employer would remit the $994.50 collected from the employee, as well as an additional $994.50, representing the employer's contributions, for a total of $1,989.00. The same person earning the same income as a sole proprietor must pay both portions, the employee and employer contributions, for the same total of $1,989.00.

If you have any employees, even temporary or part-time, you must deduct Social Security contributions, and remit quarterly reports.

RETIREMENT AND DISABILITY PLANS

Social Security retirement benefits only replace part of the retired employee's income, as do Social Security and state-mandated disability benefits. Most business owners, as well as most employees, supplement these mandatory plans with other programs. Employees may contribute to an Individual Retirement Account ("IRA"), where a certain amount of income is not subject to income tax if it is deposited into an account, where it may not be withdrawn until retirement age. Interest and dividends on the account are likewise not subject to income tax. The idea is to force saving, and to delay taxes until retirement, when the income and the tax rate are expected to be lower, with adjustments for inflation and the cost of living. Employee IRA accounts are easy to open at banks or stock brokerage firms, and are easy to maintain, and to report for income-tax purposes.

Somewhat similar plans are available for self-employed persons, and for partners and corporate owner-employees. However, these plans are more complicated to open, maintain, and report. They can save you money, and help your savings grow, but you should consult your accountant before taking any steps.

Employee pension plans can also save partnership and corporate owners much money, but they are quite complicated and expensive to initiate, maintain, and report for tax purposes. Such plans must not discriminate between owners and other employees, and similar plans must be offered to similar classes of employees. In many cases, the plans require

the approval of the U.S. Department of Labor. Do not try to do this without reviewing the proposal with your accountant and attorney.

USING SUBCONTRACTORS

If you hire a subcontractor, you must obtain proof that the subcontractor carries workers' compensation insurance. You should also require proof of liability insurance for all applicable risks. If you hire an uninsured subcontractor, you may be held liable for injuries to employees or other persons, as well as for property damage caused by your subcontractor.

HEALTH AND DISABILITY INSURANCE

There is no national program for health and disability insurance for workers and their families, nor is any such coverage required. Owners of small businesses should consult their insurance broker about this vital insurance, which is often available at reduced, but still expensive, cost through social, professional, and industry associations.

A partnership or corporation that provides company-paid health and disability insurance for the owners must also offer similar coverage for similarly employed workers.

UNEMPLOYMENT INSURANCE TAXES

Each state requires employers to contribute to funds for workers who lose their jobs without fault. These funds are administered by state agencies, which set tax rates based upon each industry's level of risk. Employers are assessed both state and federal unemployment insurance taxes, which are based on payroll. You may not require your employees to pay this tax, or reimburse you for this tax.

Income Tax

Both sole proprietors and partnerships pay their income tax on their profits via self-assessment. Directors of corporations companies pay their income tax by employer deductions, which is also the tax system used where there are employees of a business.

INCOME TAX FOR SOLE PROPRIETORS AND PARTNERSHIPS

In the case of sole proprietors or partnerships, income tax is based on the business profits as declared in the quarterly self-assessment tax return. The income tax is paid in installments (currently in January and July each year). In the case of partnerships, the profits of the business are divided equally between the partners unless the partnership agreement says to the contrary. Each partner is liable only for the tax due on his or her share of the partnership's profits.

But what is meant by "profits"? Consider this example: your total annual sales (turnover) are $75,000, but you had to spend $60,000 on stock, part-time staff wages, and other overhead. Your profit is $15,000. That amount is declared in your tax return and the $15,000 is subject to a Social Security contribution (see above). The balance would then be regarded as approximately equivalent to your wage in that you are entitled to the normal "personal allowances" (but not subject to Social Security contributions). What is left is taxed at the prevailing rates of income tax.

Note that your liability to income tax is dependent upon the profitability of your business. It makes no difference how much money you actually draw from the business, be it $50 or $500 per week! Hence the "wages" a sole proprietor or partner takes from the business are more correctly called "drawings."

ALLOWABLE EXPENSES

What types of expenditure and overhead are you allowed to deduct from your annual sales figure to calculate your taxable profits? An important distinction is made between "revenue expenditure" and "capital expenditure."

■ **REVENUE EXPENDITURE** Broadly speaking, "revenue expenditure" covers the purchase of stock or raw materials, staff wages, business rent and tax, phone bills, electricity and heating charges, advertising, stationery, business insurance, professional fees, the replacement of worn-out tools by similar tools, necessary repairs and maintenance, interest on business loans, and most vehicle expenses that relate to the business. Only revenue expenditure which is "wholly and exclusively" for your business can be deducted (or is "allowable") for income tax purposes. Items that are not allowable for income tax purposes include: your own drawings (wages), household food or other domestic expenditure, income tax, and business entertainment.

■ **CAPITAL EXPENDITURE** This covers one-time purchases of tangible assets, such as business equipment, tools, and vehicles. Only certain categories are allowable. The Internal Revenue Service has schedules of the useful life of tangible assets. The annual deduction for depreciation is equal to the cost of each asset, divided by the number of years of useful life.

There are frequently situations in small businesses where expenditure is partly for business and partly for domestic purposes. Examples include the use of a car, the use of a telephone at your home, and heat and lighting used in an "office" in your home. In the case of a car, you could keep a vehicle logbook in which you record every business trip (with date, destination, mileage, and purpose of journey). In the case of a telephone, you could also keep a simple log of all business calls you make to back up an itemized phone bill (if available). In this way you will have the necessary proof to claim the correct proportion of the charges against tax. Before you start to log anything, speak to your accountant, as you may be giving yourself an unnecessary burden.

DEDUCTING HOME–BUSINESS EXPENSES FROM INCOME

The Internal Revenue Service allows home-business expenses to be deducted from the owner's income if the business is conducted primarily from a part of the home that is used exclusively for business purposes. If these conditions are met, the pro-rated expenses may be deducted from income for tax purposes.

Several important caveats apply here. First, you may not deduct more than gross income derived from the trade or business operated from home, except if the business is operated from a free-standing structure separate from the home itself.

Second, you must use that part of your home exclusively for business. You may not, for example, deduct the pro-rated share of your kitchen, or any part of it, just because you write checks to pay your bills, or mail invoices and statements, from the kitchen table.

Third, the site must be where you regularly conduct business, not where you sometimes make telephone calls or store goods.

Fourth, taking a home-business deduction is a red flag for Internal Revenue Service staffers. You must keep scrupulous records, and expect to be audited.

Also, home-business deductions affect how certain gains that would otherwise be exempt, or subject to a lower tax rate, will be treated if and when you sell your home.

Other Insurance Considerations

Carefully review your home and vehicle insurance policies to be sure that business activities are not excluded from coverage. Discuss your insurance needs with your insurance broker, after disclosing all the relevant facts. Your honesty may result in higher premiums, but the up side that that you will be covered for these risks, which could otherwise put you out of business, and could even put you out of your home.

FINANCING AND GUIDANCE

The U.S. Small Business Administration (SBA), a division of the U.S. Department of Commerce, offers several programs providing financing for new businesses, with a particular emphasis on exporting. SBA loans are made by commercial lenders, who are willing to make the loans because most of the principal is guaranteed by the federal government.

The critical element in these loans, as well as most loans to new businesses, is the creditworthiness of the business owner, as well as the business plan.

The SBA also offers a mentoring program of particular interest to new businesses, the Service Corps of Retired Executives (SCORE). These volunteers have a lifetime of experience in business, credit, finance, or marketing, and can help new businesses develop business and marketing plans, loan applications, and grant proposals, at no charge.

SBA staffers and SCORE volunteers can also help new businesses take advantage of other guaranteed and reduced-rate loan programs, industrial development programs, grants, and opportunities for exporting, and for doing business with the government and large corporations.

BANKRUPTCY

No one starting a business wants to consider the possibility of failing; but new businesses, especially if they are poorly funded, do have a high rate of failure. Be sure you have enough funds to get your business off the ground, and take all the steps needed to protect your assets, including choosing the right form of entity and having adequate insurance.

If your business gets into financial difficulty, consult your attorney promptly. Trying to keep your business afloat, and protecting your assets, is a complex process, full of opportunities to make costly mistakes.

Bankruptcy is governed by federal law, and the proceedings are in federal bankruptcy court, but states differ as to which personal assets are exempt from being sold to satisfy your debts.

PLANNING FOR THE DEATH OF AN OWNER

This topic is even less savory than bankruptcy, but unlike bankruptcy, this will affect even the best-run business. You should discuss estate planning with your attorney, accountant, and insurance broker. Proper planning will reduce any estate taxes your estate may owe, and will also enable the surviving owners to pay your share of the business to your survivors without stripping the business of assets that belong to the surviving partners or shareholders.

Proper planning is also important for sole proprietors, to ensure that the business can be continued through employees, contractors, or consultants, until it can be sold or otherwise disposed of at the highest possible value for your survivors.

ACCOUNTING

You left your job and began your home-based business to do what you enjoy doing, and do well, not to be your own bookkeeper and accountant. However, you can reduce your accounting fees and maintain a closer watch on your income and expenses if you keep your own records. Ask your accountant to help you set up accounts, and to recommend an accounting software program to help you maintain your records.

If used regularly, these programs can help you record income and expenses, bill customers, and ensure that bills do not remain unpaid too long. Also, the programs generate reports that can help your accountant file your quarterly income tax, sales tax, Social Security, and other mandatory payments. Many programs directly link to other software programs your accountant uses to prepare these and other reports and filings, thus reducing accounting time and expense.

If you know nothing about accounting, the *For Dummies* books published by IDG, and the *Complete Idiot's Guide* series published by Que, are recommended sources of basic information. They make lively reading, assume you know

nothing, and take you step-by-step through the basics.

Other Taxes

Corporation tax is a tax on the profits of a business; it applies only to corporations, and is normally paid nine months after the end of the company's accounting year.

CAPITAL GAINS TAX

If you dispose of any asset for more than you paid for it, you have made a gain, which may be liable to capital gains tax (CGT). The tax rules are complex, as the initial value of the asset can be adjusted by previously deducted depreciation, and there may be "roll-over relief" if the proceeds are used to buy another "qualifying" asset within a set time. If you set aside part of your home exclusively for your business, you may have to pay CGT on that part when you come to sell the house; seek professional advice.

PROPERTY TAX RATES

If you set aside a room or your garage *exclusively* for business use, you may be liable for higher property tax rates on that room or garage. If there is continued domestic use of that space, business rates do not usually apply, but get professional advice at an early stage.

Moving

If you move, you must immediately notify the Internal Revenue Service, Social Security, and your state or local tax authorities. You should also notify your bank, without delay. It would also be wise to have the postal service redirect your mail to your new address and to get your phone company to redirect calls to your new number.

GLOSSARY

Allowable Expenses
Expenditure that is allowed (by the Internal Revenue Service) to be deducted from annual sales to calculate the taxable profits.

Balance Sheet
A statement of what a business owns (its assets) and what it owes (its liabilities) on a particular date. Usually prepared as part of the annual accounts at the end of the financial year.

Brainstorming
A creative technique used for generating new ideas. Individuals suggest ideas, which are recorded but not judged. At a later stage the ideas are then evaluated and developed.

Break-even Point
The point at which a business's gross margin from its sales is sufficient to cover its overhead. At this point, the business is just operating viably.

Business Angel
An individual, often a successful businessperson, who is prepared to invest money and expertise in other businesses.

Business Plan
A written report setting out details of a proposed business. Often used to raise money to start a business, or to raise money to expand or take an existing business into a new direction.

Capital Expenditure
An outlay on one-time, tangible business assets, such as equipment, computers, tools, and vehicles. For tax purposes, the whole amount is not usually deductible in the year of purchase, but over the projected lifetime of the asset through capital allowances.

Cash Flow
The movement of money in and out of a business.

Cash-flow Forecast
A prediction of the money that will flow into and out of a business. Often prepared as part of a business plan; also an ongoing business planning tool.

Depreciation
The loss in value of an item over time. The life of an item for tax purposes is set by the Internal Revenue Service.

Double-entry Accounts
A method of bookkeeping in which each transaction is entered twice, once as a debit and once as a credit.

E-commerce
The carrying out of business transactions over the internet.

Equity Finance
Backing an incorporated company by purchasing some of its shares, usually by an outside investor.

Estimate
The approximate price given to a customer in advance for doing a job. See also **Quote**.

Floating Charges
A form of security taken by a bank over the assets of an incorporated company; this asset value may "float" up and down.

Franchising
The right, under license, to copy the successful business format of another business, including its name, its products, and its image.

Goodwill
The value of a business when the physical business assets have been deducted; usually a highly negotiable figure.

Guarantor
An individual who guarantees to pay the bank in the case of a named person defaulting on loan repayments.

Invoice
A list of goods purchased (or services provided), with particulars of quantity and price. Sent or given to the customer. Less formally called a "bill."

Liquidity
The amount of funds or assets that can be readily changed into cash to meet immediate debts.

Margin
The profit made on selling goods or services. Usually expressed as a percentage.

Market Share
The portion of the total market taken by a business or its products or services.

Markup
The difference between the cost price and the selling price; markups tend to be broadly standard within a trade. Usually expressed as a percentage.

Network Marketing
A term used in direct selling to describe a multilevel system in which a salesperson receives bonuses based on the performance of those they recruit as salespeople.

Overgearing
A term describing the situation when the ratio of loans to share capital in a business is such that the profits cannot support the interest payments on the loans, and the business sinks.

Overhead (Fixed Costs)
The regular (often monthly) expenses of keeping a business running; includes electricity, telephone, insurance, and most wages.

Overtrading
Trading beyond the financial resources of a business. Overtrading can cause cash-flow problems.

Profit and Loss Account
A summary of the profits and the outgoings of a business. Usually prepared as part of the annual accounts at the end of the financial year.

Prospect
A sales term; abbreviation for "prospective customer." Used of someone to whom a salesperson is pitching a sale.

Purchase Ledger
An accounts book in which all the purchases made by a business are recorded.

Quote
The fixed price quoted to a customer in advance for doing a job. If agreed, the quote is normally binding on the seller and the customer. See also **Estimate**.

Refinancing
The process of raising additional money for an existing business, either to fund expansion or to see it through financial problems.

Sales Ledger
An accounts book in which all the sales made by a business are recorded.

Single-entry Accounts
A method of bookkeeping in which each transaction is entered once only into an accounts book.

SOHO
Small Office, Home Office.

Start-up Capital Expenditure
The one-time costs of purchasing equipment in order to start up a business.

Statement
A summary of financial transactions, usually sent by a business to a customer at the end of the calendar month. May act as a reminder of unpaid invoices.

Target Market
The section of the population that could potentially use a product or service.

Telecommuter
A person who works away from their employer, either from home or on the road, and generally uses computers and phones to keep in touch.

Turnover
Total sales made in a specified period of time.

Unique Selling Proposition (USP)
The factor that differentiates a product or service from others in the marketplace.

Variable Costs (Direct Costs)
The irregular and changing costs of keeping a business running; these usually vary directly in relation to the level of business.

Venture Capital
Money for an incorporated company invested by an outside party with the aim of getting a good return on the investment. Venture capitalists are either individuals or companies set up for the purpose.

Working Capital
The amount of short-term funds a business needs to carry out its normal work.

USEFUL CONTACTS

In addition to these national sites, check the internet and your telephone directory for organizations and government agencies geared to your industry and your locality. Also, contacting a local college, junior college, or university business department is highly recommended.

ADVERTISING AND MARKETING

American Association of Advertising Agencies
405 Lexington Avenue
New York, NY 10174-1801
Tel: (212) 682-2500; Fax: (212) 682-8391
http://www.aaaa.org

Direct Marketing Association
1120 Avenue of the Americas
New York, NY 10036-6700
Tel: (212) 768-7277; Fax: (212) 302-6714
http://www.the-dma.org

ARTS GRANTS

National Endowment for the Arts
1100 Pennsylvania Avenue, N.W.
Washington, D.C. 20506
Tel: (202) 682-5400
http://www.arts.endow.gov

BUSINESS ADVOCASY ORGANIZATIONS

Many trade and development groups advance their causes before national and state lawmakers and regulators. Two such national groups, with local affiliates, are:

National Association of Manufacturers
1331 Pennsylvania Avenue, N.W.
Washington, D.C. 20004-1790
202-637-3000; Fax: 202-637-3182
http://www.nam.org

U.S. Chamber of Commerce
1615 H Street
Washington, D.C. 20062-2000
202-659-6000
http://www.uschamber.com

CORPORATE INFORMATION

Corporations must generally register with the secretary of state of the state, and partnerships with the clerk of the county, in which they are registered. For information on public corporations, contact:

U.S. Securities and Exchange Commission
450 Fifth Street, N.W.
Washington, D.C. 20549-0304
202-942-2950
http://www.sec.gov

EXPORTING

American Management Association
1601 Broadway
New York, NY 10019
212-586-6100; Fax: 212-903-8168
http://www.amanet.org

U.S. Small Business Administration
409 Third Street
Washington, D.C. 20416
800-827-5722
http://www.sba.gov

FRANCHISING AND CUSTOMER PROTECTION

Federal Trade Commission
Pennsylvania Avenue and Sixth Street, N.W.
Washington, D.C. 20580
202-326-2222
http://www.ftc.gov

GOVERNMENT BUSINESS DEVELOPMENT AGENCIES

Department of Commerce
14th Street and Constitution Avenue, N.W.
Washington, D.C. 20230
202-482-1850
http://www.doc.gov

GOVERNMENT OFFICES

U.S. Copyright Office (Library of Congress)

101 Independence Avenue, S.E.
Washington, D.C. 20559-6000
202-707-3000
http://www.loc.gov/copyright
U.S. Department of Justice
Immigration and Naturalization Service
Office of Business Liaison
Employer Hotline: 800-357-2099
e-mail: office.business.liaison@usdoj.gov
Fax-on-Demand: 202-514-2033
National Customer Service: 800-375-5283
http://www.ins.usdoj.gov
U.S. Department of Labor
200 Constitution Avenue, N.W.
Washington, D.C. 20210
202-219-6001
http://dol.gov/elaws

Occupational Health and Safety
Administration (DOL)
202-693-1999
http://www.osha-slc.gov
U.S. Environmental Protection Agency
1200 Pennsylvania Avenue, N.W.
Washington, D.C. 20460
202-564-4700
http://www.epa.gov
**U.S. Equal Employment Opportunity
Commission**
1801 L Street, N.W.
Washington, D.C. 20507
202-663-4900
800-669-4000 (direct connection to nearest
field office)
http://www.eeoc.gov

OTHER USEFUL WEBSITES

The major internet providers and portals, such as About.Com, America Online, MSN, Netscape, and Yahoo, have useful business resource pages, and access to most information is free. In addition, the following free sites are recommended.
Angel Capital Network (Ace-Net)
http://www.sba.gov/advo
Business Advisor (federal government information)
http://business.gov
Commerce Business Daily (federal government contracts)
http://cbdnet.access.gpo.gov
Consumer Information Center
http:///www.pueblo.gov
ExpoGuide (trade show information)
http://www.expoguide.com
Inc. Magazine
http://www.inc.com
Knowledge Centers Small Office-Home Office site
http://www.knowledgecenters.org
Minority Business Development Agency
http://www.mbda.gov

National Foundation for Women Business Owners
http://www.nfwbo.org
Office.Com
http://www.office.com
Service Corps of Retired Executives (SCORE)
http://www.score.org
Small Office.Com
http://www.smalloffice.com
State Government and Legal Resource
http://www.alllaw.com
State Tax Forms
http://taxweb.com/forms
The Small Business Journal.Com
http://www.tsbj.com
Thomas Register
http://www.thomasregister.com
University of North Carolina, Charlotte J. Murrey Atkins Library
http://libweb.uncc.edu/ref-bus/buselec.htm
Women's Business Center (also young entrepreneurs)
http://onlinewbc.org

Internal Revenue Service
1111 Constitution Avenue, N.W.
Washington, D.C. 20224
202-927-5170
http://www.irs.ustreas.gov
Social Security Administration
820 First Street, N.W.
Washington, D.C. 20254
800-772-6270
http://www.ssa.gov
U.S. Patent & Trademark Office
Crystal Plaza 3, Room 2C02
Washington, D.C. 20231
800-786-9199
http://www.uspto.gov

MANUFACTURERS REPRESENTATIVES
**Manufacturers Representatives Educational
Research Foundation**
P.O.B. 247
Geneva, IL 60134
630-208-1466; Fax: 630-208-1475
http://www.mrerf.org

MARKET RESEARCH STUDIES
U.S. Census Bureau
4700 Silver Hill Road
Suitland, MD 20746
301-457-4608
http://www.census.gov

YOUNG ENTREPRENEURS
Many trade and development groups promote
initiatives by young people. In addition to local
groups and universities, you may contact
clearinghouses for such information.
Edward Lowe Foundation
P.O. Box 8
Cassapolis, MI 49031
800-232-5693
http://www.lowe.org
The Entrepreneurship Institute
http://www.tei.net
Initiative for a Competitive Inner City
727 Atlantic Avenue, Suite 600
Boston, MA 02111
617-292-2363; Fax: 617-292-2380
http://www.icic.org

SUGGESTED READING

The American Marketplace
(New Strategist Publications, 1999)
A survey of how and where we live, what we
spend our money on, and what motivates us
to do so.
Building a Website
Tim Worsley (Dorling Kindersley, 2000)
An easy-to-follow guide to Microsoft's website
building program, FrontPage 2000, aimed at
complete beginners to this software. Fully
illustrated.
**The Complete Idiot's Guide to Online
Marketing**
Bill Eager & Cathy McCall (Que, 1999)
An easy-to-use and follow guide to
using the internet to market and sell
products.

The Do-It-Yourself Business Promotions Kit
Jack Griffin (Prentice Hall, 1995)
Using advertising, media planning, and
marketing communications to promote your
business. Focuses on small-business
management.
Do-It-Yourself Direct Marketing
Mark S. Bacon (John Wiley & Sons, 1997)
How to sell using mail order, telemarketing,
radio and television commercials, print ads,
and the internet, with tips for small businesses
with small budgets.
E-Mail Marketing
*Jim Sterne and Anthony Priore (John Wiley &
Sons, 2000)*
Using email to reach a targeted audience, and
to build and maintain customer relationships.

Entrepreneur Magazine's How to Start a Network Marketing Business
(Entrepreneur Media, 1997)
A step-by-step guide to building a successful network marketing business.

Essential Manager's Manual
Robert Heller and Tim Hindle (Dorling Kindersley, 1998)
A highly readable reference book with general advice on areas such as giving presentations, communicating, and time management.

ExportAmerica
A monthly magazine from the U.S. Department of Commerce, with practical tips on every step of the business of selling U.S.-made goods abroad, from getting started through getting paid. For details and subscription information, call 202-512-1800, or see http://exportamerica.doc.gov.

Getting Started in Export
Roger Bennett (Kogan, Page, 1998)
Hands-on advice about researching overseas markets, finding customers, pricing, delivering goods, and the legalities of export.

101 Ways to Promote Your Website
Susan Sweeney (Maximum Press, 1999)
Suggests marketing tips, tools, techniques and resources to drive traffic to your company's website.

Secrets of Successful Telephone Selling
Robert W. Bly (Henry Holt, 1996)
How to use the telephone to generate leads and referrals, to close sales and to keep customers.

Selling Successfully
Robert Heller (Dorling Kindersley, 1998)
All you need to know about successful selling.

Small-Business Franchises Made Simple
William Lasher and Carl Hausman (Doubleday, 1994)
A guide to franchising businesses, especially retail operations, throughout the United States.

The Small Business Legal Guide
Lynne Ann Frasier (Sourcebooks, 1998)
A guide to the critical legal matters that can affect your business.

Small Business Legal Smarts
Deborah L. Jacobs (Bloomberg, 1998)
How to establish and protect your business.

Start and Succeed in Multilevel Marketing
Gregory F. Kishel & Patricia Gunter Kishel (John Wiley, 1999)
A guide to building a network sales business

Starting and Operating a Business in the U.S.
Michael D. Jenkins (Running "R" Media, 1999)
A how-to-guide, with printed forms and a laser optical disc.

Statistical Abstract of the United States, 1999 Issue
(U.S. Census Bureau, 2000)
Updated annually since 1878, this may be the most important fact book on the social, political, and economic aspects of American life. Available in print, CD-ROM, or downloadable (PDF file) format. The 2001 issue should incorporate the results of the 2000 national census.

Streetwise: Do It Yourself Advertising
Sarah White & John Woods (Adams Media, 1997)
How to create ads and use promotions and direct marketing, with strategies to jump-start sales.

FRANCISE DIRECTORIES

Franchise Opportunities Handbook *(LaVerne L. Ludden, Park Avenue, 1999)*
Franchise World Directory (Franchise World)

INDEX

ACKNOWLEDGMENTS

AUTHORS' ACKNOWLEDGMENTS

We would like to thank Charlotte Hingston for reading the manuscript and for her many useful suggestions, and Frank Binnie, chief executive of the Scotland Internet Society, for his insight and knowledge. We would also like to thank our hard-working editors and designer and, finally, Julie Servante and Stuart Ramsden for their kind assistance.

PUBLISHER'S ACKNOWLEDGMENTS

Grant Laing Partnership would like to thank the following for their help and participation in producing this book:
Special Photography: Mark Hamilton
Proofreader: Nikky Twyman
Indexer: Kay Ollerenshaw
Models: Augustin Luneau, Francis Ritter, Mario de Souza

Dorling Kindersley would like to thank the following for their help and participation in producing this book:
Editorial: Mary Lindsay, Daphne Richardson, Mark Wallace
Design: Sarah Cowley
DTP: Jason Little, Amanda Peers

The Types of Work model and definitions feature on page 26 © Prado Systems Limited; reproduced by kind permission of TMS Development International Ltd.

The accounts book illustration on page 86 is reproduced with kind permission of Hingston Publishing Co.

PICTURE CREDITS

2: The Image Bank; 5 top: The Image Bank; 5 centre above: The Image Bank; 5 centre: Powerstock/Zefa Photo Library; 5 centre below: Pictor; 5 below: gettyone stone; 12: Powerstock/Zefa Photo Library; 15: The Stock Market; 16: Telegraph Colour Library; 20: gettyone stone; 25: The Stock Market; 37 below: Telegraph Colour Library; 39: Telegraph Colour Library; 43: Powerstock/Zefa Photo Library; 48: Rex Features; 51: gettyone stone; 55: The Stock Market; 56: The Image Bank; 61: The Stock Market; 69: Telegraph Colour Library; 71: gettyone stone; 75: gettyone stone; 109: CoKevin R Morris/Corbis; 110: The Stock Market; 113: Pictor; 114: Telegraph Colour Library; 116: gettyone stone; 117: Lu Jeffery; 122: gettyone stone; 125: Pictor; 127: Spectrum Colour Library; 130: Telegraph Colour Library; 139: The Stock Market; 140: The Stock Market; 142 below right: gettyone stone; 143: Pictor; 146: The Stock Market; 148: The Stock Market; 152: Powerstock/Zefa Photo Library; 154: Pictor; 157: The Stock Market; 160: gettyone stone.

AUTHORS' BIOGRAPHY

After serving in the RAF, Peter Hingston started his first business in 1979, working with cars near Oxford. He sold this, and later started an electronics manufacturing business in Barbados. Then, with his wife, he launched a fashion shop in Edinburgh, a national trade magazine, and a book publishing business. All traded profitably and were eventually sold, apart from the publishing business, which he runs today. He has written six books on running a small business, some of which have been bestsellers and translated into several different languages. Peter is also a non-executive director of a large retail business in Barbados.

Alastair Balfour is a Scottish entrepreneur, private investor, and writer who works from home. He began as a business journalist on newspapers. After he was made redundant he co-founded a monthly business magazine, which grew into the leading business publishing company in Scotland. The business was sold in 1999, and Alastair is now an investor in five companies as well as maintaining a consultancy and writing career.